# THE SGML FAQ BOOK

## *Understanding the Foundation of HTML and XML*

# ELECTRONIC PUBLISHING SERIES

*Consulting Editor*
**Eric van Herwijnen**

## *Latest Titles:*

**INFORMATION RETRIEVAL AND HYPERTEXT**, Maristella Agosti, Alan Smeaton, editors
ISBN: 0-7923-9710-X

**HTML AND THE ART OF AUTHORING FOR WORLD WIDE WEB**, Bebo White
ISBN: 0-7923-9691-X

**RETHINKING HYPERMEDIA: The Microcosm Approach**, Wendy Hall, Hugh Davis, Gerard Hutchings
ISBN: 0-7923-9679-0

**MAKING HYPERMEDIA WORK: A User's Guide to HyTime**, Steven J. DeRose, David G. Durand
ISBN: 0-7923-9432-1

**PRACTICAL SGML, Second Edition**, Eric van Herwijnen
ISBN: 0-7923-9434-8

**PRACTICAL SGML**, Eric van Herwijnen
ISBN: 0-7923-0635-X

# THE SGML FAQ BOOK

***Understanding the Foundation of HTML and XML***

by

**Steven J. DeRose**
Chief Scientist
Inso Electronic Publishing Solutions

SPRINGER SCIENCE+BUSINESS MEDIA, LLC

**Library of Congress Cataloging-in-Publication Data**

A C.I.P. Catalogue record for this book is available
from the Library of Congress.

ISBN 978-1-4757-7056-8 ISBN 978-0-585-34049-4 (eBook)
DOI 10.1007/978-0-585-34049-4



*Printed on acid-free paper.*

"The name of the song is called 'Haddocks' Eyes.'"

"Oh, that's the name of the song, is it?" Alice said, trying to feel interested.

"No, you don't understand," the Knight said, looking a little vexed. "That's what the name is called. The name really is 'The Aged Aged Man.'"

"Then I ought to have said 'That's what the song is called'?" Alice corrected herself.

"No, you oughtn't: that's quite another thing! The song is called 'Ways and Means': but that's only what it's called, you know!"

"Well, what *is* the song, then?" said Alice who was by this time completely bewildered.

"I was coming to that," the Knight said. "The song really is 'A-Sitting On A Gate': and the tune's my own invention."

*Through the Looking Glass*
*Lewis Carroll*

# Table of Contents

# Foreword

Although not evident to all, many people have been waiting more than a decade for *The SGML FAQ Book* by Steve DeRose. It has been "brewing" for a long time, with many hours, months, years of research talking to people, gathering their ideas, listening to their frustrations, applauding their successes. Only Steve with his experience, credentials, wit, and enthusiasm for the subject could have written this book.

But it is also a measure of the success and maturity of ISO 8879 and its amazing longevity that allows an "SGMLer" to write such a book. We can now laugh at ourselves, even disclose our mistakes without fear of the other guy. While most would not recognize it, the revolution known as the World Wide Web would not have happened without a non-proprietary, easy, and almost "portable" way to create and distribute documents across a widely disparate set of computers, networks, even countries. HTML, an SGML application, enabled this and as a result the world and the SGML community will never be the same.

For some the term *SGML* means order, management, standards, discipline; to others, the term brings images of pain, confusion, complexity, and pitfalls. To all who have engaged in it, the Standard means hard work, good friends, savings in terms of time, money, and effort, a sense of accomplishment and best of all – fun. This book adds immeasurably to all of these. Enjoy the quote from *Through the Looking Glass* by Lewis Carroll as much as we have.

The initial intent of Steve's book was to provide answers to questions, examples and clarifications on some of the more obscure areas of the Standard. However, before it could be written, other events took over: the explosion of the Web and the opportunity and information it provided and the beginning in earnest of the second 5-year review process for the SGML standard. At the same time it became clear to many that for SGML to reach its full potential, the concepts and practice must become accessible to a broader, less sophisticated audience. Attention was focused on the true benefits of the Standard; many of which were clearly elucidated by the XML ERB in their original working papers. The intent, therefore, shifted to encompass all three areas: to aid in developing an understanding of various aspects of the Standard; to identify and comment upon constructs and restrictions that could be eliminated during the review process, and lastly to provide a birds-eye view and rationale of the need for XML.

We know the book will help you find your way around many of the nooks and crannies of SGML to enable a productive and beneficial use of this most important of all Standards. I hope his next book is on DSSSL.

Sharon Adler and Anders Berglund
East Greenwich, Rhode Island, March, 1997

The spectacular growth of the World Wide Web has given a strong push to the awareness and the acceptance of SGML, the Standard Generalized Markup Language. The principles of openness and reusability on which SGML are based, have been important contributors to the success of HTML and the Web.

The acceptance and interest in SGML can be measured by the recent surge of books on this topic. But rather than writing yet another conventional textbook, Steve DeRose decided to address the nitty gritty nuts and bolts of SGML - in particular those nuts and bolts that seem to get worn out after a bit of wear and tear.

His very popular book *Making HyperMedia work: A User's Guide to HyTime* (co-authored with David Durand) remains the most accessible text on HyTime. Now he has compiled *The SGML FAQ Book.* Using his extensive experience creating innovative SGML software at Electronic Book Technologies (now part of Inso), he has now written a text that discusses nearly all the difficult aspects of SGML. The explanations stand on a very sound theoretical basis, but above all they stem from very concrete practical cases - an attitude that I can closely identify with.

Anyone who has some SGML knowledge and has used SGML software will find this book very useful indeed. Those features of SGML that seem bizarre and esoteric and those that cause problems to the inexperienced (and experienced!) user are clearly explained. Moreover, Steve draws on his wide breadth of contacts in the SGML community and his own participation in the standardization process to place these features in their correct historical context. This helps enormously to augment the readers' understanding and effective use of SGML. In the end, everyone benefits by this, especially those who have invested much time and effort in SGML and HTML.

In some places he gives important suggestions as to how SGML could be improved - what modifications to the standard would make sense, and why. A number of these suggestions have been adopted by XML, the Extensible Markup Language proposed as the next generation markup language for the Web. I sincerely hope that the committee reviewing SGML will take note of this important work.

I have seen SGML referred to as "at worst incredibly boring, at best of academic interest". Yet using his easy to read, light-hearted style and a good dose of humor, Steve has proved that statement wrong by creating the first book on SGML that is a pleasure to read. I was unable to put it down and I hope you will share the experience.

Eric van Herwijnen
CERN, Geneva, 28 march 1997

# Preface

This book is similar, but not quite the same kind of thing as an online FAQ or Frequently Asked Question list. It addresses questions from people who already actually use SGML in some way (including HTML authors), and people who are about to use it. It deals mainly with issues that arise when using SGML in practice. But it does not focus on the most introductory questions like "What is SGML?" or "Where can I download a parser?". For those, many "Introduction to SGML" FAQs are available online, easily available via a Web search, and I have included a very brief introduction to SGML as Appendix A.

When I shared my collection of "Frequently Asked Questions" with people who make their living serving the SGML community they told me that many of the questions are ones they repeatedly hear. SGML experts spend many hours teaching these details, sometimes repeatedly because some questions don't seem important — *until you run into them.* So one benefit of this book is learning more of the art of document creation and management, both by general reading before questions arise and by specific reference when a question arises. For the latter use, the appendixes, glossary, and index are particularly important.

A second benefit of this book is that it provides a common theme to its answers, that you can apply in your use of SGML, HTML, and related languages in general. The fundamental answer to many of the questions boils down to "simplify": many questions do not show up if you use the simple, elegant core of SGML without worrying about optional features. This pattern is true of many other technologies, too.

This book owes much to a genre I first encountered through *C Traps and Pitfalls* (Koenig 1989), and again in *VHDL: Answers to Frequently Asked Questions* (Cohen 1996), *C Programming FAQs* (Summit 1996), and *C++ FAQs* (Cline and Lomow 1995). Books such as these enhance effective, reliable use of the languages they describe. Like this book they also frequently advocate simplicity as a key way to avoid incompatibilities, errors, and other problems. C and SGML are similar in that each has already become successful, even dominant, in its own field. Thus fears that if someone hears there are questions about SGML they will flee to PostScript, troff, or ODA (ever used ODA?) are unjustified, just as fears that if someone hears about C's more complex aspects (such as "operator precedence" rules) they will flee to Forth, assembler, or BASIC.

The credo of this book, so far as it has any, is simply "SGML doesn't need to be complicated". SGML has the potential for complexity at certain points. But much of the complexity comes from optional parts and can be avoided (like a radio kit I painstakingly put together once, only to find that I could pull out half the components before it actually failed). SGML methodology and its primary benefits suffer no loss even if you skip many features, which speaks well for the quality of SGML's overall design. Many of the questions discussed involve those optional parts, and therefore can be avoided by judicious designers and authors. This principle informs the two key goals in this book, both of which you will see reflected in the answer to nearly every question:

1. Answering questions that you may actually encounter as an SGML user, to help you get "unstuck" and be as productive as possible in using the language.
2. Showing proactive ways you can simplify your use of SGML, and get its very substantial benefits with minimal complexity.

The latter sounds a lot like the Web, and perhaps it is no coincidence that the Web revolution has been fueled in large part not merely by SGML, but by a very simple tag set (HTML) that also requires only a small subset of SGML capabilities. In the late 1980s people laughed whenever Lou Reynolds said that SGML would eventually be "bigger than spreadsheets". Then came the Web, and now SGML *is* bigger than spreadsheets, even without counting its high-end features.

Why did the SGML tag set (or "DTD") called HTML win so big? The software applications and the network hardware and infrastructure that make remote data access practical are obviously crucial. But the data representation pulls it all together: a Web without HTML, that merely let you download PostScript or troff or GIF, would be only slightly more compelling than manual ftp or emailing documents around (Gopher is very much like that). The same strengths that made SGML win so big in a different forum (large publishers of all kinds) also help fuel the Web. Specifically, SGML provides a basis for HTML that is:

1. *Portable,* making data independent of computer system, software, output medium, window size, screen resolution, formatting details of various software, etc.
2. *Transportable*, because the simple choice of keeping document files in plain text has many technical benefits (involving network byte order, character set and encoding independence, avoidance of machine-specific memory addresses, etc.).
3. *Editable*, even with no special software (not that anyone wants to, but most Web authors can deal with pointy brackets at need).
4. *Open,* developed and documented so that anyone can learn it and implement it
5. *Flexible*, so anyone can invent their own document types (that's why HTML could be created as an application of SGML in the first place).

6. *Redundant* in its syntax, so that error recovery is possible. This is a subtle point (and not all SGML systems take advantage of it), but details such as having element types in both start- and end-tags increase the possibility of detecting and recovering from errors, much as redundant bits on Compact Disks can keep the music intact even if the disk is scratched.

SGML provides these strengths to HTML as well. Technology acceptance often involves finding which capabilities are crucial through real use, and then finding the least complicated way to achieve them. None of the benefits above requires the "complicated" bits of SGML. You can achieve them without having to worry about **DATATAG**, **#CONREF**, **#CURRENT**, or fancy minimization, and HTML does just that.

HTML comes fairly close to expressing the essence of SGML, the parts of it that SGML experts have come to value over the years. However, HTML lacks one crucial thing from the list above: the flexibility to create any document structure you want. *No* one set of tags will ever be enough. People who need to create poetry, parts catalogs, or nearly any other specialized document do not have the tools in HTML. They can often create the appearance by overloading existing tags, but catalog publishers cannot create a `PRICE` tag on their own — and the appearance is only enough if *all* they must do is display the data in the same form. If (as is increasingly common) an application involves not just formatting but also searching, then tagging prices merely as being boldface doesn't help. While very useful, adding a `CLASS` attribute does not solve the problem because it leaves the first-class idea of document structure as a second-class citizen in the language, and that limits processing capabilities in many ways.

The key is to have the best of both worlds: a simple language that nevertheless allow authors to create and represent new *document structures*. This means trivially simple syntax and grammar rules, but sophisticated vocabulary and structural power. In SGML terms, this translates to using relatively few features but retaining key capabilities such as creating your own tag sets, appropriate to your own document types. The questions and answers in this book will help you use SGML and gain its advantages while retaining the simplicity of HTML. If you use HTML, you'll learn a lot about why things in HTML are the way they are, and what to watch out for when trying to build truly portable HTML documents.

The existence of questions or of potential simplifications such as this book discusses should not be taken as some kind of "black mark" on SGML or HTML: a book such as this deals with how to *use* them effectively, not how to *avoid* them in favor of something else. In FAQ Books such a reminder seems to be required, and I can say it no better here than Steve Summit said it for C:

> ...this book is not intended as a "hatchet job" on the C language. It is all too easy to blame a language (or any tool) for the difficulties its users encounter with it or to claim that a properly designed tool "ought" to prevent its users from misusing it. It would therefore be easy to regard a book like this, with its long lists of misuses, as a litany of woes attempting to show that the language is hopelessly deficient. Nothing could be farther from the case.
>
> I would never have learned enough about C to be able to write this book, and I would not be attempting to make C more pleasant for others to use by writing this book now, if I did not think that C is a great language or if I did not enjoy programming in it. I *do* like C, and one of the reasons I teach classes in it and spend time participating in discussion about it on the Internet is that I would like to discover which aspects of C (or of programming in general) are difficult to learn or keep people from being able

to program efficiently and effectively. This book represents some of what I've learned....

Like C, SGML has proven itself by soundly defeating both standard and proprietary alternatives in every major arena, and its developers can be justly proud of it. SGML has been embraced as an industry-wide standard in countless areas: aerospace, telecommunications, computer hardware and software, auto, power and fuel, finance, pharmaceuticals, libraries and academia, semiconductors — in each case it has helped save huge amounts of money through data longevity, portability, and even paperless publishing and distribution. It also makes data far more able to survive beyond whatever software may be used on it in some particular month. Then came the Web, which derives much of its power from the data portability provided by HTML, which is an application of SGML.

Alan Kay once commented that the Macintosh was "the first personal computer good enough to be criticized". In a similar way SGML was the first markup language good enough to be criticized, or even to be the subject of study and analysis.

**Note**: To be thorough, I should note that the Mac had a precursor in the Xerox Star, as SGML had precursors such as Shaw's document model, Reid's Scribe system, and Goldfarb's GML, all of the late 70s. Indispensable summaries of the history of document processing systems, hierarchical and descriptive markup, and related topics are in Reid (1981) and André, Furuta, and Quint (1989).

Like all technical innovations C, the Mac interface, and SGML are human efforts subject to human limitations in their designs. SGML is not perfect, or even "the best that was possible given the state of the art in 1986". Nevertheless, the committee that created SGML accomplished an astounding feat: a language with almost unprecedented breadth of application, that has had enormous impact (even though some of it goes unseen, beneath the surface), and that has required unusually little maintenance or repair. Structurally and semantically SGML is very powerful and continues to suffice *ten years* later for an enormous range of tasks. This is primarily because of its conceptual approach: SGML implements a very powerful and compelling core model for electronic documents called "descriptive markup" (this term was in use at least as early as 1979, when Reid and Goldfarb both spoke on it at the GCA GenCode conference).

SGML has proven very effective as a document creation, management, and delivery solution. It also has a significant and unusual advantage because you can avoid nearly all the inelegant bits by subtraction: not using certain options. Even better, there are usually elegant ways to accomplish the same things so no functionality is lost. Such simplification also makes it easy to build smaller, cheaper, and faster software, that has fewer bugs, is more easily maintained, and can be built with off-the-shelf tools computer scientists use to build other languages. College sophomores commonly build a Pascal or C compiler in a single semester course (the parser itself commonly takes a week or two, and a fully functional document markup parser need not be any harder).

> **Note:** The aspects of SGML that are often considered less elegant are largely details that appear to have been added to accommodate concerns that were legitimate priorities at the time but have become less relevant over the last decade: keyboarding convenience in the absence of authoring software, compatibility with early systems, or accommodating past implementation strategies. Whatever the history, experts in formal language and system design have now had time to find areas where SGML could increase in elegance with no decrease in function, just as happens for C and other technologies. SGML is undergoing its official review as this book is being written, and it is likely that an amendment will enhance and simplify SGML in just these areas.

The beauty of SGML is that it gives a simple, portable means of transmitting descriptively structured *documents* between systems and people. It gives a way to avoid the distraction of putting system- or application- or processing-specific instructions inside documents, and lets authors operate at the more conceptual level of "what is it?" rather than "what did I last want to do with it?" These strengths have everything to do with the structures SGML represents, and little to do with which optional features of SGML may be used to represent them. Or as early SGML committee member Sharon Adler puts it, they have to do with SGML *methodology* as opposed to SGML *syntax*. That said, it is important to remember that *standardizing* on a syntax is still crucial for practical data interchange, and so SGML's status as a full ISO standard is a benefit.

Many SGML experts have made these dual points about the ingenuity of SGML's methodology and the potential for useful simplifications of its syntax. An important recent example is the World Wide Web Consortium's SGML effort, which has now formalized a powerful yet radically simpler subset of SGML called XML. XML was developed by SGML experts in close cooperation with the SGML committee, and is *not* a new language (it didn't need to be). It does not conflict with, supplant, or undermine SGML or HTML. It is simply a subset of SGML that retains the structural power and flexibility, but leaves out a lot of syntax complexity. The fact that XML is a true subset is underscored by the fact that several SGML system vendors demonstrated support for it within a week of the draft specification becoming available, and it looks likely that major Web browsers will support it as well (check the Web for up-to-date information on implementations). The XML subset should make SGML more accessible to authors and implementers alike. Because it so closely reflects the union of sophisticated functionality and simple syntax, some excerpts from the actual XML specification are included in Chapter 8 of this book.

There are many new things to do with structured documents that go even beyond what SGML can support — not because of syntax limitations but because the structures go beyond SGML's model. They are a topic for another book, though I mention a few in passing and Barnard et al. (1995) mentions some in more detail. But for now, I look forward to SGML continuing to grow simpler and more widespread and for its powerful methodology to continue making the world's literature and other documents more useful and accessible to more people. XML is not the end; it is not the beginning of the end; but perhaps it is the end of the beginning.

## Acknowledgments

Many friends deserve thanks for helping me to finish this book. Chief among them is David Durand, who knows every question in here backwards and forwards, and has added immeasurably to my understanding of SGML, hypermedia, and many related topics. Had his dissertation not intervened he could have written most of this book himself, and might have done so. The students he and I have taught in various forums have sharpened our awareness of what SGML and HyTime users find difficult, and I thank them as well.

The SGML, HTML, and XML author, designer, and developer communities have taught me much, and many of their members have become close friends. Many scholars working with electronic document and hypermedia systems have as well, and have helped in other ways such as providing articles, technical advice, and other information. Sharon Adler, Anders Berglund, and Robin Cover helped in many ways. Several early members of the SGML committee have given me their perspectives on early SGML history and the process of standardization that occurred.

Carl Harris at Kluwer Academic Publishing found an especially thorough, diverse, and qualified group of reviewers, who provided indispensable feedback on the book in two major cycles and several minor ones. Each one of them put in far more substantial work than merely a "review". Most sent extensive comments and suggested additional questions. They deserve special thanks, and the entire organization and content is far better because of their help. The major reviewers are listed in the next section; some additional reviewers also helped. Noah Landow ably provided the cover art as he did for *Making Hypermedia Work.*

Beyond all these friends, though, most of all I am grateful to my wife Laurie and our sons Todd and Brian. They have supported me unfailingly through a year that was quite stressful enough even without a new book.

Steven J. DeRose, Ph.D.
Seekonk, MA
March, 1997

# Reviewers

SHARON ADLER
DAVID BARNARD
ANDERS BERGLUND
MICHAEL BROWN
ROBIN COVER
HARRY GAYLORD
DEBBIE LAPEYRE
JOHN LAVAGNINO
CHRIS MADEN
EVE MALER
GAVIN NICOL
LIAM QUIN
PETER SHARPE
MACKENZIE SMITH
C. M. SPERBERG-MCQUEEN
B. TOMMIE USDIN
ERIC VAN HERWIJNEN
WAYNE WOHLER

# Organization and Conventions

## Prerequisites

This book is not primarily a tutorial on SGML, but Appendix A gives a very brief overview of the basic ideas. Some experience of HTML or another application of SGML is helpful, and the first several chapters should be easily accessible to nearly any HTML or SGML author. Those chapters cover many of the most common practical questions. To understand them you only need to understand a few basics such as:

- the difference between tags, start-tags, element instances, and element types
- constructs such as elements, attributes, entities, and so on
- the difference between character data and the markup that gives information about it
- basic ideas such as separating formatting from document structure.

The middle chapters require a little more knowledge, such as how to refer to external entities for graphics in HTML and/or SGML, how to at least read DTDs (they declare what elements and other constructs can appear in certain kinds of documents), and how to manipulate files with various tools such as editors, global change commands, regular expression languages, or similar devices. A few more details such as the SGML delimiters and their names (**STAGO**, **TAGC**, **PIC**, etc.) are also useful (a table is supplied in Appendix B).

To get through the last few chapters a reader should be able to use more advanced SGML terms such as "**NET**-enabling start-tag" and "nested ignored marked section". No computer programming skills are required, though computer scientists will often see additional reasons for various statements.

Readers needing instruction, review, or reference on SGML are encouraged to read Eric van Herwijnen's *Practical SGML*, Martin Bryan's *SGML: An Author's Guide,* and

Charles Goldfarb's *SGML Handbook.* Several more books on SGML have appeared recently, or are about to. Some references appear in the Bibliography.

## Organization

This book is organized according to various ways different people use SGML. It starts with questions for authors who actually create marked-up documents, then goes on to questions applicable to DTD designers, and finally addresses a few for SGML system implementers. The chapters and the audiences they address are listed here.

**Authors** or others doing actual markup, for whom the first several chapters are especially applicable:

1 Authors working with SGML-aware software that insulates them from many SGML details (particularly syntax and minimization). In theory there should be very few SGML-specific questions for this group; just questions about particular DTDs ("Is this a `BOOKTITLE` or a `NAME`?"), or about the software itself ("Where's the Insert Element command?"). In practice, however, software doesn't protect authors completely and so questions about particular details of SGML syntax creep in. This chapter tries to provide a relatively painless introduction to those details and how to handle them.

2 Authors working without such software (even from time to time) for data conversion, testing, or other tasks. They are generally comfortable with basic pointy-brackets and SGML document syntax, but need not know much about DTDs, external entities, and other SGML constructs. Nearly any HTML author will find at least some of these questions familiar.

3 Authors or data conversion specialists who must transform SGML data, convert non-SGML data to SGML, or do other markup-intensive tasks. Because they handle a lot more data, and try to do it systematically, they get bitten faster by any inconsistencies in their data, and have to manage special cases and details that much better. Webmasters and HTML publishers that convert data from other forms into HTML will feel at home here.

4 Authors and Editors who must use some DTD syntax, for example to declare entities for external data or to modify existing DTDs. They are right on the edge of becoming DTD designers, and must learn some parts of DTD syntax in order to expand their use of SGML to include external data objects, add "just one extra" attribute, and so on. Webmasters concerned about the differences between versions of HTML will find some relevant questions here.

**Designers** of Document Type Definitions, who decide how documents may be structured, and what SGML constructs are used to express the structure:

5 DTD Builders in general, who design document types and markup conventions.

6 DTD Builders who are also concerned with more complex aspects of document design, constraining and validating data in special ways, setting up stylesheets, etc.

**Implementers** of SGML-based applications or systems. They must deal with another level of complexities to get their systems just right, and to pick which optional parts of the standard they will invest to support.

7 SGML systems designers, whether they are creating advanced DTDs and SGML declarations, or perhaps writing stylesheets, configuring software products and installations, or writing parsers. They are concerned with more complex aspects of document design, constraining and validating data, creating variations on SGML's syntax using SGML declarations, etc.

This book has some notes for other groups such as implementers, standards experts and markup theorists, but these are separated from the main text in "Note" boxes. The book would be far thicker and more technical if it really addressed these groups. Instead, it is mainly for actual practitioners of SGML (including HTML authors, who run into many of the questions quite often). Computer scientists, formal language experts, standards mavens, and the like will find it informative, though more likely as a means of clearing away encumbrances to understanding the point of SGML, which I consider to be treating documents as ***structured objects*** rather than formatted page images (see Coombs et al. 1987 for more on this).

Some questions arise in many different kinds of situations, and so may not be in the place you might expect. As one example, a question often arises about "inherited" attributes: ones that default to the value the like-named attribute has on the parent element (or another ancestor element). Different people are affected in different ways by the answer (which is that at this time SGML provides no such capability): authors may have to respond by inserting extra attribute values, DTD designers may choose to impose conventions, and implementers and others may have other responses. This inherited-attribute question is covered in a later chapter for DTD builders (in Question 6.8) because they seem to me the most likely group to run straight into the limitation and have to deal with it, but other authors would no doubt make other choices.

Where my intuition for placement inevitably differs from that of some readers, I hope that the extensive cross-references, glossary, and index will help. It is unlikely that all the answers will be unanimously agreed upon, but each of them has arisen in actual experience and most have been reported widely and repeatedly as actual user questions, so I believe they deserve presentation. Many have been discussed in the comp.text.sgml newsgroup, an active online forum for discussing SGML. I indexed, reviewed, and searched the archives of the list as I developed this book, and am grateful to the many people who participate in the group for their insights.

## Typographic and other conventions

To distinguish descriptions of SGML itself from occasional discussion of possible alternative syntactic constructions that SGML could adopt in the future, this book uses indicative language for SGML: "SGML does x". It uses subjunctive language when discussing an alternative language or version: "A language might/would/could do y".

Unless otherwise stated, examples assume Basic SGML documents, except for arbitrarily high limits on **NAMELEN**, **LITLEN**, and other quantities (I have not attempted to shorten all SGML names to 8 characters). Basic SGML documents are defined in Clause 15.1.1 of the SGML standard. They use only SGML's reference concrete syntax, and only the **SHORTTAG** and **OMITTAG** features, plus **SHORTREF** which this book doesn't use. Statements that have significant exceptions when these values are changed are usually qualified by the word "normally", for example "Normally, '<' is a delimiter." This does not imply that other settings are "abnormal"; indeed some changes are very common and useful, such as increasing the maximum length for tag names.

The typographic styles used to distinguish different kinds of keywords, examples, and other text objects are these:

- Although SGML element type and attribute names typically ignore case, this book follows common practice and shows them in fixed-pitch capitals: "The `CHAPTER` element".
- Entity names are also shown in fixed-pitch, but not all in capitals because entity names normally distinguish case in SGML.
- SGML reserved words as well as names appearing in the SGML declaration such as delimiter and feature names, appear in bold fixed-pitch capitals: "An **`RCDATA`** marked section".
- Sample SGML data may appear quoted (if short) or in boxes with a shaded background. It is always fixed-pitch: 'A tag such as "`<P>`" can have attributes'.
- Examples of alternative markup to support some capability in an amended SGML or a future markup language appear in different boxes from SGML examples, and the text points out the difference.
- Examples of invalid or erroneous SGML usage (that is, counter-examples) appear like other SGML examples but have "`<!-- WRONG -->`" at the beginning. Some of these examples could probably be made valid by creating enough unusual context (or at least by putting them inside comments!), but they are not valid in the context described in the text.
- SGML examples sometimes have portions indented to clarify the nesting relationships of elements. This may or may not be permissible in reality, depending in part on the DTD, since SGML has various rules for where whitespace is significant (see Question 1.8). In the few cases where the positions of line-breaks are important to the discussion, they are marked by the "¶" symbol.
- For brevity, examples often use an ellipsis ("...") to mark where additional SGML text has been omitted. Some examples would not be valid without some extra content, even though it is omitted if not relevant to the example.
- References to ISO standards use the word "Clause" and a number regardless of whether the portion is a full clause, a sub-clause, or a smaller unit.
- Quotations from ISO standards are set in sans serif type like the SGML standard itself uses: "only as provided in this sub-sub-clause, and only if the omission would not create an ambiguity, and if "OMITTAG YES" is specified". Quotations from the SGML standard incorporate Amendment 1.
- References to other parts of this book use the word "Chapter" or "Question" and a number: "See also Question 3.4".
- Digressions on technical points appear in separate boxes and start with "**Note:**".
- Web page addresses are shortened by omitting "http://" at the beginning (other schemes such as "ftp:" are retained).

# 1. For Authors and Document Editors Using SGML Tools

When you use an SGML-aware tool to edit SGML documents, the details of how SGML actually *represents* those documents may be hidden: as an author you may never need to know that "<P>" means anything special to SGML. However, some cases can come up where these details intrude. How often this happens depends on the particular tools you are using, and is usually more a question of the tool's style than of its quality.

Many of the questions in this chapter come up when your tool doesn't perfectly insulate you from the details of SGML syntax. For example, you may be typing in text and the system refuses to insert some character or sequence of characters you type. It may beep, give a more- or less-helpful error message, or something. Questions seldom arise when "all is well" in your editing session, so this chapter doesn't focus on concerns such as how to choose what tag to use, how to adjust formatting for different types of elements, or how to accomplish various editing functions. Rather, this chapter addresses a number of questions that come up when SGML syntax rules, perhaps unexpectedly, affect editing. SGML software varies in how well it hides these issues and therefore in how likely you are to run into them.

There are really two kinds of SGML-aware editing software (all this applies to HTML and HTML editors as well):

- The first kind hides things as much as possible, representing elements and other SGML objects graphically, perhaps with the tag name in an icon or bubble. This kind might be called a "GUI" or "WYSIWYG" editor (although "What You See" should not be *all* you get in SGML!). Typically, a new element would be created by choosing it's type from an "Insert Element" command, or something similar.

- The second kind lets you type and see the raw internal form of SGML, but checks the document and reports any errors as you go along. This kind is often built on top of a generic editor, for example emacs. Typically, a new element would be created by literally keystroking its type name along with the special characters SGML uses to mark tag names as opposed to text content (for example, "<P>").

Depending on the particular editing tool you're using you may run into these questions more or less often. The closer the tool stays to the "real" SGML representation that goes on underneath the interface, the more you will have to know about and deal with that representation.

This chapter tries to avoid pointy-brackets, since these are less important if you're using SGML-aware editing software at least of the first kind. However, it does show what your editing actions are likely to produce underneath, because when the software isn't doing what you hoped you may end up having to look under the SGML hood, and by seeing it here first you'll be more able to tell the spark plugs from the air filter. Even if you generally use a WYSIWYG tool, you will probably see raw SGML occasionally (at least, most people seem to, especially on the Web), and it's worth knowing the basic rules for how it fits together.

## 1.1. What characters or sequences of characters can't I just type in content?

SGML reserves certain characters and sequences of characters to mark the beginning and ending of various constructs, such as elements. For example, you may want a character such as "<" as a literal less-then sign, or to mark the beginning of a tag for an SGML element such as a paragraph. Thus if you type it into a place where it could serve either purpose you may get some kind of error signal.

Some SGML systems hide this detail well, but not all do. The issue is intrinsic in SGML because it is a side-effect of a feature of SGML that is, on the whole, a strength. Unlike most word-processors, SGML represents documents in a way that *can* be read even without SGML software. Unless you've been totally insulated from SGML representations by your software and have also somehow managed not to use the World Wide Web, you've probably seen things like:

```
<P>This book is about <EM>SGML</EM> users.</P>
```

This example represents a `P` element (the usual shorthand for "paragraph") containing some text and a `EM` element (shorthand for "emphasis"). The less-than sign signals to the computer that a tag is starting instead of just more text. Characters or character strings that signal information like that are called "delimiters", and each one in SGML has a name, such as "Start-tag open" or **STAGO** for the "<" shown at the beginning of start-tags above. The names make it possible for a DTD designer to change what actual strings perform each function, though it is a bit unusual to do so.

The main characters to be concerned about are "<", "&", and in very limited contexts "]", but all the strings that mean special things to SGML in content are shown here (other strings are special in certain other contexts, the most obvious being ">", which serves to end a tag when inside one, but is not special in content).

| String | Delimiter | Purpose |
|---|---|---|
| < | **STAGO** | Start a start-tag |
| </ | **ETAG** | Start an end-tag |
| <? | **PIO** | Start a processing instruction |
| <! | **MDO** | Start a markup declaration (including comments) |
| & | **ERO** | Start an entity reference |
| &# | **CRO** | Start a character entity reference |
| ]]> | **MSC+MDC** | End a marked section |
| / | **NET** | End an element (only in special circumstances) |

All but two of these cases start with either "<" or "&". "]]>" is important but very uncommon, and "/" is only a delimiter in very limited circumstances (see Question 1.5). So remembering three basic cases is usually enough. To use these sequences as data content, at least in certain contexts, you need to substitute something else for at least their first characters. The usual substitutes are "`<`" for less-then, "`&`" for ampersand, and "`[`" for left square bracket.

Most of the delimiters are only recognized "in context" of a certain kind, so you don't actually need to replace them with substitutes all the time. For example, the start-tag open delimiter "<" is only recognized if followed by a character that SGML allows at that point, such as a letter (which could start a tag name). If followed by a blank or certain other characters it is not "in context": "`< P >`" is data, not a start-tag.

The general rule that you should replace any less-than or ampersand in content (or any not followed by a space) will stand you in good stead. You may substitute in a few case that you don't technically need to, but you will almost never miss one that you do. If you also remember to take care of "]]>", the only snag left is if you use substitutes in the very rare contexts where they are not recognized, such as "**CDATA**" contexts (for details on those see Question 2.4).

You already have the essential answer to this question, so you can go on to another question if you wish. The next couple pages, however, fill in more details about just what those "contexts" are, broken down for the various delimiter characters and strings. If you want to know exactly when you can and can't use these strings literally without having to use a substitute, read on.

## Details on when you need to avoid delimiter strings

There are many advantages to representations that embed markup right in content. Many of them involve portability across various software and computer platforms, data longevity, version independence, and so on. On the other hand, there is a cost. Because "<" has a special meaning, if you try to type a literal "<" right into your text it may fall in a place where the computer takes it as starting a tag. If that happens you have to put in some substitute instead of a literal "<".

Depending on the tool you're using, you may insert an entity reference like those mentioned with a special command, or just type it as shown. An "entity reference" pulls in some other data (such as a less-than sign). Since the data is hidden behind the entity reference the computer needn't count it as markup. Some editing software may do the substitution for you automatically when you type "<", and display it as "<" unless you request something else. Thus you might never see this distinction.

However, there are cases where things may not go so smoothly. If your editing tool is of the second kind described above (one where you see the raw SGML form, but the tool continually checks it and reports errors), you will likely see "`<`" and may wonder why. This is especially true because SGML rules do not require *every* "<" to be substituted for; only ones in certain contexts. If your editing tool is of the first kind, you may see a special representation of the less-than sign or you may not, but a question may still arise because there are a few very special contexts where SGML doesn't even permit the standard substitution: if you hit one of those cases even a system that generally does the substitution automatically will have to complain instead.

Of course computers (being as smart as they are) can't "just know" when you want a literal less-than sign as opposed to a tag, or intuit your intent in the other cases that come up. Because of this SGML provides some rules about just *when* "<" means "less-than sign" and when it means "start a tag" (likewise for other special characters). This section describes some of those rules.

> **Note:** A table of all the SGML delimiters is in Appendix B. Those not listed above are recognized in other contexts, but not right in content ("**CON**" mode). For example, ">" (**TAGC**) is used to close start- and end-tags, and so is recognized as a delimiter only when *inside* a tag.

## Basic contexts where "<" needs to have a substitute

A "<" that is not literal character data is part of what is called "markup": the signals that tell the computer about how the document is structured and how it might be processed. If you want to understand the rules that determine when SGML will or won't find "<" objectionable, read on; otherwise skip to the next question, knowing you can (almost always) solve the problem by substituting "`<`".

The first rule is straightforward:

- If the next character after the "<" is a character that can start a tag name, the "<" is markup. Unless the DTD designer changed the settings, the characters that can start a tag name are simply the Latin letters A-Z. Normally capitalization makes no difference for tag names (throughout the book, "normally" means "unless the DTD designer changed something in the SGML declaration"). In non-English-speaking countries the list is often expanded to include additional letters or other symbols.

This is why software may wait and complain when you type a letter *after* the "<", instead of complaining as soon as you type the "<". It doesn't matter whether the tag name is OK or not: "`<ZHADJ>`" still is markup even if the DTD declares no element type called `ZHADJ`. In that case it's an error, so typing that string into content may result in some kind of error message.

"<" followed by a space is the most obvious case where the "<" is taken literally instead of as markup: "`< P >`" is not a start-tag. In that case there is no need to substitute "`<`".

> **Note:** A user recently asked on comp.text.sgml why they got no error messages for things like "`<3>`" in their documents even though they had never declared an element type named "`3`", and "`<3>`" sure looks like a start-tag for an element of type "`3`". The answer is that an element type name can't start with a digit, so the "<" is taken as literal data and no error is reported.

All these rules only apply in places where a start-tag could be recognized. Inside a quoted attribute value, for example, tags aren't allowed and so "<" isn't special (see the next question for more details on attribute values).

There are some other related cases where less-than is special: "<" is not only the string for opening start-tags, but also the first character in several other delimiter strings SGML uses for other purposes. A substitution is needed for them too (SGML's shorthand features, called "minimization", also add a few more cases described later):

- "`</`" starts an end-tag, but only given a similar rule about following context. It must be followed by a character that could start a tag name, or a couple other special cases involving minimization.
- "`<!`" starts various other SGML markup. In this case the requirement is that it be followed by some SGML construct that makes sense there, such as the start of a

comment ("<!--"), a marked section ("<!["), or a named declaration (indicated by a letter, as in "<!ELEMENT").

- "<?" starts a "processing instruction", which is another kind of markup much less common than tags. In this case it doesn't matter what character follows the "<?".

These are the basic cases where you can't type "<" (unless your software automatically protects you by substituting something else for it). The rules so far will likely cover most of the cases you see. However, there are possible additions: your DTD designer or document administrator may have changed one or more of the strings that are reserved to indicate markup, in which case you'll need to find out what they changed them to. Perhaps they changed "<!" to "{{" so that you can freely type "<!", but then you can't type "{{--", etc. Delimiter changes are very uncommon, however; most SGML applications stay with the normal delimiters.

> **Note:** The rules about what characters must immediately follow a delimiter for it to be recognized as a delimiter instead of as literal data content are called "contextual constraints". They are defined in Clause 9.6.2 of the SGML standard.

## Other contexts for "<"

SGML has several shorthand methods for expressing markup, designed in the days when markup had to be typed by hand (see next Chapter). A couple of these "minimization" methods add more cases where "<" must be escaped depending on the following character. If you are using a WYSIWYG SGML editor minimization is probably not an issue and you needn't care what shorthand the editor uses as long as it handles your "Insert Element" request correctly (most such editors use *no* shorthand). However, if you're using the other kind of SGML editor, or if you type certain strings into content that would be taken as markup, these cases may arise:

- A start-tag can sometimes be shortened to just "<>" (see Question 2.1 for the rules on what element type SGML fills in for you). There is never a *requirement* to shorten it, and most SGML editing software never writes out documents that do (though most accepts abbreviated forms when *reading* a document). If the feature that allows this (called **SHORTTAG**) is turned on, then "<" followed by ">" must be taken as markup, not data. Substituting "<" for the initial less-than sign resolves the conflict.

- If (and only if) SGML's **CONCUR** feature is used, then a less-than sign followed by an open parenthesis also counts as markup. This feature is very uncommonly used, so you may not have to avoid "<(".

## Other characters that must be substituted for

Similar rules apply to the ampersand character, "&" because it is used for marking up entity references. These are used to include data that isn't stored literally in-line in the document, for example "<" to refer to a less-than sign. Another familiar use of entity references is as a way of getting untypable special characters in HTML, such as "©" for the copyright symbol ("©"). Because of this reserved use "&" has to be replaced when it is followed by a letter, which could start an entity name. The usual replacement is "&".

Like "<", "&" is special in a few other contexts too. The main one is when it is combined with "#" to form a delimiter used to refer to characters by their computer code numbers or a few special SGML names. For example, on many systems "`A`" will get a capital A — though it's not a very easy or portable way to get an A. The end result is that "`&#`" is markup if it's followed by a letter *or a digit* (unlike various other delimiters which do not allow digits).

> **Note:** When used to mark an entity reference the ampersand is called the Entity reference open or **ERO** delimiter. The "**&#**" is similarly called the Character reference open or **CRO** delimiter.

The only other character string that normally has to be substituted within documents (ignoring Document Type Declarations for now) is "`]]>`". This is because it is used to signal the end of a "marked section", and in SGML that signal is recognized even if no marked section is in use (see Question 2.9 for more details). You can substitute "`]]>`" or various other alternatives if this string comes up.

The slash character ("`/`") must also be replaced with a substitute ( "escaped"), but in extremely limited circumstances. It only matters if you started some prior element with a start-tag that ended in slash instead of greater-then: "`<P/`" instead of "`<P>`". This is called a "**NET**-enabling start-tag" and is discussed in Question 1.4. But if you don't do start-tags that way you don't need to substitute anything for slashes in content.

### When to use substitutes

It is worth remembering that all these conditions only specify when you *must* use a substitute, such as for the ampersand in "`R&D`". You *may* use one nearly any time. If you need the content "`a < b`", the space after the "<" means you don't *need* to substitute "`<`", but it doesn't hurt to do so. So one tactic is just to replace *all* the literal less-thans and ampersands in your documents (and all right square-brackets as well, though the sequence "`]]>`" is rare enough that people sometimes skip that step).

Escaping these characters by substituting entity references everywhere works fine, with one exception: contexts where recognition of the entity references (such as "`<`") is suppressed, for example within a **CDATA** marked section, **CDATA** entity, or **CDATA** element (though not a **CDATA** attribute — see Question 2.4). In those rare cases the "`<`" will not be recognized as marking an entity reference, so cannot be used to get the desired effect. The related **RCDATA** constructs are similar except that entity references are still recognized. Some very sophisticated SGML software may manage all this for you; if you are fortunate enough to use such software you needn't bother learning which element types or other constructs in the DTDs and documents you use are of type **CDATA**.

> **Note:** References to special-character entities such as "`<`" and "`&`" are usually the easiest way to deal with any of the cases where a character or string that you want as literal text content would otherwise be taken as markup. However, there are other ways as well, described in Question 3.7.

## 1.2. When must I quote attributes?

Attributes are part of start-tags in SGML, and typically express properties or characteristics of the element that is starting, such as the `ACCESS` attribute below. "`ACCESS`" is the attribute's name, and "`PUBLIC`" is its value. The value may or may not be quoted, and may refer to entities (such as to get a quotation mark inside quotation marks). There are some special SGML terms distinguishing the more complicated cases, but we'll skip them for the moment:

```
<P ACCESS="PUBLIC">Today's lottery number will be announced
<TIP ACCESS="PRIVATE">and it will be 134217727.</TIP></P>
```

As with any other part of SGML, using a character-based representation for structure means that certain characters are reserved. In attributes, SGML has several rules you should know unless your authoring systems completely hides them. It is not trivial for software to do this perfectly, so you may well run into difficulty with a few attribute values from time to time. The basic rules are these:

- An attribute value needs to be quoted if it contains any characters that cannot occur in an SGML **NAME**. Normally (that is, under the reference concrete syntax settings), name characters include the 26 Latin letters (upper and lower case), digits, period, and hyphen (element types, attribute names, and entity names are all SGML **NAME**s).

> **Note**: One nice aspect of this rule is that any attribute the DTD designer set up to only allow a choice from a "menu" of values will never need quotes. That is because the values allowed in such cases are always SGML **NAME**s, and contain only the permitted characters.

- Either single (`'`) or double (`"`) straight quotes may be used, but not distinct open- versus close-quotes ('...' or "..."), or two single quotes as a way of typing each double quote (`''`).
- If you need single quotes inside an attribute value you can enclose the value in double quotes, and vice versa; but the only way to get both kinds in the same attribute value is to use an entity reference.

> **Note**: Technically, there is another way to get both kinds of quotes inside of attributes, but this chapter skips it because it requires quite advanced features and is almost never used.

- Entity references in attribute values are always replaced; there is no way to suppress it (since "&" is used to mark entity reference but is not a name character, any attribute value that does contain an entity reference must be quoted). Because of this you may need to substitute "`&`" for "&" in attribute values (again, your authoring system may automate this). See Questions 1.2 and 1.9 for more details.

Quoted attribute values are called "attribute value literals". Implementers sometimes assume that unquoted attribute values (not attribute value literals) can contain any characters other than space and ">". Space is clearly not allowed because it separates one attribute from the next, while ">" would clearly end the entire start-tag, and therefore the attribute as well. This assumption, however, is wrong, because any value that contains non-**NAME** characters must be quoted. Thus the quotes around the attribute value below are required:

```
<ENTRY ALIGNCHAR=",">98,6</ENTRY>
```

Some SGML systems report the error and then recover from it gracefully, but if you need to deal with a system that fails to report this kind of error, be careful to quote your attributes even when that particular system doesn't complain or your documents may not work in any other systems later.

## 1.3. What entities can I use in attributes?

Because entity references are always recognized in attribute values, it is not uncommon to see "`&`" in attribute values as a way of including a literal ampersand. Other entities can be referenced as well. However, all the restrictions on attribute values still apply after the reference is expanded: if you refer to an entity that contains a whole chapter (say, "`&chap1;`"), the attribute is treated as if the whole chapter were there in the attribute value. Unless your chapter is unusually succinct this would violate several rules governing the length and content of the attribute value. Questions 1.11 and 1.12 discusses how attributes can be used to *name* such entities without actually referring to them and pulling in their whole content as part of the attribute value.

In many DTDs various attributes are declared a bit more freely than the designer may have wished. Attributes are declared **CDATA** if they must contain anything but **NAME** characters. As discussed in Question 2.4, **CDATA** for attributes does not prevent recognition of entity references. Also, a **CDATA** attribute allows any value at all (subject to a maximum length), and so SGML itself cannot validate constraints on the form of such an attribute. There is no way to declare (for example) that a `CHAR` attribute must take a *single* character argument. This is a general limitation of the declared values, as discussed in Questions 1.9 and 6.9. With such attributes, authors must simply be careful to make their data conform not only to the SGML validation rules, but also to the intended conventions.

> **Note:** One user took advantage of the permissiveness of **CDATA** attributes to specify `WIDTH="real wide"`, `WIDTH="big"`, and similar attributes in their tables. The table DTD required numbers and units: `WIDTH="1.2I"`, `WIDTH="3M"`, etc., but had to declare `WIDTH` as **CDATA** because it was the only declared value loose enough. The user was quite surprised when the software failed to format their tables well, since the attribute values were "valid". But there's a very big difference between syntactic validity and semantic correctness. Moving information between attributes and subelements can sometimes help you get additional validation as discussed in Question 5.10, but even that can never completely guarantee that data is correct and meaningful.

In practice there is an additional limitation on what entities you can reference from attributes. Much otherwise-conforming SGML software supports entity references in attribute value literals only in limited ways, perhaps because some cases can be difficult to manage. The most important example is that many systems do not work well if you reference an **SDATA** entity from an attribute. **SDATA** entities are commonly used to represent various special characters, such as international characters not available in your local character set.

One example comes up with tables. The SGML Open Consortium surveyed just what vendors do and don't support from the much-used "CALS" table markup (which originated in a DTD for military equipment manuals). One feature of these tables is the ability to line up the information in a given column by some character, such as to line up columns of numbers at the decimal point regardless of how many digits each has. However, the character to line up need not be the decimal point: any character may be specified using the `ALIGN` and `CHAR` attributes. This is an important feature because not all countries use "`.`" as the decimal point character:

```
<TABLE>
   <TGROUP>
      <COLSPEC COLNAME="country" WIDTH="5*">
      <COLSPEC COLNAME="pop" WIDTH="5*"
         ALIGN="char" CHAR=",">
   </TGROUP>
   <ROW>
      <ENTRY COLNAME="country">China</ENTRY>
      <ENTRY COLNAME="pop">1400,0 M</ENTRY></ROW>
   <ROW>
      <ENTRY COLNAME="country">India</ENTRY>
      <ENTRY COLNAME="pop">800,0 M</ENTRY></ROW>
   <ROW>
      <ENTRY COLNAME="country">USA</ENTRY>
      <ENTRY COLNAME="pop">250,3 M</ENTRY></ROW>
   <ROW>
      <ENTRY COLNAME="country">France</ENTRY>
      <ENTRY COLNAME="pop">50,01 M</ENTRY></ROW>
</TABLE>
```

Although most products handle such cases fine if a single printable character other than single or double quote or ampersand is used, SGML Open discovered that virtually no software could do anything useful if the attribute referred to an **SDATA** entity (the kind of entity generally used to access special characters). For example, if you were to specify "`CHAR="…"`" in order to line up columns at ellipses ("..."s), all surveyed software would fail. Fortunately, aligning on characters other than period, comma, and a few others is uncommon enough that this is not a substantial problem in practice.

## 1.4. Can I use "/" in attributes?

SGML imposes certain rules on when attributes should be quoted, as discussed in the previous question. Some authoring systems quote attributes automatically, in which case authors may not need to know the rules; but many do not. In that case, an unquoted attribute value with any non-name characters (say, in data being imported) usually leads to the parser immediately reporting a syntax error, and the problem gets solved. But in one special case there is usually no syntax error: if the first non-name character is "/" then the start-tag simply ends earlier than intended, and the rest of the attribute list becomes character data. This occurs because of an SGML capability known as the "null end-tag" or **NET**.

SGML duplicates a feature of a long-lost IBM word processor called Janus, which had the distinction of showing a tagged view and a formatted view simultaneously (see André, Furuta, and Quint 1989). This was done in the days before window interfaces — ingeniously using two separate monitors. In SGML as in Janus, a start-tag that ends with "/" instead of ">" means that a later "/" occurring in text content will be taken as the corresponding end-tag. The following forms thus represent the same element structure:

```
<EMPH>very</EMPH>
<EMPH/very/
```

In certain cases, a slash that is meant to be part of an attribute value can therefore lead to wildly wrong results. In the following real-life example, an author neglected to put quotes around the attribute value "42/a", and so "/a>" is not taken as part of the start-tag's attribute, but as the **NET** delimiter and two characters of content. No syntax error results, so the logical error is likely to go unnoticed until a reader of the document complains about seeing a mysterious "a>" in the text they are reading.

```
<p ln=42/a>Intended content of paragraph.</p>
```

This kind of error is very common in HTML files because some HTML parsers deviate from the SGML standard by accepting all characters except space and ">" in unquoted attributes, and because URLs nearly always contain slashes:

```
<!-- WRONG -->
<a href=//xyz.com/skating/lakeplacid97/ad/BrMII/lutz.gif>
```

Fortunately complete URLs have a colon before the first slash (for example beginning "`http:`") and so will generate a syntax error because the colon is not an SGML name character. However, partial URLs may not include the colon, and thus can lead to surprises. The simplest way to avoid this problem is to always quote your attributes.

## 1.5. Why did adding a "/" in content change my document structure?

Typically, SGML authoring systems do not prevent inserting slashes in text content. This is because the slash character is only meaningful to SGML under certain very limited conditions. However, it may happen that a document created with such slashes is modified later, or saved in a way that raises those conditions, making the slash into markup instead of data. In that case the structure can radically change, because in just the right context a lone slash in content can be treated as an end-tag.

The special condition is that some open element has been started with a "**NET**-enabling start-tag". Such a start-tag ends with a different delimiters: for example, "`<P/`", which changes the meaning of a later "/" in content from data to markup (see Clauses 7.4.1.3 and 7.5.1.3 of the SGML standard and the previous question here). If content with "/" happens later to be pasted within the element (from another file, another editing system, or wherever), that act of pasting changes the end-tag's location to be wherever the "/" falls. This may or may not lead to a syntax error, but will nearly always have an unintended effect on the document's structure.

For example, pasting the seemingly-innocuous `P` into the `SEC` here would cause the `SEC` to end prematurely, namely between the `1` and `2` (the slash is also no longer part of the character content). If **#PCDATA** is allowed in `SEC` then no syntax error necessarily arises, though surely the meaning is not what the user intended:

```
<SEC/
   <P>It's about 1/2 mile back up the road.
```

This is less common in a WYSIWYG SGML editor, but a very easy error in less-graphical ones. The reverse error can also arise because an innocuous slash in content can become an end-tag without being moved, for example if someone adds a **NET**-

enabled container *around* it, or moves the element containing it into a **NET**-enabled container elsewhere.

Note: Much the same questions may arise with the **MSOCHAR** and **MSICHAR** function characters. **MSOCHAR** (Markup Scan Out) is a locking shift: it turns markup recognition off completely until the next **MSICHAR** (see Clauses 9.7 and 13.4.4). If one of these characters unintentionally occurs (I have heard of, but not seen, one occurring intentionally), it may have surprising effects on later markup. The result will be even more surprising if the character occurs within a marked section, or if you accidentally carry it into one when you copy and paste some content later. Unlike undesired delimiters, these are function characters and have no default values; thus they can be ignored unless you encounter an SGML declaration whose author assigned them.

The easiest ways to completely avoid unintended **NET**s are to ask your DTD designer to turn off **SHORTTAG**, or to always quote all attributes. The first option has a drawback because the most useful aspects of SGML minimization are certain parts of **SHORTTAG** and so turning them *all* off is not ideal. The SGML review and revision process going on now will likely provide ways to turn each kind of minimization on or off separately; should that happen your DTD designer could avoid the **NET** question simply by turning off **NET** minimization.

Note: Defining **NET** out of existence by assigning no concrete character string at all to the **NET** delimiter role in the SGML declaration would solve the problem, but this is not possible in SGML because there is no way to specify it in the SGML declaration. A DTD designer could define **NET** to be some bizarre string, such as "`"!&^%&@#@`" or perhaps even a string containing special characters outside the 7-bit range, thus making it highly *improbable* that the delimiter will ever accidentally occur. However, there is no guarantee.

## 1.6. My SGML comments somehow turn into errors. What's happening?

SGML uses two hyphens as the delimiter to mark off comments ("`--`"). So when you insert a comment it will get stored in SGML with two hyphens at each end. But two hyphens is also a common keyboarding convention, used to type the long- or em-dash used to separate parts of a sentence — like this one. If you are trying to type a comment delimiter in a non-WYSIWYG SGML editor or in a word-processor from which you plan to export SGML later, you may find the software translating two dashes into a special em-dash character without asking. Some will even change "`-->`" into a right-pointing arrow character. The (erroneous) SGML could look like this:

```
<!-- WRONG -->
<!-- This comment is long—>
```

This should raise the mechanical ire of your editor or parser because the long dash is not a valid comment delimiter in SGML (neither is a pair of them, should that case arise). This error also can come up when you paste data from other programs into your SGML documents, or when you (or someone else) run a later program on your SGML to spell-check it, "clean it up" somehow, insert ligatures, hyphenate, or whatever.

**Note:** It is possible that no error will be reported. In the example above the comment stays open, and it could happen that the next double hyphen in the document is followed by ">". In that case the comment just closes there, and perhaps no later error will arise.

Nearly every SGML book I have seen contains typographical errors of this kind involving comment delimiters, perhaps because there are many comments in examples. Even books or chapters that SGML experts reviewed thoroughly have suffered at the hands of non-SGML-aware typesetters after the last review. Unfortunately, most editing and final page layout programs do not know about SGML and may do such transformations even when they shouldn't.

A truly SGML-aware system is not likely to make this mistake in the markup it is handling, but it may still do it in content where markup recognition is suppressed such as in examples of SGML usage (that is why the problem is widespread specifically in SGML books). This occurs because an SGML tool does not think of that content as being SGML: it's just an example. So if a document contains

```
<![ CDATA [
<p><!-- this is a sample SGML comment -->
]]>
```

it may well show up in print with long dashes rather than two hyphens. Even authors or typesetters who know about the SGML issue may introduce the problem: they may construct a clever program that leaves hyphens intact in markup while changing them in content, yet still forget content that is specifically SGML examples. Some editor interfaces and some fonts also make it difficult to see the difference on-screen, which makes the error harder to catch.

Using some other string for the comment delimiter (**COM**) prevents the problem:

```
<!* comment *>
<!// comment //
  // more comment //>
```

DTD designers can make this change via the SGML declaration (assuming their parser supports the option of variant delimiters). Even so, as discussed in Question 7.3 they cannot set the comment start and comment end delimiters separately, so a comment syntax like the one shown below is not possible in SGML (the SGML review going on now may add the delimiter distinction, making such syntax possible in the future):

```
<!-- WRONG -->
<! /* comment */ >
```

The only other workaround is to be careful: be sure to turn off any software features that affect "- -", and be thorough about your proofreading even to the very last stage. And be sure to tell anyone who might handle your data, so that they don't run into the same problem.

The next question discusses why you can't just put "- -" inside of an SGML comment; Question 7.8 discusses a different issue with hyphen, that arises because it is an allowed character in SGML names as well as appearing in delimiters like **COM**.

## 1.7. Why can't I type "- -" inside a comment?

Authors often assume that comments in SGML involve just an opening delimiter "<!--" and a closing delimiter "-->", but this is not exactly correct. Actually the comment just runs from one double hyphen to the next, and one or more such comments is then placed between the "<!" and the ">" (making a "comment declaration"). Because of this, "--" is not allowed inside a comment.

If the assumption just described *were* true, "-->" would logically be the only thing not permitted within comment text: "--" without a following ">" would be perfectly fine inside a comment and be taken just as a literal part of the comment's text. Although that might be analogous to how many computer languages do comments, SGML's comment syntax is slightly more complex. The "<!" is a separate delimiter used to start all kinds of "markup declarations" (the building blocks document type designers use to create new sets of tags or DTDs). A markup declaration is ended by ">". Comments themselves go *inside* those markup declarations and are of the form "--...--", where "--" is a separate SGML delimiter just for comments.

> **Note:** The delimiters involved are: "<!" (called **MDO** for Markup Declaration Open), "--" (call **COM** for Comment), and ">" (called **MDC** for Markup Declaration Close). Even some HTML systems have implemented comments the incorrect way, which can lead to inconsistent results when comments with "--" inside crop up. See Question 7.1 for much more information on SGML delimiters.

Because of this two-layer structure a comment is really ended by two dashes, not by two dashes plus ">". Since this is true, comment text cannot contain "--". The case to avoid is accidentally using "--" to separate parts of a sentence within a comment:

```
<!-- WRONG -->
<!-- Comments are--usually--simple. -->
```

This will not work without escaping the **COM** delimiter somehow (such as using **MSSCHAR** — see Question 3.7); it is better to avoid putting dashes inside comments.

After a comment ends, the markup declaration remains open until the ">". This structure does allow you to put any number of comments in a single markup declaration so long as there is nothing but whitespace between them:

```
 <!-- part 1 --     -- part 2 --
   -- part 3 -->
```

It is also allowed to have *no* comments inside the markup declaration, in which case it amounts to an empty markup declaration ("<!>").

> **Note:** The empty markup declaration does not have any other real meaning in SGML. It does cause another rule about when the **MDO** delimiter is recognized. It can be used to separate a special character from its following context, as a way of getting the character literally. For example, if you are in an editor that shows you actual SGML markup you can put "<P>" into content as data rather than as a tag, by substituting either "<P>" or "<<!>P>".

A comment is considered part of a markup declaration because comments are very commonly needed inside declarations. Given that, requiring that comments always go inside markup declarations is symmetrical, even though authors sometimes ask why a comment declaration does not declare any markup.

Questions can also arise if someone confuses the syntax to produce:

```
<!-- WRONG -->
<!--...--!>
```

This is incorrect in SGML, although it is symmetrical. Fortunately the " ! " falls outside the comment proper and is not whitespace, so it produces an immediate syntax error and is easy to catch.

Some versions of some Web browsers have implemented comments in a different way from either of these. On seeing "<!" they merely skip to the next ">" regardless of what intervenes. Such a program will accept the *incorrect* comment above, which is perhaps less painful than if it failed to accept *correct* comments; but then you cannot have ">" inside comments (or in markup declarations, which are essentially treated as if they were comments). This means that you cannot "comment out" undesired tags. For example, with the (valid) input shown below, an incorrect program would take the ">" after "P" as ending the markup declaration, and then you'd get " -->" as leftover content in the document:

```
<!-- <P> -->
```

Errors can be avoided by always remembering that "--" is not allowed inside comments. The SGML review is considering adding a "simple comments" setting to the SGML declaration, so DTD designers can turn off the multiple-comment capability and make the syntax correspond to the common user perception. If that happens, then making sure that setting is used will help avoid surprises.

## 1.8. When can I use whitespace?

Whitespace characters such as spaces, tabs, and carriage-returns or newlines can be used almost anywhere in SGML documents. However, they are only treated as actual data in certain places; otherwise they are ignored. Since the rules are complex, some SGML authoring systems restrict where you can type whitespace characters. Many more details are covered in Question 2.5 because they arise mainly for authors without SGML-aware editing software. This question discusses some basic distinctions, namely:

- Whitespace that occurs inside markup rather than in content, such as within tags and attributes.
- Whitespace in two different kinds of content, called "element" and "mixed".

### Whitespace inside markup

Spaces within SGML constructs such as start- and end-tags are said to be *in markup*, while ones down in the text are *in content*. Spaces in markup rarely have any meaning other than their use to separate things. For example, no SGML system I know of will process the tags on each line below differently, and no DTD claims to expect distinct processing (though in theory they could):

```
<P TYPE=TOPIC>
<P    TYPE    = TOPIC    >
<P
TYPE
=
TOPIC
>
```

An SGML-aware system would not typically distinguish such cases, such as by displaying the first P element above in bold, the second indented specially, and the third another way; or by indexing them in different ways. The SGML standard does not prohibit such distinctions, but it is generally agreed that they are not meaningful, and very few SGML systems bother with them.

> **Note**: This tendency excludes one trivial case: a program whose specific goal is to copy a file with no changes. Such a program may *preserve* spacing distinctions, as might a program to copy an SGML document with changes, such as renaming some or all P elements to PARA. In the same way, a vanilla editor like WordPad or vi will show the lines exactly as shown above, since they do no SGML-aware processing of the data at all.

## Whitespace inside quoted attributes

Within quoted attribute values spaces are generally discarded as well. For example, an **ID** attribute can be specified in any of these ways and not count as different:

```
<SEC ID=SEC32A>
<SEC ID="SEC32A">
<SEC  ID = "   SEC32A
"  >
```

The SGML standard actively declares that quoted attribute values are "normalized" by applying the three steps below. This applies regardless of their declared value type (see Clause 7.9.3).

1. Replacing entity references
2. Ignoring entity ends and record starts.
3. Turning other whitespace characters (such as record ends and tabs) into spaces.

For attributes declared to be **CDATA** this is all that happens. So in this example:

```
<!ENTITY tei.ed         "CMSMCQ
    LB">
<!ATTLIST  X
   RESP     CDATA        #IMPLIED>
...
<X RESP="   SJD DGD     &tei.ed;">
```

the RESP attribute's value ends up as shown below:

```
   SJD DGD     CMSMCQ      LB
```

However, for all types other than **CDATA** even more whitespace is normalized, "by replacing a sequence of SPACE characters with a single SPACE character and ignoring leading or trailing SPACE characters". This is useful because extraneous spaces do not get in the way of **ID**, **IDREF**, or other comparisons and searches. Also, attributes whose values include lists of tokens become simplified, with the tokens each separated by single spaces. So with the same example except that RESP is declared **NAMES** instead of **CDATA**, the attribute value ends up as shown below:

```
SJD DGD CMSMCQ LB
```

If *all* spaces were discarded the attribute above would end up as "SJDDGDCMSMCQLB", which would be wrong. But beyond their function as separators whitespace characters mean little or nothing in attribute values.

### Whitespace in content

In content the issues become more complex. SGML distinguishes two kinds of content (Clause 7.6), although the distinction is commonly ignored except when whitespace questions come up. The types are:

- **Element content**: This applies to element types that when used may only contain other elements, but not **#PCDATA** (text content). Most large or high-level elements have element content.
- **Mixed content**: This applies to element types that when used may contain **#PCDATA** as well as elements. Elements that only allow **#PCDATA** and no subelement type also have mixed content in SGML terminology; there is no special term for "**#PCDATA**-only content".
- **Declared content**: This applies to element types that have special restrictions on their content, such as always being **EMPTY**, or suppressing the use of delimiters (as commonly needed within examples).

Whitespace is treated differently in element content versus mixed content. For **EMPTY** declared content whitespace is obviously irrelevant. When markup is suppressed (declared content "**CDATA**" or "**RCDATA**" whitespace is treated as in mixed content.

In element content whitespace is considered to amount to "s" separators and "If it is considered part of an s it is ignored". The underlying rules are found in Clauses 7.6, 6.2.1, and 6.2; see also Question 7.9 and Clause 7.6.1. What the rules amount to for the user is that whitespace in element content can be inserted freely, but should not show up in the displayed form of documents. The rules reflect two principles:

- First, since **#PCDATA** is not permitted in element content (by definition), if whitespace was not ignored it would produce an error, which would not be helpful.
- Second, authors who type markup without benefit of SGML software like to be able to lay it out legibly by inserting extra space between elements, such as starting each tag on a new line. This means whitespace gets inserted solely for ease of typing, and it makes sense for SGML to discard such whitespace (the other obvious choice would be to count it as data and leave it up to stylesheets or formatters to avoid putting in extra blank lines if they are not wanted).

In mixed content SGML tries to apply the same abstract idea: whitespace is said to be ignored when it is "attributable to markup", or more simply, when SGML figures it's there for that same reason of laying out the hand-typed SGML document to look better when completely unformatted. The rules for which line-breaks are "attributable to markup", however, are generally considered the most complicated feature of SGML — it may still be practical to name all the people that understand them.

More of the details are discussed in Question 2.5, but a few parts of the rules are summarized here. Record boundaries in SGML files appear as abstract record start (**RS**) and record end (**RE**) characters during parsing. Except with certain uses of SGML's advanced **SHORTREF** feature, **RS** characters are always ignored, so only **RE**s are much of an issue. Exactly which **RE**s are ignored is complex, but generally a single **RE** (in effect, a single line-break) at the very beginning and end inside an element is ignored. So the two P elements below count as the same:

```
<P>hello</P>
...
<P>
hello
</P>
```

The full rules get a little more complicated because some things can intervene between the start- or end-tag and the **RE**. For example, a processing instruction or a comment doesn't count as separating the line-break from the start- or end-tag (SGML authoring systems may provide special commands for inserting each of these):

```
<P><!-- still the same -->
hello
<?pagebreak></P>
```

Note, however, that if any *data* occurs, that does count as separating the line-break from the tag, and then the line-break then is *not* ignored:

```
<P> <!-- still the same -->
hello
<?pagebreak> </P>
```

There are also some rules about multiple line-breaks occurring together (thus producing empty lines) in the middle of elements. SGML does not ignore tabs or spaces in mixed content as it ignores some **RE**s; this fact leads to an important case: the common method of laying out lists with leading spaces on each line will lead an SGML parser to pass back all those spaces. See Question 2.5 for more details on SGML's whitespace handling rules.

Some authors avoid these rules entirely by removing all line-breaks before processing (they typically change each to a space, not to nothing, so that wordsdon'tjoinup). Others use software features to delete extra whitespace during formatting (some software may do it automatically). Most SGML authoring systems try to prevent problems from the beginning, either by preventing authors from typing in line-breaks at all or by eliminating them later. However, they cannot do this where text content is actually allowed: they have no way of telling for sure whether you "really meant" the whitespace or not.

The safest way to avoid these issues is not to use line breaks in SGML input. This is seldom difficult except for a very few element types, such as poetry and program code examples where it may be a pain to put every line in a separate element, such as the HTML PRE element. Some (but not all) SGML systems provide a special stylesheet setting that causes line breaks and other whitespace to be preserved in such elements. Some other SGML editing systems prevent typing in line-breaks without some special action, in which case your documents need not be affected by the whitespace rules.

## 1.9. Can I prevent entity recognition in attributes?

No. Entity references are always recognized in attribute values, even those of type **CDATA**. The usual way to get around this is to substitute "`&`" for any needed ampersand characters (suppressing markup with special function characters is also possible, but rarely done).

SGML provides an attribute declared value called **CDATA**. However, this term means something different for attributes than anywhere else it is used in SGML. All attributes (regardless of their declared values) have entities replaced, much like **RCDATA** content. Declared values are better viewed as testing the value that results after all other processing such as entity replacement, whitespace normalization, and case-folding occur.

No declared values affect delimiter recognition in attribute values. The meaning of the **CDATA** keyword generally involves suppressing markup recognition; but applying that notion to the declared value **CDATA** would be incorrect. The only way to suppress markup recognition in attributes is with the rarely used "markup scan suppression" characters discussed in Clause 7.5 and Question 3.7. It is better to think of declared value types (including **CDATA**) as constraining attribute value *after* all entities are replaced.

> **Note**: There are potential uses for a way to suppressing markup in recognition within attributes, as well as for declared values that reflect additional SGML constructs. See Question 6.10 for more on this.

The most common question thus arises when someone defines a **CDATA** attribute in hopes of permitting ampersand as a literal character within it. This eventually leads to a syntax or logical error:

```
<!-- WRONG -->
<P TYPE="important&easy">
```

The simplest work-around is to reference an entity to get the desired ampersand. The usual entity is named `amp`, so the example above could be expressed as:

```
<P TYPE="important&amp;easy">
```

Although **CDATA** does not suppress recognition of entity references in attributes, it does affect on how whitespace within attributes is treated, and whether letters are forced to uppercase. These treatments cannot be separated. For example, you cannot get case-folding without getting whitespace normalization, or permit non-name non-digit characters without giving up case-folding. To prevent a delimiter string such as ampersand from being taken as the start of an entity reference inside attributes, you must substitute something else, such as "`&`".

## 1.10. Why aren't my cross-references working since I started using special characters?

SGML **IDs** and **IDREFs** may only contain **NAME** characters, normally letters, digits, period and hyphen. They also normally ignore case distinctions: "`chap1`" and "`ChAP1`" count as the same. Sometimes authors or DTD designers want to use additional characters. One way to get this effect is to change the DTD so it declares attributes that are conceptually **IDs**, to actually be of declared content **CDATA**. But a side-effect comes up, because **CDATA** not only permits many extra characters, but also regards case distinctions. So after this change, those two values are no longer considered the same and cross-references based on them will fail.

Such redefinition is tempting as an easy way to allow extra characters, but can be confusing because your logical **IDs** are no longer syntactically **NAMEs** as true SGML **IDs** are. One often sees DTDs that started out using **IDs** but later changed to **CDATA**; usually the attributes stay named ID, RID, or similar because that is what they are conceptually and because authors quite reasonably don't want to go back and change all their documents:

```
<!ATTLIST  XREF
   ID       CDATA         #REQUIRED
   TYPE     NAME          #IMPLIED>
```

But after such a change it is very easy to forget that the change made the attributes case- and whitespace-sensitive. That may lead to hyperlinks that fail later on because the destination's **CDATA** attribute doesn't exactly match the case of the origin's. Software that just obeys the parsing rules then cannot locate the intended destination; it must do some extra work on its own.

To alleviate this problem some software products search for **IDs** first in all upper-case as they "should" be, and if that fails they try again without case-folding to catch any that were declared **CDATA**. Some other software does not do this by default, but can be set up to do it, or to do *all* searches ignoring case, regardless of the destination's type. In other situations the only workarounds are to resist the temptation to use **CDATA** (and re-define one's names to fit), or to provide some proofing process for ensuring that the case does not actually vary. For more on this issue see Question 4.3.

## 1.11. Why don't I always put "&" in front of an entity name in an attribute?

The attribute declared value **ENTITY** lets you provide the name of an entity as a complete attribute value. This just *names* or *mentions* the entity, and does not *reference* it in the way that would occur if you put "&" and ";" around it (which is also possible within attributes. That is, naming an entity in this way does not make the SGML parser go out and get it and take the entity's replacement text as the real value, as it would if the ampersand were present (see Clause 7.9.4.3).

If the entity were a chapter, pulling it all in as the attribute's value by including the semicolon could be quite an error. There is a world of difference between the first P tag below and the others:

```
<!ATTLIST  P
   ENTNAME ENTITY        #IMPLIED
   TYPE    CDATA         #IMPLIED>
<!ENTITY   fangorn       "Hello, world"
...
<P ENTNAME="fangorn">
<P TYPE="&fangorn;">
<P TYPE="Hello, world">
```

In the first case, the value defined for entity `fangorn` is irrelevant to parsing; the `ENTNAME` attribute has a 7-character value, not a 12-character value. Some application might later retrieve the `fangorn` entity (for example when the user clicks to follow a hypertext link), but that is long after the SGML parsing is done. On the other hand, the `TYPE` attribute in the second `P` has a 12-character value, and the application will typically never know that it was any different from the third case shown.

**Note**: This is closely related to what philosophers and linguists call this a "use/mention" distinction, and it can be quite important in human language as well as in SGML.

This distinction is not a limitation, merely a real but subtle difference that may take a while to master. Mentioning entities rather than referring to them directly is very useful, but some SGML systems cannot make use of **ENTITY** attributes as well as they ought to. This is because they only get what is called the "ESIS" information about the SGML structure, and this does not include information about which attributes are of type **ENTITY** and therefore candidates for entity retrieval after parsing. Some software does handle this case, by retaining extra information ("beyond ESIS") such as the external identifier for referenced entities. The "groves" that DSSSL introduced to formalize SGML document trees can also include that information (see Question 5.11).

It is important to keep in mind whether you really want the value of the entity fetched and made part of the attribute value, or whether you just want the name and reference information about the entity kept for later use (for example in hyperlinking). Keeping these two notions very clear will help avoid problems. Also, it is worth checking just what your software can do with entity mentions, to be sure it can do what you need.

## 1.12. What kind of entities can I mention on ENTITY attributes?

The previous question discussed the distinction between *referring* to an entity from content or an attribute, versus merely *naming* an entity in an attribute of type **ENTITY** or **ENTITIES**. Clause 7.9.4.3 of SGML restricts such attributes to naming **SUBDOC** or data entities (such as **NDATA**, **SDATA**, **CDATA**, and **PI**). If you name any other kind of entity an SGML parser should report an error.

Most entities that authors want to mention in this way are **NDATA**, which are typically associated with external data objects such as a multimedia presentation or graphic to be retrieved and displayed somehow. To do this you would create an entity name for the external data file or other object, and then insert that name as the value of the particular attribute. The DTD designer usually provides the declarations needed so that you can tell SGML what **NOTATION** the entity is in (such as JPEG), and a stylesheet that causes the entity to be retrieved and displayed at the proper time.

**SUBDOC** is another kind of entity that can be named on an **ENTITY** attribute, and is used to mention another SGML document. As with other **ENTITY** attributes this does not cause the entity to be retrieved as part of the document that names it. However, systems can be built to retrieve and display the mentioned document at viewing-time as a "live quotation".

> **Note:** **SUBDOC** entities do have the limitations that they must use the same SGML declaration as the referencing document, and must be complete SGML documents, not specific sub-parts. This affects their use in multilingual settings and for quotation, especially the active type that hypermedia experts call "transclusion".

Naming an **SDATA** entity might be useful in a DTD for tables, so the table could have columns aligned on any character at all (not just a decimal point, the most common case). This might also help assure that the value be a single character, though there is no real guarantee (see Question 1.3 for more on such cases in tables).

**PI** entities (used to store "processing instructions") could also be useful, such as to specify processing information that applies to an element. For example, the CLASS attribute in HTML can point to a stylesheet entry, as can the REND attribute in the Text Encoding Initiative *Guidelines*. A style specification can be thought of as a kind of "processing instruction", and using a **PI** entity to name it has some advantages:

- As compared to inserting processing instructions in content, a **PI** named on an attribute is clearly associated with the element as a whole rather than appearing ("<?...>") at a point location somewhere near the start-tag (some processing effects like a forced page-break may want exactly the opposite meaning, and so would logically go in content).
- As compared to just stating a style name on a **NAME** or similar attribute, using a **PI** entity allows declaring and validating that the names used represent the right kind of information.
- As compared to putting the whole rendition description in a **CDATA** or similar attribute, using a **PI** entity allows re-use of similar descriptions, and allows isolating the processing instruction content from the document.

However, beyond all of these authors frequently want to name plain old SGML text entities on attributes: not entire documents, just portions of SGML content such as a paragraph to be quoted or linked. Such portions are commonly called "fragments", and they cannot be named on **ENTITY** attributes as such. It is often useful to quote portions of external documents, but that can only be done by "promoting" such an entity to either **NDATA** or **SUBDOC**. A fragment is not an entire document: SGML allows SGML text entities to start and stop almost anywhere, without regard to element, marked section, or other boundaries. See Question 2.13 for more on this.

To get the most benefit from naming SGML text entities, for example to support retrieving them and displaying them, they would have to be parsable without benefit of all the preceding context of their "home" document (or documents!). This involves some technical subtleties for SGML in general, but SGML Open fragments and XML documents do have this useful property, so if your SGML system supports these then you may be able to do this.

Otherwise the usual workaround for naming entities that aren't of permitted kinds is to declare a special notation named something like "SGML" or "FRAGMENT", and then declare the entities as **NDATA** of that type. This does generally work if the entities obey the necessary syntax constraints for parsing. On the other hand, a **NOTATION** that happens to be named "SGML" means no more to an SGML parser than one named "TIFF" and so a reference to data in it will not cause the SGML content to be parsed. Clause A.2.1 of HyTime provides such **NOTATION** declarations for SGML and HyTime itself (though it prefixes the **PUBLIC** identifiers with "+//"; the form here is that specified by ISO 9070):

```
<!NOTATION SGML         PUBLIC
   "ISO 8879:1986//NOTATION
   Standard Generalized Markup Language//EN">
<!NOTATION HyTime       PUBLIC
   "ISO/IEC 10744:1992//NOTATION
   Hypermedia/Time-based Structuring Language//EN">
```

Given that, one can just declare some SGML data to be mentioned as being in that **NOTATION**. However, that entity cannot also be referenced from content unless you declare it again *without* the **NDATA** suffix (as a data entity, it would not be parsed). If the data does constitute an entire document conforming to some DTD then **SUBDOC** will serve for both cases, but that is not always the case.

```
<ENTITY chap1.s         SYSTEM "c:\sgml\chap1.sgm"
                        NDATA SGML>
<ENTITY chap1           SYSTEM "c:\sgml\chap1.sgm">
```

### Interaction of ENTITY and NOTATION attributes

A more sophisticated use of **ENTITY** attributes is for an element that can only name graphical entities, but that has one **ENTITY** attribute for a PNG or TIFF form (for speed) and one for a CGM (for precision, scalability, or other needs). This can be done by declaring multiple **ENTITY** attributes or a single **ENTITIES** attribute. However, SGML is unaware of any intended restrictions on what **NDATA** types can go with which attributes or attribute portions. One cannot duplicate the **NOTATION** information on the element, because a **NOTATION** attribute is expected to specify the (single) **NOTATION** of the *element's* content, not of any entities it happens to mention.

> **Note**: The SGML review could remove or loosen the entity type restriction, or provide a way to declare what types of entities could be named on any given attribute, or provide intrinsic support for SGML fragments, but it is not certain.
>
> **ATTLIST** declarations could also be amended to add a way to declare just which types of entities may be named on a given attribute, or which **NOTATION**s are allowed for which **ENTITY** attributes, as is done for **NOTATION** attributes.

At present, authors must handle any constraints on particular uses of **ENTITY** attributes as application conventions, built or managed outside of SGML proper (though hopefully by the same overall program).

## 1.13. Why don't my special character ("SDATA") entities work?

This probably means that your **SDATA** entities are not set up correctly for the system you are on. The solution is to obtain SDATA entity definition files that are set up for the particular software system you are using. SDATA entities are one of the few places SGML reserves to handle system-to-system variation, and they generally need to be replaced for each different system.

How special characters work varies greatly from one country and one computer system to another, and SGML's **SDATA** feature inherits some of that non-portability. Question 5.20 discusses this question further, because the solutions get a bit technical.

# 1.14. I moved a section of my document and a lot of attributes changed values. Does this have something to do with "#CURRENT"?

Among the "default values" for SGML attributes is the value **#CURRENT** (Clause 11.3.4), and it can result in this kind of behavior. **#CURRENT** means that if an element instance doesn't specify an explicit value for the attribute, the value is taken to be whatever value was *last* specified for that attribute. So if A was declared to have default value **#CURRENT**, then the last two P elements in this example are considered to have A=1:

```
<P ID="P1" A="2">...</P>
<P ID="P2" A="1">...</P>
<P ID="P3">...</P>
```

Thus, if you move any of these element around relative to the others you may find that P3's value for the A attribute changes. In other words, simple editing can have surprising effects. For example, assume that the SECURE attribute below has default value **#CURRENT**:

```
<P SECURE="SHARED">Welcome to Lotto-Web</P>
...
<P SECURE="SECRET">Tomorrow's lottery number is 459230.</P>
...
<P>And the day after, the number will be 062862.</P>
...
<P SECURE="SHARED">Buy lots of tickets.</P>
```

The third paragraph is SECRET because of **#CURRENT**. However, editing can easily make it non-secret unless the person doing the editing is expert and very careful. For example, any of these changes will make it SHARED:

- making the second paragraph SHARED
- moving the third paragraph to be first, second, or last
- pasting the last paragraph between the second and third
- creating a new SHARED P before it.

None of these will result in a syntax error except moving the endangered paragraph so early in the document that *no* element that sets this attribute precedes it (this is because with **#CURRENT**, the very first occurrence must always give an explicit value).

An author is likely not to notice these effects, because there is no limit on the size or structure of the gaps (shown as "...") between **#CURRENT** attribute instances. Authors might expect that if they merely copy the "ad" as shown below, the CHAP break "resets" SECURE, but in SGML it does not. It is especially easy to assume this without realizing it when each chapter has a different author. So in this example a simple edit has made information insecure:

```
<P SECURE="SHARED">Welcome to lotto-Web</P>
<CHAP>
<P SECURE="SECRET">Tomorrow's lottery number is 459230.</P>
<P SECURE="SHARED">Buy lots of tickets.</P>
</CHAP>

<CHAP>
<P>And the day after, the number will be 062862.</P>
<P SECURE="SHARED">Buy lots of tickets.</P>
</CHAP>
```

This happens even if CHAP declares a SECURE attribute. As discussed in Question 1.15, **#CURRENT** attributes share their "current" value across different element types if (and only if) they share the same SGML **ATTLIST** declaration. Thus, with these declarations CHAP and P share the same "last value" at all times (they can still have different content models):

```
<!ATTLIST  (CHAP, P)
   SECURE  (SECRET | SHARED)        #CURRENT>
```

while with this form they would have two completely unrelated values:

```
<!ATTLIST  CHAP
   SECURE  (SECRET | SHARED)        #CURRENT>
<!ATTLIST  P
   SECURE  (SECRET | SHARED)        #CURRENT>
```

Even with shared values, however, CHAP does not override P. So in the last example the second CHAP would inherit SHARED from the last P in the first CHAP, regardless of whether the preceding CHAP sets SECURE, SHARED, or nothing.

In general, the best solution is simply to avoid **#CURRENT** attributes. If you must use a DTD that uses them, it is best to decide on a strict convention for how to do so. It is always possible to reduce the long-distance interactions by setting the attribute's value explicitly more often, or even on *every* instance. In some cases it may be possible to set the value once and leave it in effect for the rest of the document (though in that case **#FIXED** attributes would be a better choice, as discussed in Question 5.15).

## 1.15. I changed an attribute on one type of element and affected another one. What's happening?

This can happen when the attribute involved is assigned a default value called **#CURRENT**, as discussed in Question 1.14. This means that if you don't specify a value for the attribute on some element the SGML parser must fill in the value using the value *last specified* for that attribute. It does not matter whether the last specification was near or far away, inside the same chapter, or anything: just the last element. The last specification can even be on an element of a different type, depending on how the DTD designer set things up.

It is tempting to assume that this "last specified" idea works by attribute name, so that if two element types each have a TYPE attribute that is declared to be **#CURRENT**, then after one element sets TYPE, the next element that has a TYPE attribute would default to "TYPE="REPAIR"" (pardon the pointy-brackets here):

```
<TASK TYPE="REPAIR">...</TASK>
<WARNING>...</WARNING>
```

If WARNING has a TYPE attribute, it may or may not inherit its value from the TASK element before it, depending on the DTD. The DTD designer decides this by defining the TYPE attributes in one of two different ways: either together in a single declaration, or in two separate declarations. If they are declared together, then the value inherits across types; if not; it doesn't.

This makes more sense when you consider that there is no reason the second **ATTLIST** declaration above even had to allow the same set of possible values as the first: the DTD designer could conceivably want to set up WARNING elements to take a TYPE attribute with values HARMFUL or FATAL, while TASK elements take a TYPE attribute that must be either REPAIR or TEST. In that case inheriting across the element types would make no sense.

One might instead assume that these attributes are separate for every element type: that a TASK element could never affect the like-named attribute on a WARNING element. That is also incorrect.

The actual rules for this are found in Clause 7.9.1.1 of the SGML standard. It says that two or more element types can share a single **ATTLIST** declaration, and in that case the attributes they declare do share their "last specified" or "current" values across instances of the various element types. The DTD would define a shared attribute this way:

```
<!ATTLIST   (TASK | WARNING)
   TYPE     (INSTALL | REPAIR | REPLACE) #CURRENT>
```

As an author, you cannot tell which is the case without looking at the DTD or its documentation, or asking someone who does. Shared and unshared attributes look exactly the same in the document instance. So be sure to check with your DTD designer if this question comes up.

## 1.16. Can I name a file on an attribute to link to it?

This is an interesting question because the answer is opposite in theory and in practice. In short, "it depends" on what the DTD designer set up.

In SGML there is a way to refer to data objects that are not physically part of the document: as entities. To use such data objects you declare the external data as an entity, and then refer to it from an attribute whose type is **ENTITY**.

> **Note:** "Not physically part of the document" usually means "not in the same file", but not necessarily. A single entity could be spread across multiple files, or multiple entities could be packed into one file. It can even happen that there is no "file" involved, if the entity's information is stored in some other way entirely.

In an authoring system this typically means you use commands such as

- "Define new notation", if the DTD designer hasn't already defined the data format you need to SGML (such as GIF, WAV, or whatever). Hopefully, the needed **NOTATION**s are already set up for you.
- "Define new entity" (to give the name, location, and type or **NOTATION** of the external data object, like a graphic);
- "Insert element" (to create a place to hold the name of that new entity); and
- "Set attribute" (to add the specific entity's name to that new element).

What actually goes into the SGML representation is a little more detailed. It corresponds very closely to those same things, and you can see the names of the different parts in the representation, which will end up looking something like this:

```
<!NOTATION GIF          PUBLIC
                        "-//Compuserv//Bitmap format//EN">
<!ENTITY   GOLD         SYSTEM "c:\thombs\eagle.gif"
                        NDATA GIF>
<!ENTITY   SILVER       SYSTEM "c:\eldredge\axel2.gif"
                        NDATA GIF>
<!ATTLIST  FIG
  OBJECT   ENTITY       #REQUIRED>
...
<FIG OBJECT="GOLD">
```

This is in some sense the "right" way to refer to a file from an SGML document; and most SGML systems support it. However, many DTDs take a short-cut that leaves out the first two steps. This is not the best practice, but you may encounter a situation where you must just insert an element and then put an actual filename on an attribute, with no declarations. Inside this looks like:

```
<!ATTLIST  FIG
  FILE     CDATA        #REQUIRED>
...
<FIG FILE="c:\thombs\eagle.gif">
```

This is less complex in terms of the amount of typing, the number of declarations involved, and various other measures. It has a few other advantages, too:

1. Authors don't need to learn DTD syntax and add entity declarations just to insert graphics. Good editing software ought to hide this behind a reasonable interface anyway, though not all does.
2. Often this type of **ENTITY** declaration is the only thing in a document's internal declaration subset, and they are easy to process there. However, *other* things that could occur in that subset can make it harder to optimize implementations in certain ways (such as pre-processing declarations to save time on re-uses). A parser that wants to optimize subsets has to do more work to make sure it can do so safely, and so some may optimize only when there is *no* internal subset present.
3. The shorthand approach puts all the data relevant to the data object together in one place, making errors less likely over the long haul.
4. Most SGML software can deal with filenames, since the **ENTITY** declaration ultimately resolves to some kind of storage object identifier anyway. Thus, the shorthand *works*, which may suffice.

Because of these advantages the shorthand is quite tempting, and is used very frequently. Nevertheless, it has some drawbacks and using it may lead to surprises if you don't know about them in advance:

1. SGML doesn't ***know*** that the attribute's value identifies external data. Thus an SGML aware program to gather up all the relevant data objects (such as to mail them somewhere) would miss them.
2. There is nothing explicitly saying what format the data object is in (in this case, GIF). The "`.gif`" extension can be used for this, but again, SGML doesn't know about extensions, and extensions are not entirely portable across various operating systems.
3. Since to SGML such as attribute is just a string, the SGML parser itself cannot validate that it is a correct filename. A later application could do this check, and for reliability's sake this is often very important to do.
4. If the value that goes on the attribute is really a filename instead of something like an FPI, it will break whenever the document moves to another computer system. Also, the points of breakage end up scattered: someone can't just scan through **ENTITY** declarations and update all filenames conveniently in one place.

Given all the tradeoffs, it is usually wiser to go the extra mile and really declare each data object as an entity.

## 1.17. Can I include ">" in a processing instruction?

Processing instructions specified inline in an SGML document cannot contain ">".

Processing instructions (**PIs**) are used to insert specific commands to be passed to particular software operating on SGML documents, as opposed to the structural markup intended to be communicated by the tags and element structures.

">" ends a **PI**, so the following examples are not allowed. Also, because entity references are not recognized inside processing instructions substituting ">" does not express the same thing (SGML will not resolve it to a literal ">"). Not even numeric character references are recognized inside **PIs** (such as ">" to refer to the character with that number, which is normally greater-than).

```
<!-- WRONG -->
<TABLE>
<?XYZ breakchar='>'>
...
<BLOCK.QUOTE>
<?XYZ if margin > 2 newpage>
```

It is possible to define your own substitute to use within **PIs**, although SGML itself cannot apply it or check it for you. One way is to have the application interpret an SGML-*like* syntax after the SGML parser hands it the **PI**. For example, even though SGML doesn't see any entity references in the example below, the **PI** is valid as is: the parser will simply hand back ">" as a literal part of the **PI**. An application on top of SGML can scan for certain strings (in this case ">"), and replace them with anything it wants:

```
<?XYZ if margin &gt; 2 newpage>
```

It is important to emphasize that even though this looks like an SGML entity reference inside the **PI**, it is not one. An SGML parser recognizes no delimiters at all within **PI**s except for the “>” that ends the **PI**. Therefore the ampersand does not start an entity reference; if it ends up replaced by “>” that is only a convention applied by some later process. Such a process could just know about “gt”; or could know about character numbers;, or could even talk more closely to the SGML parser, and know about all declared entities.

**Note:** The actual string assigned to the processing instruction close delimiter could also be changed from “>” to reduce conflicts. Also, it may be possible to set up your SGML system to use the rare “markup scan suppression” characters to prevent a “>” from being recognized (on which see Question 3.7).

Another workaround is to move such processing instructions out into separate **PI** entities instead of placing them inline. Setting this up is better left to the DTD designer. But once set up, since SGML knows where **PI** entities begin and end it need not scan them at all and there is need to prohibit delimiter strings within **PI** entities:

```
<!ENTITY   set.bc.gt    SDATA "XYZ breakchar='>'">
<!ENTITY   cond.page    SDATA "XYZ if margin > 2 newpage">
...
<TABLE>&set.bc.gt;
...
<BLOCK.QUOTE>&cond.page;
```

If a processing instruction is expressed by a **PI** entity instead of inline, it can contain anything. Processing instructions that return data (and so should be contained in **SDATA** entities according to Clause 8) depend on each system's characteristics for what they may contain.

**Note:** At least one SGML authoring system used to write out documents with “>” in quotes within some of its **PI**s — fortunately this was fixed long ago.

XML exercises SGML's feature of changing delimiters to make it less likely for authors to run into the processing instruction close delimiter by accident (see Question 7.1 for some related questions about changing delimiters). In XML the **PIC** delimiter is “?>” instead of “>”, because it makes the **PI** delimiters symmetrical and because it is far less likely you will need “?>” inside a **PI** than that you will need just “>”; but there is still no guarantee.

The easiest way to avoid any potential conflicts with **PIC** is to avoid processing instructions.

**Note:** Processing instructions are fairly rare in SGML as it is used today. A few are provided by most vendors for system-specific functions or for formatting hints like forced page breaks. The various vendors' **PI**s generally do not collide (see the next question on why), and documents usually work adequately even in systems that completely ignore them.

# 1.18. Why don't my processing instructions work in all SGML programs?

The last question in this chapter is also the easiest: Processing instructions are specifically meant to be a place to put non-portable, system-specific data. Any information that is truly part of your document rather than "asides" directed toward some particular processor, should not be in a **PI**.

For example, if you are busily formatting your SGML document for print and want to force a page break at a certain point to make the layout look nicer, then a **PI** is appropriate. Your authoring system likely has a command to "Insert Page Break" that inserts a **PI** in some form that particular piece of software understands.

On the other hand, if you are putting ancient manuscripts into electronic form and you want to record where the actual page breaks happened in the manuscript because that may be important historical information for your audience, then you should not use a **PI**: it's not a processing instruction. Since in this case the page break is "real" information, it should be expressed with an element

> **Note**: The DTDs from the Text Encoding Initiative provide modules to support many details of this kind when they are needed. See Chapter 18 of the TEI *Guidelines*.

Even though **PI**s are system-specific it's reasonable to expect systems not to trip needlessly over each other's **PI**s. Each system should at least detect all **PI**s, and decide for each one whether it understands it. It should then ignore any it doesn't understand (except for preserving them untouched in case you are moving your SGML data back and forth, and perhaps warning you that they are there!).

In current practice this usually works fine, because most software that generate **PI**s at all *always* prefixes them with an identifying prefix. Usually it is an abbreviation of a company name or product, such as in the table below.

| Prefix | Organization |
|---|---|
| `BKM:` | IBM BookMaster |
| `EBT` | Inso Electronic Publishing Solutions (formerly EBT) *Dyna*Text |
| `Pub` | ArborText Adept |
| `SO` | The SGML Open Consortium |
| `XML` | The Extensible Markup Language |

Because of these prefixes products can tell their own **PI**s apart from those understood by other products, and behave accordingly. They still may not execute other product's **PI**s (sometimes it would make no sense to, for example if one tool is a formatter and one is a retrieval engine), but at least they don't get confused. The XML specification requires such a prefix. It is wise to declare the prefix as a **NOTATION** and provide a reference to some documentation of the range of **PI**s supported and their meanings.

# 2. For Authors and Document Editors Who Commonly Deal With Raw SGML

If you are not using an SGML editor that understands and hides all the markup (say, showing tags as buttons or icons instead of as strings with pointy brackets), you will meet all the "syntax" details of SGML head-on: you'll quickly need to learn just when "<" is part of a tag and when it's part of your text data, and other rules. You use your knowledge of the rules to avoid outright syntax errors, but more importantly to avoid accidentally creating an SGML structure that is technically *valid*, but not at all what you *intended*. That is, if you type some punctuation in the wrong place you might think it represents a tag when it's really data, or vice versa. If you're using SGML's minimization features, especially **OMITTAG**, the parser may infer enough other tags to get the document back to validity — but they may not be the tags you meant.

One common example of this "unintended validity" comes up when authors use an element they thought was allowed in a given place, but it actually isn't. Perhaps they intend to put a SIDEBAR in a SEC, but the DTD only allows them in CHP elements as shown below. When a parser finds the SIDEBAR shown, it will close the SEC (leaving it empty except for its TI) and the rest of the intended SEC contents will be part of the CHP. This will not produce an error until the SEC end-tag shows up far later (if it is omitted, probably no error at all will be reported). Few parsers will tell you at that later point, just *when* the SEC was assumed to close, and this can lead to questions such as "Why didn't I get an error message for this?" or "Why did the error message happen so far away from the error?"

```
<!ELEMENT  CHP          O O (TI, (SEC | P | SIDEBAR)*)>
<!ELEMENT  SEC          O O (TI, P*)>
<!ELEMENT  (TI, ABSTRACT, P, SIDEBAR) - - (#PCDATA)>
...
<CHP>
...
<SEC><TI>The sower</TI>
<SIDEBAR>Responses vary.</SIDEBAR>
<P>...
```

Another example, pointed out by C. M. Sperberg-McQueen, occurs when you insert an element you think is not allowed within the current element, assuming it will force the preceding element closed. One such case is assuming that NOTE will force a HEAD to close, which may not be true in the DTD. If the preceding element's content model is looser than you think, some following elements may quietly be subsumed into it.

This is the sort of question covered in this chapter. Many details about what *characters* you can and can't type were covered in the last chapter, because some current SGML editing tools don't hide those issues completely (in a few cases it would be hard for them to do so). But the issues in this chapter are less likely to show up for you if you never see a pointy bracket, so are discussed here for those readers who more frequently deal with SGML document syntax directly.

## 2.1. Is "<>" really a tag?

This is called an empty start-tag. It is permitted when the **SHORTTAG** option is set to **YES** in the DTD. If the very first start-tag in the document is empty, it opens the document element (such as BOOK). For other situations Clause 7.4.1.1 assigns it two different meanings, depending on how the **OMITTAG** option is set:

**YES** it opens "the most recently started open element [type]".

**NO** it opens "the most recently ended element [type]".

New users often ask why the double rule exists. They ask either when they first learn it, or when they switch **OMITTAG** on or off. Since what tag SGML infers differs depending on that switch, authors can end up creating a document with unintended elements in various places. Similarly, if after using "<>" **OMITTAG** and **SHORTTAG** are turned off, each "<>" becomes just literal data content instead of a tag at all, and no syntax error need arise.

The surest way to prevent any such misunderstandings is not to use this form of minimization. If possible, having the DTD designer turn it off is a good way to ensure that it is not used.

The SGML rule seems to arise because of a (not unreasonable) assumption about just how one might use **OMITTAG** in practice. Consider the case of paragraphs that can contain text and subelements other than paragraphs, but not nested paragraphs. If **OMITTAG** is **NO** you must have *some* explicit form of every start- and end-tag such as shown below; the tags can never be entirely missing. Because you *must not* have omitted the end-tag for the previous P, that previous P is definitely ended before you get to the "<>", leaving a containing element such as SEC open. So to get the desired effect of opening a new P, some definition basically like the second one above is necessary:

```
<SEC>
  <P>Text of <EMPH>important</> paragraph one.</>
  <>Text of paragraph two.</>
  <>Text of paragraph three.</>
</SEC>
```

On the other hand, if **OMITTAG** is **YES** the apparent assumption is that you *will* omit those end-tags entirely. So in the example below the "<>" occurs with the previous P still open, and so a rule like the first one above is needed to get the desired effect. The example also shows why any smaller internal elements (like the EMPH) must be closed first.

When end-tags are omitted one can scarcely predict what the last element *closed* might have been (in this case it would be the EMPH, but if the EMPH element had not happened to be there it might well have been the previous CHAP). The first rule ensures that an SGML parser will open a P, which will in turn force the previous P closed (because the declaration for P does not allow nested P elements).

```
<SEC>
   <P>Text of <EMPH>important</> paragraph one.
   <>Text of paragraph two.
   <>Text of paragraph three.</>
</SEC>
```

So this example works fine; but the convention does impose some practical constraints:

- If P allowed an embedded P, the start-tag would be inferred correctly but the **OMITTAG** rules would not force the prior P closed. In that case the example above would lead to a stack of nested Ps, not a sequence of Ps all at the same level.
- If the author does not omit the end-tag for a P, then when the following "<>" is reached "the most recently started *open* element" is something else like SEC, so that "<>" will serve to open a new SEC (this may or may not lead to an error report, depending on how SEC is declared).

One other consequence of how SGML defines empty start-tags is that the structure of a document can change drastically if the user turns **OMITTAG** on or off in the SGML declaration. The change may produce myriad syntax errors (with **OMITTAG YES**, error reporting is frequently imprecise because parsers often cannot be certain there is an error until long after the error occurred). Or the change may simply alter document structures without resulting in errors. The result depends on a variety of circumstances such as how the DTD and document instance interact and where "<>" is used.

Authors can avoid confusion by *always* omitting end-tags before "<>"; DTD designers can by designing content models with this in mind. Even so, few authors will likely understand the subtle effect of *failing to omit* an end-tag: that the result will likely be syntactically valid (parse without errors) even though it is incorrect. Since SGML provides no way to declare that an element type's end-tags *must* be omitted, the parser cannot help to validate the necessary convention (a larger program that *contains* the parser could, but that part of its functionality would be beyond SGML). Thus, the safest course is to avoid this type of minimization.

## 2.2. When can I omit a start-tag?

Probably one of the most frequent questions in SGML is "when can I omit a start-tag?" The brief but not very useful answer is "whenever the SGML parser can figure out that the element type it starts is required". This section fills in a bit more detail.

In practice, many authors do not bother learning the detailed rules. Instead they enter all the start-tags, which is always permissible, is easily understood, and usually looks clearer on-screen anyway. In typical SGML-aware systems an "Insert Element" command that manages start- and end-tags all at once so the question never arises; authoring systems also typically write out all tags with no minimization, making the question irrelevant. But when authors deal with raw SGML, it can be tempting to save keystrokes by omitting as many tags as possible. Because of this it can be very important to understand the rules for how SGML decides what tags to fill in for you. Its rules guarantee that there is only one correct start-tag for a parser to infer at a time, and it will be *consistent* (it would be hard to avoid that — this is a computer, after all); understanding what it will do, however, is the subject of this section.

## Simple cases

There are a few obvious cases where you can't omit the start-tag, regardless of what else is going on:

- If the DTD designer has turned off the **OMITTAG** feature entirely.
- If you have to specify some attributes, either because they have default value **#REQUIRED** or because you want to give them some non-default values. In such cases you need the start-tag as a place to hang the attributes.
- If the DTD says you can't omit the start-tag for a given element type (it has "-" and not "O" for its first minimization flag). Such a setting applies to all contexts and instances of a given element type. The reverse, however, is not true: see below and also Question 4.1 for details on why you might not be able to omit a tag even though the DTD flag says you may.

The SGML standard gives detailed rules in Clause 7.3.1. These rules do result in the obvious cases already described; some of the other restrictions they impose may deserve additional explanation, as given below.

## Declared content elements

Elements with declared content (**CDATA**, **RCDATA**, or **EMPTY**) are prohibited from omitting their start-tags. *The SGML Handbook* (p. 309) states that the restriction is because "there is no way to know that the parser must respond differently unless the start-tag is there". See also Question 3.3 on end-tags for **EMPTY** elements.

Given the rule, one must always include the start-tag, even though a parser *could* infer such start-tags much as it does for other cases of start-tag omission if the rules allowed. For example, a system could infer the omitted XMP start-tag easily enough in a case like this, since it would know "Tags..." is not valid otherwise:

```
<!ELEMENT  EG           O O (TITLE,XMP)>
<!ELEMENT  XMP          O O CDATA>
...
<EG><TITLE>Example 1</TITLE>
Tags look like <P>.
</EG>
```

The difficult cases are more subtle, for example when such a parser would see "<TITLE>" and then what might be an entity reference (say, "<"):

```
<EG><TITLE>Example 1</TITLE>
&lt;P> is how tags look.
</EG>
```

The difficulty is that there are two reasonable rules that could be made for what to do in such cases. SGML's choice to disallow minimization in this and similar cases may be simpler than allowing it and stating a choice between behaviors:

1. Open the required XMP first, and then take the "<" literally; or

2. Recognize the entity reference first, and continue parsing in the entity (which might start with "<XMP>", with another entity reference, or with something else, that would cause the parser to infer "<XMP>" at that point).

### Empty (but not **EMPTY**) elements

Another case ruled out is omitting the start-tag when the element type does not have declared content **EMPTY** (as discussed above), but all of its content is optional and an element instance just *happens* to be empty. In such cases the start-tag is always required, regardless of what the DTD says about permissibility of omitting tags and regardless of whether the situation is ambiguous or not.

*The SGML Handbook* notes (p. 310) that it would look funny to see an end-tag with no start-tag or content (end-tags with content but no start-tag *are* allowed), or to see nothing at all representing an element. So in the end this case is allowed:

```
<!ELEMENT CHP           O O (TITLE,SEC)>
<!ELEMENT TITLE         O O (#PCDATA)>
...
<CHP>Introduction<SEC>...
```

but these cases are not:

```
<!-- WRONG -->
<CHP><SEC>...
<CHP></TITLE><SEC>...
```

Omitting a start-tag immediately before an active **SHORTREF** delimiter is also ruled out, though we're not focusing on **SHORTREF** here. The details are generally similar to the other issues with delimiters after omitted start-tags.

> **Note:** A parser could implement such omission by starting the element on seeing either its end-tag (if its end-tag were not omitted), or something that is not allowed inside it (if both the start-tag and end-tag were omitted). This alternative does not seem to introduce any ambiguity.

### Contextually required and optional elements

The most complex issue, and the most common, however, is an SGML rule that a start-tag may be omitted when an "element is a contextually required element and any other elements that could occur are contextually optional elements".

One sub-case of this rule is particularly easy: if there is only one possible "next" element and it must occur, then it is contextually required and naturally it is the one inferred. In this example where `TITLE` is required at the start of `CHP` and nothing else is permitted there, `TITLE` can have its start-tag omitted:

```
<!ELEMENT  CHP          - - (TITLE, SEC*)>
...
<CHP>Introduction</TITLE>
<SEC>...
```

Perhaps surprisingly, however, "contextually required" does *not* mean that the element must be the next element. It could be that any number of other elements may intervene, but that after them the required element must still occur, such as the `REQD` element here:

```
<!ELEMENT  FOO           - - (A?, B*, (C|D)*, REQD)>
```

This is a reason for the phrase "and any other elements that could occur are contextually optional elements". REQD begins to be contextually required immediately after the start of FOO, and continues to be so until it has occurred (or until some error arises, such as closing the FOO element prematurely).

Authors sometimes expect that in an **AND** group, if all but one of the element types has occurred already then the remaining one would become contextually required. But this is not the case. That is, you cannot omit the start-tag for Z here:

```
<!-- WRONG -->
<!ELEMENT  Q             - - (X & Y & Z)>
<!ELEMENT  (X|Y|Z)       O O (#PCDATA)>
...
<Q><X>hello</X> <Y>there</Y> not allowed</Z></Q>
```

The SGML standard's definition is expressed in terms of the tokens (GIs and parenthesized groups) and operators that make up content models in element declarations. The full story requires following out some definitions: Clauses 4.59, 4.60, 4.61, 4.62, and 4.159, but boils down to "required" meaning basically "inevitable, even if not immediate", and "optional" meaning anything *else* that is permissible (this summary is imperfect, but the other cases are rather technical).

## One last case: inferring containers

Authors commonly want to make hierarchical documents out of flat ones. That is, to take markup that has few or no containers, and infer containers. This is discussed in detail in Question 5.1, but in short, even though container structures facilitate many kinds of useful processing and data management, data is extremely common in and out of SGML in which "headings" are marked as various levels but the large objects *which those headings label* are not marked up. A common convention is to name such heading tags simply H plus their (conceptual) level number:

```
<H1>Introduction</H1>
<H2>Origin and Goals</H2>
<H2>Relationship to Existing Standards</H2>
```

In such a document the markup does not represent the structures that the headings head, and does not represent the fact that H2 is a different level than H1 except by a naming convention: human readers might guess those things from the tag names, but particular tag names mean nothing to SGML.

Flat markup may have been encouraged by systems such as IBM's GML starter set, which influenced many early DTDs (although GML could be set up to handle containers, and sometimes was). It had tagging like "`:H1.Introduction¶`", where the title ended at end-of-line as if the end of line were a **SHORTREF**. Thus you couldn't really tell whether H1 was a container with an unnamed title element with both tags omitted, or whether H1 was a heading, with no container present.

The non-binding sample DTD in Annex E of the SGML standard accommodates such markup in that it makes H1 a container, whose title is a required H1T (both of whose tags can be omitted if the next thing after the title is something like a P, as opposed to just **#PCDATA**). The BookMaster system and the early Association of American

Publishers DTD show some similarities as well, though in the latter the H elements are clearly headings.

> **Note**: The IBM GML starter set also influenced HTML. Working at CERN (the European Center for Nuclear Research) in the mid 1980s, Anders Berglund (an early member of the SGML committee) developed a tag set based on the GML starter set plus some enhancements. This was the document system in use at CERN central computing facilities when Tim Berners-Lee and Robert Cailliau were there and developed HTML and the Web (see Berners-Lee et al, 1992 and 1994); it was also used to typeset the SGML standard itself. A comparison shows close similarities between HTML and that enhanced starter set: HTML has different names for some elements; combines cross-reference tags into A and LINK (and introduces URLs); adds BASE, ISINDEX, META, FORM tags, and a few other types; and omits tags for tables of contents, appendixes, some heads and captions, and front-matter items such as author, date, etc.

A lot of flat data comes from word processors that only support paragraph-level objects. But whatever the history, this situation comes up quite frequently both for authors who have to work with data they receive in this form and for data conversion staff who need to transform it into more hierarchical forms to facilitate more powerful processing of all kinds.

Although descriptive markup of any shape is far superior to markup that merely represents formatting instructions, among descriptive markup systems flat markup is less useful in many respects than hierarchical. This is not the place to go into all the issues with nested lists, tables of contents and outliners, context-based formatting and retrieval, structured version control, and other capabilities that it makes easier (see Coombs et al. 1987, DeRose et al. 1990, or Chapters 2 and 3 in DeRose and Durand 1994 for more details). There are very good reasons to want those larger containers, and it is unfortunate that SGML did not make it easy to infer containers from their titles. As the discussion on this gets a bit more technical it is found later, in Question 5.1.

## 2.3. When may an end-tag be omitted?

The rules for when an end-tag may be omitted are far simpler than the rules for start-tags. Whether that is the reason or not, end-tag omission is used far more frequently than start-tag omission.

The first and simplest case is that end-tags can be omitted at the very end of the document. When the parser finds end-of-file (fussily, the end of the document entity), it should close anything left.

The second case is like it: omitting any but the last end-tag when closing several elements all at once:

```
<CHP>...
   <SEC>...
      <SUBSEC>...
         <P>...
</CHP>
```

Because SGML elements must "nest" properly, closing the CHP must be taken as closing anything left inside the CHP (in this case P, SUBSEC, and SEC). Otherwise you could end up with non-hierarchical structures like the invalid case shown below:

```
<!-- WRONG -->
<B> <I> the quick brown fox </B></I>
```

It is possible to create markup systems that support non-hierarchical structures, but processing them can be very difficult (hierarchies have many nice technical characteristics). They are needed for certain sophisticated applications (see Barnard et al. 1995 and 1996), but the case shown above is merely an error.

Occasionally authors will try to save a tag or two by using markup like that shown below instead of using two separate `I` elements (the second enclosing just "`fox`"):

```
<!-- WRONG -->
<B> the quick <I> brown </B> fox </I>
```

Most Web browsers survive such markup (which is good), without reporting an error (which is questionable), and then do wildly inconsistent things with it (which is bad). One respected browser displays "`fox`" in bold, which seems a bit odd since it clearly follows an explicit end of `B`.

The final case is slightly more complex: An element ends if the parser sees something that can't occur there. The most common use of this is for elements that cannot contain other instances of themselves. Typically, nearly all element types are "non-recursive", for example, paragraphs cannot directly contain paragraphs and chapters cannot contain chapters. For such elements, any time you have a sequence of like elements in a row, **OMITTAG** can deal with leaving out end-tags:

```
<SEC>
<P>
<P>
<SEC>
```

The detailed rules for when end-tags can be omitted are in Clause 7.3.1.2 of the SGML standard.

## 2.4. What do "CDATA", "NDATA", "SDATA", and "#PCDATA" mean in SGML?

These keywords are used in many places, especially **CDATA**. They refer to particular constraints on how an SGML parser interprets the information it sees, such as what delimiters are recognized. A question frequently arises because **CDATA** in particular means different things in different uses:

- A **CDATA** *element* suppresses markup recognition (including entity references), so that strings which would otherwise be taken as delimiters, are instead taken as data. This effect continues until "</" (the **ETAGO** delimiter) occurs in context: basically, before a letter or ">" (see Question 1.1 for details).
- A **CDATA** *entity* suppresses markup recognition entirely until the entity ends (this is signaled in some special way by the software, not by running into a reserved string).
- A **CDATA** *marked section* suppresses markup recognition until "]]>".
- A **CDATA** *attribute* means any data characters are allowed. As in all attribute types, entity references are replaced in quoted attribute value literals.

The **CDATA** keyword thus applies to all four of these constructs, although with slightly different meanings appropriate to the different contexts. Other keywords that specify special parsing constraints likewise apply differently (or not all all) in those different context.

- **RCDATA** only applies to elements and marked sections, and works like **CDATA** in those cases except that it does not suppress recognition of entity references. This makes it more useful because with **CDATA** there is no way to include the string that would end the construct, such as "]]>" or "</" but with **RCDATA** you can do so by using an entity. **CDATA** *attributes* work more like **RCDATA**, since entity references are recognized; there is no **RCDATA** type for attributes.
- **NDATA**, **SDATA**, and **PI** apply only to (some) entities, and in these cases the SGML parser itself doesn't try to parse the data at all, so any string can occur. **NDATA** is related to **NOTATION** attributes but not quite the same; **PI** has a syntax of its own ("<?...>") as well as being a kind of entity.
- **#PCDATA** applies only as part of an element's content model, and is the typical "parse this text" case. "**PCDATA**", however, is a reasonable way to describe the parsing behavior within **INCLUDE** marked sections and within SGML text entities, even though they do not go by that name.

> **Note:** Complete symmetry may not be desirable, but the diversity could be reduced since in principle any of these parsing types could apply to any syntactic construct.

The main reason that authors need to know which of these types they are working with is that the type constrains what strings count as markup in the construct. For example, in **#PCDATA** (such as typical paragraph text content) many delimiters are recognized, and to get those strings as data instead they must be escaped (see Questions 1.1 and 3.7). But in **CDATA** very little markup is recognized: in a **CDATA** marked section only "]]>" must be avoided. **NDATA**, **SDATA**, and **PI** entities can contain anything, since SGML treats them purely as data and does not parse them to look for *any* SGML delimiters.

## 2.5. When are line breaks ignored and what does "ignored" mean?

Question 1.1 discussed some questions about just where whitespace is prohibited, permitted, and permitted but ignored. But what happens to whitespace that *is* "ignored", or that is not? And what are the rest of the details about just when it happens? This question addresses more complex aspects of whitespace.

The simplest general answer is that few systems use ignored whitespace for anything (other than a few effects it triggers during parsing itself, that authors can frequently ignore), but that some systems provide formatting directives that designers can apply to non-ignored whitespace. For example, many formatters provide a "verbatim", "preformatted", or "as-is" setting in stylesheets so that the content of certain elements can be laid out in lines exactly as it appeared in the input. This is good for program listings and a few other things, and can be pressed into use for rudimentary tables and artwork in a pinch. For more on this see Question 5.6.

**Note**: There is some debate among DTD designers about whether this is good practice. On the one hand it seems a little un-SGML-like to express structurally important units such as "lines" of code only via layout, and many tools do not support layout-dependent formatting well; on the other hand it seems tedious to surround every line of such examples to make `LINE` elements, and a bit of overkill to introduce the **SHORTREF** feature only to do the same thing. But all the practices can be found, and all do work adequately: the details of how authors manage such elements depends on the DTD design.

Whitespace can also be used as part of **SHORTREF**s. Though this book does not discuss that feature much, one simple example the SGML standard gives is using them to match empty records (record start immediately followed by record end) in order to infer something like a paragraph tag (see Clauses 11.5-11.6):

```
<!ENTITY   start-p "<P>">
<!SHORTREF textmap
   "&#RS;&#RE;" start-p>
<!USEMAP textmap book>
```

Obviously this is mainly useful in cases of manually keyboarded or scanned data, but can also be used to accommodate presentational markup such as found in email where markup is expressed by various whitespace conventions rather than tags or other (meta-) information. However, many systems for inferring markup from presentation do analysis more complex than matching literal whitespace or other strings, and having done that they just insert full markup. Many such systems are used to turn email, news, and scanned text into HTML, SGML, and XML. See Coombs et al (1987) for more on this notion of presentational markup.

## RS and RE ignoring

Barring recognition via **SHORTREF**, **RS** and **RE** are usually ignored. In practical terms "ignored" means the character is not considered part of the literal data content, and so should not be displayed to the user in a formatted form of the document.

*The SGML Handbook* (p. 322) characterizes the intent as being "if the record end is there solely because of something in the markup, it is ignored...." Clause 7.6.1 of the SGML standard states the rules. In data content all **RS**s are ignored unless they are "interpreted as markup". The main way an **RS** would be interpreted as markup is if it is used in a **SHORTREF** as described above (though there are a few other possibilities).

This rule is one reason an SGML system must include a layer (called the "entity manager") that discards record boundaries (regardless of how they are discovered) and inserts **RS** and **RE** instead. As noted above, UNIX systems use *only* Line Feed to represent record boundaries. Because the numeric code for Line Feed is 10, the same as the normal value assigned to **RS**, without a separation layer an SGML system using the reference concrete syntax would consider the Line Feed to be an **RS**, and discard it.

Some SGML users have had the experience of seeing the last word of every line join up directly to the first word of the following line whenever they load a UNIX file. For example, this would end up displayed as "This is somebody of text.":

```
<P>This is some
body of text.</P>
```

> **Note:** This is a UNIX-specific problem. DOS and Windows files separate lines using a Carriage Return (CR) *and* a Line Feed (LF), which works pretty well since they look like an **RE** followed by an **RS** (except for the detail that a CR and LF are both associated with the same line, whereas **RE** and **RS** are associated with adjacent lines). Macintosh files use just CR, so it makes no difference if a system discards LF as if it were **RS**.

Although few SGML systems lack an entity manager anymore, the author or SGML publisher still has a few things to watch for:

- First, some systems that deal with SGML only as an import format *do* lack an entity manager and so are prone to this problem.
- Second, even a perfect SGML system must be told *somehow* what to expect in the files it receives.

An entity manager must somehow be told that it is being fed a UNIX-style file as opposed to DOS, Macintosh, or other kind of file. Without being told that it cannot tell what information in the file to recognize as line breaks, and so cannot insert **RE** and **RS** in the right places. Entity managers typically default to assuming files are in whatever form is natural for the system the parser is running on: this is often correct, but may fail when a file is mailed or moved across from another system, potentially leading to the lines-joining up problem.

## RE ignoring

The rules for **RE** are also in Clause 7.6.1, and are more complex. Markup such as **SHORTREF**s and entity references is handled first. Then SGML applies some rules to decide whether the author created the line-break to lay out their SGML source, or to really create a conceptually significant break in the data. The former are said to be "attributed solely to markup". To decide this, the rules indicate that a parser must apply certain rules.

The rules cause certain **RE**s to be ignored. In particular, the first and last **RE** in each element is usually ignored, as is any **RE** that "does not immediately follow an **RS** or **RE**". If an **RE** is the *absolute* first or last thing in any element, it definitely will be ignored. The reasons for saying "usually" apply to other cases: an **RE** is not ignored if certain things come between it and the nearby event that would otherwise cause the ignoring.

The first rule is that the *first* **RE** in each element is retained if an **RS**, data content, or a "proper subelement" comes before it in the element. If nothing comes before, or only other kinds of things come before, then it is ignored.

A *proper* subelement is any direct subelement that is valid *because* it is allowed by the current element's content model explicitly, not because it is an inclusion exception (it may be allowed for both reasons). As an author you can only tell this by consulting the DTD or its documentation (or someone who has consulted one of these). It is also possible for an editing program to give you this information, but that is not common. The distinction of proper as opposed to. improper subelements is discussed in more detail below.

The second rule is basically the same as the first, but flipped end-for-end: the *last* **RE** is retained if an **RS**, data content, or a proper subelement comes after it in the element.

The third and last rule is also similar: an **RE** in the middle but not right after another **RE** or an **RS**, is retained if data or a proper subelement comes between it and that preceding **RE** or **RS**.

As an example of how these rules work out, an **RE** immediately following a start-tag or immediately before an end-tag is ignored, as shown below (**RE** is represented by "¶"):

```
<P>¶
Some REs are ignored.¶
</P>
```

In addition, an **RE** is ignored even if things *other* than those mentioned in the rules intervene, such as:

- Comments:

```
<P><!-- hi -->¶
Some REs are ignored.</P>
...
<P>Some REs are ignored.¶
<!-- hi --></P>
```

- Processing instructions:

```
<P><?break>¶
Some REs are ignored.</P>
...
<P>Some REs are ignored.¶
<?break></P>
```

- Marked sections that do not resolve to data (though note that changing such a marked section from **IGNORE** to **INCLUDE** may cause the **RE** to come back):

```
<P><![ IGNORE [ anything ]]>¶
Some REs are ignored.</P>
...
<P>Some REs are ignored.¶
<![ IGNORE [ anything ]]></P>
```

These are understandable: non-content, non-element items simply "don't count". The **RE** following them is still considered to "immediately" follow the start-tag, and so is ignored. The rationale seems to be support for typing things like this without getting an extra line-break:

```
<P><!-- very important paragraph! -->¶
Some REs are ignored.</P>
<P><?xyz keep-together>¶
Some REs are ignored.</P>
```

Any number or combination of these things can intervene and the **RE** will still be ignored. The other thing that can intervene *without* causing the **RE** to be kept instead of ignored, is an improper subelement (a proper subelement would cause the **RE** to be retained). This distinction is the most subtle part of these rules, and is described next.

## Proper and Improper Subelements

The messy case is that word "proper". In addition to all the cases above, an *included* subelement (such as FOOTNOTE might typically be) is not considered "proper", and doesn't prevent the **RE** from being ignored. This remains true no matter what occurs down inside that included subelement (possibly including its own line breaks). So another case where **RE** can still be ignored is illustrated here:

- Improper subelements:

```
<P><FOOTNOTE>¶
See also Space (1999)¶
for further discussion.¶
</FOOTNOTE>¶
Some REs are ignored.</P>
```

The **RE** following the end-tag for FOOTNOTE (which is the first one *directly* within the P element) may be ignored or not, depending on how the DTD is set up:

<table>
<tr><td>Improper</td><td><pre><!ELEMENT BOOK      ANY +(FOOTNOTE)>
<!ELEMENT P         (#PCDATA | EMPH)*>
<!ELEMENT FOOTNOTE (#PCDATA)></pre></td></tr>
<tr><td>Proper</td><td><pre><!ELEMENT BOOK      ANY>
<!ELEMENT P
   (#PCDATA | EMPH | FOOTNOTE)*>
<!ELEMENT FOOTNOTE (#PCDATA)></pre></td></tr>
<tr><td>Proper</td><td><pre><!ELEMENT BOOK      ANY +(FOOTNOTE)>
<!ELEMENT P
   (#PCDATA | EMPH | FOOTNOTE)*>
<!ELEMENT FOOTNOTE (#PCDATA)></pre></td></tr>
</table>

Only when the subelement(s) before the **RE** is permitted by virtue of the content model is the subelement "proper", and only proper subelements count as intervening between an **RE** and the start or end of an element. Thus, a proper subelement immediately after a start-tag prevents an **RE** immediately following that proper subelement from being ignored; an improper subelement in the exact same place does not prevent such ignoring.

Although DTD designers may know these facts about all the element types, authors may not, so it is very important for DTD designers to consider all the cases that will arise, and make sure authors will not find themselves in confusing circumstances.

> **Note:** There is some disagreement among experts over some complex cases. For example, when the very first thing within an element is an entity reference, experts differ on how to treat an **RE** which is the first thing within the referenced entity.

The rule for **RE**s and subelements near the end of elements applies in analogous cases:

```
<P>Some REs are ignored.¶
<FOOTNOTE>See Clause 7.6.1.</FOOTNOTE></P>
```

These cases are not the most complex involving the proper/improper subelement distinction. So far, you could tell whether a subelement is proper or not merely from its ancestry. This is because applicable inclusion and exclusion exceptions are completely predicable from nothing more than the list of element types that are open at any given point. But there are cases where you must also know just *where* a subelement is in the parent's content model in order to decide whether it is proper or not. For example, the rule for P could have been:

```
<!ELEMENT  P              - -  (FOOTNOTE?, STUFF*)>
```

In this case a FOOTNOTE occurring first inside a P is proper. But assuming BOOK made FOOTNOTE an inclusion exception as above, a FOOTNOTE occurring after any STUFF subelements would be only valid, not proper. Some further complexities arise if FOOTNOTE is the subject of exclusion as well as inclusion exceptions.

**Note:** In particular, exclusion exceptions override any content model mention except for required elements. For example, if a content model says FOOTNOTE? no FOOTNOTE is permitted if an exclusion exception for FOOTNOTE also applies.

## Summary for authors

SGML has a lot of rules about where line-breaks can occur. As an author, you do not have control over how the rules apply in your DTD (unless you *also* happen to be the DTD designer). The best overall rule is to avoid putting line-breaks in your files entirely. Some SGML editing software even enforces this practice. If your software has such an option it is probably a good idea to turn it on.

If you really want to include line-breaks in your SGML source and want to be sure of where it will affect your results, you will need to:

- work through and understand the rules,
- learn enough about your DTD(s) to know which elements are proper and improper in which contexts, which elements have mixed or element content, and so on, and
- discover what semantics your SGML system can apply to whatever **RE**s are left after the rules apply so some are ignored (for example, whether you can set up the stylesheets to retain line-breaking in code or similar example elements, etc).

Short of this, you can apply very strict conventions on where you insert line-breaks: A single line-break immediately after a start-tag, or immediately before an end-tag, is always ignored. Line-breaks inside tags (but not within quoted attribute values) are also insignificant except that they cannot occur in mid-token, such as dividing an element type or attribute name in half.

## Summary for technophiles

Parser writers resolve these rules into a thing called a "finite state automaton", which is a way of implementing context-specific parsing rules. This section shows such an automaton for SGML. Skip ahead unless you are a technophile. For those remaining, the diagram below shows how a typical SGML parser would decide which **RE**s to discard, given what data has been seen in the current element. The thicker arcs indicate when an **RE** is passed back as data (not ignored). This diagram is based on work by Pierre Richard, who has written several SGML parsers of which the best known is

YASP. A copy of such an automaton would be kept for each element open at any given time (conceptually — there are various performance enhancements to use):

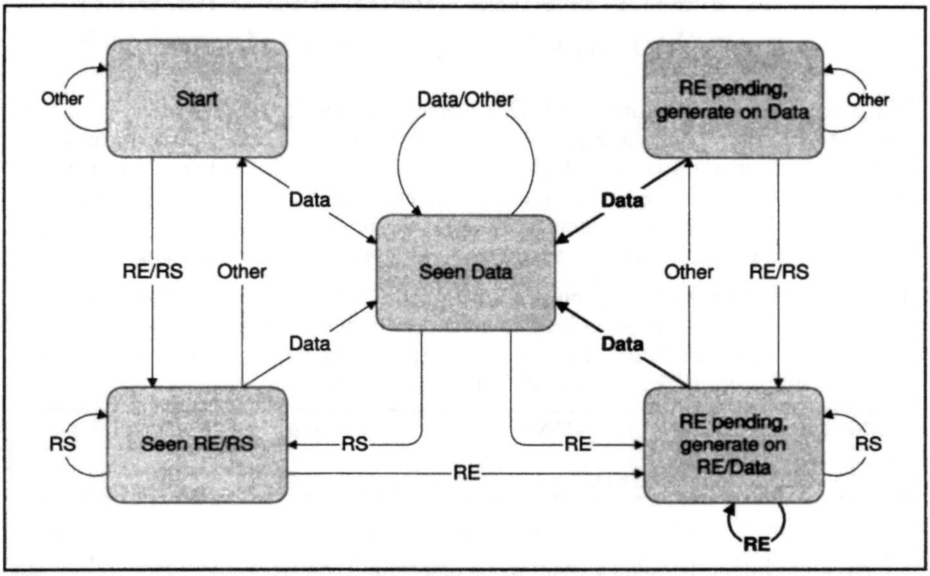


Interested readers should also read the excellent 1992 technical report on SGML record boundary handling from Exoterica Corporation, listed in the Bibliography.

SGML's rules about ignored **RE**s are considered by some to be its most arcane feature. Since they involve individual authors' preferences about how to lay out SGML source files in a non-GUI editor, various strategies have been proposed for simplifying them.

The first solution is the best: the SGML review may add an option to simply turn them off **RE** deletion in mixed content: a parser would hand back all the **RE**s and let later process decide what to do with them. A formatting process could get rid of them if desired, or could turn all the **RE**s into spaces like a parser does with whitespace in attribute values. A different modification has also been proposed, for every element type to declare whether it is "**RE**-ignoring" or not, but this would add complexity, such as for authors to reason out just which **RE**s disappear. Should such a change be made authors can. However, ask their DTD designers to ensure that *all* **RE**s are ignored (or that *none* are ignored), thus easing the author's task rather than making it more complex.

A second solution takes advantage of the fact that short of such an amendment, the bulk of the complexity can still be avoided if DTD designers use no inclusion exceptions in a DTD. The proper/improper distinction is not used anywhere else in SGML, so if there are no inclusion exceptions, there can be no improper elements, and authors need not figure out which elements are improper.

David Durand has proposed a third solution that nicely solves many of the problems with less disruption than either of the previous solutions: Tell the entity manager that the CR and/or LF characters in your files (if any) do not constitute line boundaries. Then it will not see any line-breaks in your entities at all, and will not insert any **RE** or **RS** pseudo-characters. All the rules become moot. Whitespace normalization can still apply to the CR and LF characters if you add them as separator characters in the SGML declaration. This general approach is sometimes known as "**RE** Delenda Est".

## 2.6 Why are my entities interpreted differently depending on where they are referenced?

When you refer to an entity, the SGML parser retrieves it and acts basically as if its contents had occurred in the place where the reference was. However, there are various contexts where markup is not recognized in the usual way. If you refer to an entity in varying contexts the contexts may impose different constraints on markup recognition. This can result in different elements being interpreted as present. This can happen without any error being reported, especially if you use a great deal of tag minimization.

As discussed in Question 1.1, you can refer to the "<" entity (whose replacement text is normally "<") in order to include literal less-than signs in your documents. Thus, such a reference is not exactly the same as typing a literal "<" in the same place — if it were then substituting "<" wouldn't make any difference.

```
<!ENTITY   lt          CDATA "<"    -- literal less-than -->
...
<P>The equation a&lt;b, means a must be smaller.</p>
```

But why is the "<" inside the entity treated differently? There are actually two reasons:

- First, an SGML rule called a "contextual constraint" (clause 9.6.2) says that "<" only counts as opening a start-tag when it is followed by a name start character. The end of any entity (including lt) counts like a character, and is not a name start.
- Second, the entity is often declared to be of type **CDATA** and inside **CDATA** entities no markup is recognized at all.

The current question comes up because **CDATA** entities are not the only context where markup is not all recognized. An entity's replacement text can contain strings that represent markup that is in context, and not be declared as **CDATA** or any other type that would suppress markup:

```
<!ENTITY   e           "<WARNING>Unplug first.</WARNING>">
```

If you reference this entity in a typical context the entity is expanded, the tags are recognized, and SGML sees a WARNING element and 13 characters of data content (assuming those things are allowed, no error arises):

```
<!ELEMENT  P           - -  (#PCDATA) +(WARNING | FN)>
...
<P>&e;</P>
```

This is a very common usage, such as to organize a book by putting the entirety of each chapter in a separate (probably external) entity; markup *should* be recognized in such situations. However, there is no reason you cannot refer to the same entity from a place where markup recognition *is* suppressed, such as from an **RCDATA** element or marked section (there are no **RCDATA** entities):

```
<!ELEMENT  XMP              - - RCDATA>
...
<XMP>&e;</XMP>
<P><![ RCDATA [ &e; ]]></P>
```

In these contexts the references are recognized and resolved, but the apparent tags in the entity's replacement text are not recognized, so no `WARNING` element occurs in the document. This is because the other contexts suppress recognition of the **STAGO** delimiter ("<") at the beginning of the entity's replacement text.

To get this entity treated the same in all contexts, you need to take other measures. If you want it never to represent a `WARNING` element (only literal text instead), you can declare the entity itself to be of type **CDATA**:

```
<!ENTITY    e          CDATA
            "<WARNING>Unplug first.</WARNING>">
```

If you want the markup in this entity *always* recognized, there is no way to accomplish it. Unlike inclusion exceptions, which can be overridden by their opposite, once some structure like a marked section or element has imposed an **RCDATA** parsing constraint it cannot be overridden.

## 2.7. What happens if I refer directly to an NDATA entity from within content?

An SGML parser does not parse the contents of a data entity such as **NDATA**. So (barring bugs) it should be possible to refer to one from content without confusing the parser. This will be true even if the first bits of some graphics file happen to look like potentially-valid SGML data and/or markup. However, there is no requirement that an SGML system do anything user-visible when such a reference occurs, so it is not generally considered a good practice.

There is nothing to actually prevent this usage:

```
<!NOTATION gif PUBLIC "+//...">
<!ENTITY    fig1        SYSTEM "c:\pix\fig1.gif" NDATA GIF>
...
<P>As you can see, &fig1; the sky is blue.</P>
```

A parser may or may not actually go and get the image in this case, though even if it does it will not try to parse it. It is not an SGML requirement that systems do anything in particular to present such an image, and some parsers do not give applications full information about entities that are referenced this way. In particular, some systems do not provide a way to attach processing specifications to such references so you can control what happens.

A logical behavior for a *formatter* would be to retrieve the entity, find and invoke a processor that understands it, get some display rectangle back, and show that at the point of reference. For small inline graphics this is often the desired behavior; larger objects sometimes would receive special treatment such as their own set-off display areas or a "thumbnail" inline that affords access to a higher-resolution version. Systems that support such references typically create special hooks so stylesheets or other specifications can decide whether to ignore the entity, show it inline, provide a link to it, or whatever.

> **Note:** A system may use a special kind of node for this, with the name, **PUBLIC**, and **SYSTEM** identifiers of the entity and its notation. For example, DSSSL uses a special grove node with access to such information. The ESIS specification (see glossary) also states that for a reference to an **NDATA** entity a parser should return the entity name, entity text, and any applicable notation name, identifier, and attributes (though not the entity name). However, for a reference to any internal entity other than **SDATA** or **PI**, and for the boundaries of external SGML text entities, "nothing is passed to the application"; so applications that follow ESIS may have some difficulty doing anything with those.

It is generally better practice to avoid such references altogether, although there is no way to set up SGML to prevent it. This completely prevents the problem of systems that do not support such references well.

The better alternative is to use an element with an attribute of type **ENTITY**. This is usually far more effective because the object has a full-fledged SGML element associated, and so can use all the processing options that implementations provide for elements. It also provides a nice place to hang a caption for the graphic or other data, and a text-form alternative that can be provided to visually impaired readers (see also Questions 1.11 and 1.16):

```
<ELEMENT   FIG          - - (CAPTION, ALT)>
<!ATTLIST  FIG
  ENT      ENTITY       #REQUIRED>
...
<FIG ENT="fig1">
  <CAPTION>A sunny day in Providence.</CAPTION>
  <ALT>Gray background with large water droplets.</ALT>
</FIG>
```

The good news is that there is a very good practice available for dealing effectively with such entities. The not-so-good news it that many DTD designers and authors don't use entities at all for **NDATA**. Instead, they put actual system identifiers or filenames on an attribute, and omit declarations:

```
<GRAPHIC FILE="c:\aaa.tif">See figure #1</GRAPHIC>
```

Even though such usage is commonplace (the largest example being the HTML A element, which does essentially this), it is not the best practice in SGML terms. This is because SGML has no way to know that such an attribute is really a system identifier, filename, or similar important construct, and so cannot help manage or validate the data as well as it otherwise could. For example, an SGML-aware packer will not go out and fetch such data objects and pack them up, which can lead to readers being surprised when they try to view a graphic that never made it to the receiving system. These problems could be overcome in particular implementations that went the extra mile, but it would be easier and more consistent if all systems worked the same way, which they should if the method SGML already knows about is used instead.

This approach also has the potential problem that an SGML system has no way of knowing what **NOTATION** applies (and adding a second attribute of type **NOTATION** to specify it is not correct — see Question 5.14).

The better practice is to instead declare each data object as an entity and name it (not reference it!) as needed. Since the distinction between filenames and entity names in attributes is determined by the DTD, authors need to know which way the DTD is set up. If it is not the better practice, then persuading the DTD designer to change the DTD might be in order. If it is the better practice, then authors should also be provided with a good interface for creating the **ENTITY** declarations that are needed: they shouldn't have to learn all about declaration syntax just for this one case.

## 2.8. What can I put inside elements with declared content CDATA or RCDATA?

An element whose declaration specifies declared content **CDATA** or **RCDATA** is commonly used when one wishes to have text content that may contain SGML delimiters such as "<" and "&". Most SGML markup is not recognized within such elements (entity references are recognized within **RCDATA** elements). However, such elements are ended by an end-tag, so delimiters like "</" that could start an end-tag *are* recognized when in context (namely when followed by a character that makes sense in that role, as discussed in Question 1.1).

These declared content types are frequently used for EXAMPLE and similar elements, where authors may wish to include math or computer program text containing less-than signs, or include SGML samples (for example, in a book about SGML that is also done using SGML). For example:

```
<!ELEMENT  xmp           - - CDATA>
...
<xmp>In SGML, tags use pointy brackets, e.g. "<P>"</xmp>
```

Authors typically realize immediately that the end-tag of such an element may not generally be omitted, and that an end-tag for the element will be recognized even though little or no other markup will be. Those also familiar with SGML minimization would not likely be surprised to discover that a minimized end-tag(s) such as "</>" or "</</>" also terminates a **CDATA** or **RCDATA** element, or that a **NET** delimiter terminates it if it began with a **NET**-enabling start-tag. Authors might also predict correctly that an end-tag for some larger containing element would also work (they might assume this to be true only when **OMITTAG** is on).

Authors might also expect that such an element can be ended only by a full end-tag, for example "</XMP>". Nearly everyone is surprised to learn that an **ETAGO** delimiter followed by an explicit name *other than* any currently open, still counts as markup. In such a case SGML parsers will report an error.

Intuition on this matter is so strong that the HTML DTD declares itself non-conforming in this respect, as quoted below (see ftp://ds.internic.net/rfc/rfc1866.txt). Note that HTML does this primarily as a concession to erroneous early implementations, and declares such nonconformance to be "deprecated", which is just the opposite of recommended!

```
<![ %HTML.Deprecated [

<!ENTITY % literal "CDATA"
        -- historical, non-conforming parsing mode where
           the only markup signal is the end tag
           in full
        -->

<!ELEMENT (XMP|LISTING) - -  %literal>
<!ATTLIST XMP
        %SDAFORM; "Lit"
        %SDAPREF; "Example:&#RE;"
        >
<!ATTLIST LISTING
        %SDAFORM; "Lit"
        %SDAPREF; "Listing:&#RE;"
        >

<!-- <XMP>               Example section          -->
<!-- <LISTING>           Computer listing         -->

<!ELEMENT PLAINTEXT - O %literal>
<!-- <PLAINTEXT>         Plain text passage       -->

<!ATTLIST PLAINTEXT
        %SDAFORM; "Lit"
        >
]]>
```

The SGML standard's definition of this construct in Clause 7.6 states that such an element is ended "only by an **etago** delimiter-in-context (which need not open a valid *end-tag*) or a valid **net**." *The SGML Handbook* (p. 59) states that "Only the correct end-tag (or that of an element in which this element is nested) will be recognized", which seems to suggest that an *invalid* end-tag (that is, for some other element type) is *not* recognized.

In practice, most SGML parsers take "</" in context as the end of a **CDATA** or **RCDATA** element. If followed by the GI for an element type that is not currently open, the tag is considered an error. So in practice end-tags cannot occur within such elements even if they do not name some element that is actually open.

> **Note**: Most parser writers I have discussed this with do not prefer this implementation. However, they either consider it the correct interpretation or they believe that compatibility with other parsers is a high enough priority that they must implement it the other way.

**CDATA** elements pose another question as well, because the keyword means a different thing than for **CDATA** marked sections, **CDATA** entities, or **CDATA** attributes. This is discussed in Question 2.4.

The safest practice is not to use "</" at all inside **CDATA** or **RCDATA** elements. In order to make it possible to avoid that string the element needs to be of type **RCDATA** (substituting "`</`" would not work within **CDATA**). Because of this, **RCDATA** is almost always a better choice.

## 2.9. What does a marked section end ("]]>") mean if it's outside of any marked section?

It is an error. Clause 9.6 defines the marked section close or **MSC** delimiter ("]]") to be recognized in content, as long as it is followed immediately by **MDC** (">"), but whether or not it is inside a marked section. Clause 10.4 declares its occurrence outside a marked section to be an error, as here:

```
<!-- WRONG -->
<P>Marked sections are closed with "]]>"</P>
```

This has the advantage that fragments of SGML need not be accompanied by information about how many marked sections are pending as of their start in order to be parsed correctly. Such information is only needed for validation. It also prevents authors from using the string in contexts that they *later* surround with a marked section, which if allowed could lead to their new marked section having a premature demise. However, these appear to be the only advantages.

Authors can easily forget to substitute something for "]]" when it occurs in content (the most obvious cases would be in equations or computer program examples, but the string could come up in other contexts, too). Some programs intended to protect SGML delimiters when converting data into SGML simply do not check for this string, although they do check for "<" and "&". This can lead to later surprises. See Question 7.6 for some related but more technical questions about marked section delimiters.

## 2.10. Can I put marked sections inside other marked sections?

There are five different status keywords for marked sections. **INCLUDE** and **IGNORE** permit other marked sections to occur within marked sections that use them, as does the little-used **TEMP**. **RCDATA** and **CDATA** do not allow other marked sections to be nested in them. Any type of marked section can *be* embedded in another; it is the outer marked section's type that determines whether nesting is allowed. There are cases where nesting can lead to unanticipated results, so it should be used with caution.

> **Note:** A marked section may have any number of keywords, and only the highest-ranking one applies. The ranking in Clause 10.4.2 is **IGNORE** (highest), **CDATA**, **RCDATA**, and **INCLUDE**. **TEMP** is not assigned a rank, and the grammar rules consider it part of a status keyword specification but not strictly a status keyword.

### INCLUDE and IGNORE

The two most important status keywords, **INCLUDE** and **IGNORE**, allow nesting. Nesting is entirely intuitive for **INCLUDE**. However, it is worth noting that because of nesting an **IGNORE** marked section is not quite *totally* ignored: it must be parsed enough to recognize not only its end ("]]>"), but also any marked section start.

It's actually a little bit harder than that. An **IGNORE** marked section may include another marked section, which may allow further nesting:

```
<![ IGNORE [
   It was a controversial decision.
   <![ IGNORE [
      I believe that
      <![ %flip; [
         it prevented more problems than it created.
      ]]>
   ]]>
]]>
```

You might expect that in such cases SGML examines the status keywords of the nested marked sections, expands any parameter entities there, and so on. However, Clause 10.4.2 says that the status keywords of a nested section are "ignored". Since "]]>" cannot occur as literal data within any marked section (even **CDATA** ones), failing to distinguish the keywords of nested section should not often pose problems. This rule can, however, prevent you from placing a marked section around an *element* containing "]]>", even if the element itself has declared content **CDATA** or **RCDATA**.

One subtle case that can be troublesome, however, is if you have a **CDATA** or **RCDATA** marked section that contains what looks like a marked section start:

```
<![ CDATA [
   A marked section starts with "<![" and ends later.
]]>
```

This works fine until an author or later editor happens to enclose it inside a larger **IGNORE** marked section. If they are blocking out a large section they may not notice the marked section way down in the middle. Because the SGML parser then must "ignore" the status keyword of the (now nested) marked section, it cannot know that the it is **CDATA**. Because of that it cannot know to ignore the quoted string, and must take it as marking the start of another (doubly-nested) marked section. In this case the parser will open an extra marked section:

```
<![ IGNORE [...
   <![ CDATA [
      A marked section starts with "<![" and ends later.
   ]]>...
]]>
<P>This paragraph unintentionally left out.</P>
...
<XMP>A marked section ends with "]]>".</XMP>
```

The P is still within the **IGNORE** marked section, as is whatever follows. The marked section bounaries will likely never balance out at all unless "]]>" happens to occur inside a later **CDATA** element such as the XMP here (see Clause 4.33). Even in that case the document structure would likely be wildly different from what was intended. The parser may detect an error somewhere, but it would not likely be near the actual error and may not happen at all, especially if **OMITTAG** is on.

**Note**: A more esoteric problem arises if parameter entities are used on a nested marked section, and (as many parsers allow) they do not just contain status keywords, but keywords plus the following "[" and further content (a case can be made that SGML requires this to be allowed by parsers). Any marked section delimiters in such a parameter entity will be missed if the marked section becomes embedded in another, producing interesting effects.

A final detail about nesting marked sections is that SGML prohibits the entity-end signal from occurring within an **IGNORE** marked section (Clause 10.4.2). Thus, the following is valid if the `obstat` entity is set to **INCLUDE**, but becomes invalid if it is **IGNORE**, or if a larger **IGNORE** marked section is added later:

```
<!ENTITY   q            SYSTEM "c:\tng\{1|10|42|61|94|132}">
...
<![ %obstat; [ &q; ]]>
```

### TEMP

The status keyword **TEMP** also allows nesting. The meaning of **TEMP** is limited, as it has no effect on what markup is recognized or on what content is ignored. A **TEMP** marked section (see Clause 10.4.2) "identifies the section as a temporary part of the document that might need to be removed at a later time". Thus its effect on the element structure is no different from **INCLUDE**: the distinction between the two is purely conventional. It does not address versioning issues such as distinguishing levels of **TEMP**-ness or the effectivity of multiple revision-sets or document editions. These must all be built at a higher level, so **TEMP** is seldom used in practice.

### RCDATA and CDATA

**RCDATA** and **CDATA** marked sections cannot contain nested marked sections because part of their effect is to suppress recognition of the **MDO** delimiter (which therefore cannot be used to open another marked section). This makes the way a parser must handle marked sections vary greatly depending on their keywords, so changing the status keyword of a marked section can have vast and long-lasting effects. For example, say an author is debating whether to include the following historical paragraph in some document and so puts it in a marked section:

```
<P><![ %flag; [
"<P>" is the HTML start-tag for paragraphs, but some early
HTML applications implemented it as if it were EMPTY, and
became confused if they saw "</P>." ]]>
```

Because the sentence contains strings that look like SGML markup, the marked section status keyword must alternate between **IGNORE** and **CDATA** or **RCDATA**, not between **IGNORE** and **INCLUDE**. If an author should slip and use **INCLUDE** the quoted characters will be taken as tags instead of content, producing the wrong result. If the examples used ubiquitous tag names like `P` and if **OMITTAG** is on, it can happen that no error is detected.

The probability of mistakes increases because changing "`%flag;`" must be done in a declaration far away from the place where the effect of that change occurs, and because a single parameter entity typically controls many marked sections, only some of which might *also* require **RCDATA** treatment.

Another side-effect of changing status keywords is analogous to the nesting problems with **IGNORE** discussed above: the scope of marked sections can change. For example, if a marked section that contains a nested marked section changes from **INCLUDE** or **IGNORE** to **CDATA** or **RCDATA**, then the end of the inner marked section becomes the end of the outer marked section, and the former end of the outer marked section becomes an orphan delimiter, which is an error as discussed in Question 2.9.

In the example below, changing from **IGNORE**, **INCLUDE**, or **TEMP** to **RCDATA** or **CDATA** would cause an error. Checks for this particular error are sometimes forgotten by implementers, in which case the document could end up containing "<! [ INCLUDE [" as literal data content — most likely not the desired effect.

```
<![ %flag; [
   Some <![ INCLUDE [ very important ]]> text. ]]>
```

The best way to avoid any of these complex cases is to avoid nesting marked sections at all. If you do nest them, be extremely careful about mixing types, about enclosing big areas inside of **IGNORE** marked sections to "comment them out", and about putting marked sections around declared content elements.

## 2.11. Can marked sections cross elements?

Although it is not widely known, marked sections form a tree structure almost entirely separate from a document's element structure, and can indeed cross element boundaries arbitrarily. A marked section is not required to contain any start-tag just because it contains the corresponding end-tag, or vice-versa. However, it is risky to create imbalanced (or "asynchronous") marked sections because they introduce very complex interactions that are hard to manage.

The markup shown below is an example of an imbalanced marked section:

```
<P>One paragraph
<![ INCLUDE [ </P><P> ]]>
or two? </P>
```

When this case was raised for discussion at the SGML '91 conference, an early member of the SGML committee leapt up and declared that such structures are not permitted in SGML; but indeed they *are* permitted and completely valid.

In the example above there are two paragraphs. However, if **INCLUDE** changes to **IGNORE** there is only one. This provides an excellent "acid test" for an SGML editor's marked section support. On the other hand few may care whether their software is proof against this particular acid or not. Many count the everyday benefit of preventing unintended use greater than the rarely-experienced cost of precluding intended use, and so would prefer that imbalanced (or "asynchronous") marked sections be considered an error or warning and reported to them.

The case just shown is actually an unduly simple one. There is no requirement that markup inside a marked section be "anti-balanced" as shown above, such that ignoring the marked section has only a very localized effect on the element structure. The content of an **IGNORE** marked section need not resemble valid SGML at all. So long as it doesn't contain "]]>" or "<! [", anything at all can go there:

```
<![ IGNORE [ <P><Q><R> ]]>
<![ IGNORE [
   <#FOO><?GAK> <!ELEMENT        foo ANY>
  <P!? <<<<<<
]]>
```

A trap, however, awaits authors who do this, because it is easy to cut and paste *parts* of things accidentally, producing unexpected results, especially if a marked section is long or if clever software is available to hide marked sections from view (similar to the "hidden text" option in many word processors). For example, selecting the second `P` element from the first example in this section and pasting it elsewhere may cause one of several things to happen:

- If there is no marked section open at the paste location, the user has added a probably unexpected "`]]>`" to the document. This should yield an error message since the delimiter string will be recognized despite the fact that no marked section is open (see Question 2.9).
- If there is an **`INCLUDE`** or **`IGNORE`** marked section open at the paste location, the user has caused it to end earlier than it did before, and the old end-point has been orphaned. If **`IGNORE`**, an unbalanced end-tag has been inserted, which *may* produce an error here or possibly much later.
- If there are several marked sections open, all of their delimiters shift up one level (changing all the scopes), and the last one's close delimiter becomes orphaned.
- If there is a **`CDATA`** or **`RCDATA`** marked section open, its close (and any containing marked sections' closes) are affected as just described, and in addition the "`<P>`" within the just-pasted data is no longer a start-tag.

Because of the many dangers, the marginal usefulness, and the lack of universal support for marked sections that cross element boundaries, it is good practice to avoid them.

## 2.12. Can entities cross or be crossed by element, tag, and other boundaries?

Much like marked sections, entities can cross element boundaries. That is, an entity can start in one element and end in another as shown here:

```
<!ENTITY   weird        "</CHP> <CHP> <CT></CT> <P>">
...
<P>So that is how it works &weird; sometimes</P>
```

The second part, in the document instance, looks like one paragraph with an entity reference that might be to some text. But hidden inside that entity reference is the end of an entire chapter and the beginning of the next, including a required but empty chapter title! This kind of markup can be extraordinarily frustrating to figure out, especially because it is not usually as obvious as this example. Instead, odd structures arise by interaction of entities with and without markup, referenced in contexts that do or don't suppress markup recognition, with **`OMITTAG`** filling in gaps that would otherwise raise error messages.

Clause 9.4.3 points out that this ability to cross boundaries can be misused, and recommends against using entities in any way "that obscures the markup". Common practice avoids it even more strongly, although there is no SGML setting or option for actually turning the capability off so it gets reported as an error.

A note in the Clause makes the phrase "obscures the markup" a bit more specific. The rules boil down to this table:

| Construct | Constraint |
|---|---|
| Tag | Opening and closing delimiters must be in the same entity. |
| PI | Opening and closing delimiters must be in the same entity. |
| Declaration | Opening and closing delimiters must be in the same entity. |
| Literal | Opening and closing delimiters must be in the same entity. |
| Other delimited text | Opening and closing delimiters must be in the same entity (SGML does not define "delimited text", though it is mentioned by some definitions in Clause 4). |
| **CDATA**, **RCDATA**, **IGNORE** marked section | Content must start and end in the same entity. |
| Other (**INCLUDE**, **TEMP**) marked section | Content *should* start and end in the same entity. |
| **CDATA** or **RCDATA** element | Content must start and end in the same entity. |
| Other element | Content *should* start and end in the same entity. |
| Other element | Start-tag and end-tag should be in the same entity, or "should be the replacement text of entities whose references are in the same entity". |
| Other marked section | Marked section start and end should be in the same entity, or "should be the replacement text of entities whose references are in the same entity". |
| Declarations | Parameter entities cannot start or end in mid-token (this part follows from how the ps and ts separators are defined in SGML, as discussed in Question 7.9). |

These rules arise because entity replacement is "lexical" rather than "syntactic". This means that it is a character-replacement operation, rather than a way to specifically include document sub-structures (such as sets of elements). As discussed above for marked sections, this approach does make optimizations such as pre-compiling and indexing entities more difficult, and requires that parsers maintain quite separate lists of open entities, elements, and marked sections.

## 2.13. How do SUBDOC entities relate to documents that refer to them?

In contrast to the lexical or string-oriented character of other entities (on which see Question 2.12), **SUBDOC** entities provide a *syntactic* inclusion facility. This means that a **SUBDOC** entity cannot be an arbitrary span of SGML. A **SUBDOC** must constitute a complete document, conforming to some DTD in every respect.

**SUBDOC** entities are more constrained than other (more "lexical") entities, since they must be syntactic wholes. This is useful since it prevents unwanted interactions between the referring and referenced entities, and can help pin down errors more easily by preventing mistakes from affecting distant data.

> **Note**: A restriction to being exactly a single element (including any subelements and content within it) would still be a syntactic mechanism and gain some of the consequent benefits, but such a fragment cannot be a **SUBDOC** entity (except possibly by coincidence). A method for dealing with such fragments is discussed below.

However, **SUBDOC** introduces a very strong separation: a **SUBDOC** entity is really no more closely related to its referring document than any other document, so is not a "sub" document in the sense of being an integral part. This poses a number of difficulties such as that **IDREF** links cannot be validated or used between a main document and any **SUBDOC** entities. Perhaps because of these limitations, **SUBDOC** has not seen wide use.

## Setting up SUBDOC entities

**SUBDOC** has been suggested as a way to be able to organize SGML portions smaller than whole document. To do this you must pick each element that is to be a separate organization unit and extract it into an entity, adding a declaration and reference or mention behind. Then you must "promote" each such element to be a valid **SUBDOC** entity. Promoting involves modifying a DTD so the extracted element conforms to it.

For example, if you are extracting a SEC from out of a BOOK you might start with a DTD like this:

```
<!DOCTYPE  BOOK [
<!ELEMENT  BOOK          - - (FRONT, BODY, BACK)>
<!ELEMENT  SEC           - - (ST, P*)>...
]>
```

It is often suggested that all you need to do to successfully extract a valid **SUBDOC** is to change one token in the **DOCTYPE**: in this case, BOOK to SEC. This sometimes works, because of several details such as:

- All the element types that have instances in the new **SUBDOC** should already be declared in the DTD.
- SGML ignores extraneous element declarations (some systems issue a warning).

However, the simple approach will only work for some basic cases. The changes required to the DTD may be far more extensive because SGML includes several kinds of long-distance dependencies, that all must be somehow removed before you can do such a promotion. You must take care of all these details:

- A **#CURRENT** attribute value in one **SUBDOC** entity can't affect elements in another, so the first instance in each promoted element *must* be supplied (see Question 5.16).
- **IDREF** references cannot cross **SUBDOC** entities, so any such references from the document to the part that is being made into a **SUBDOC** (or vice-versa) must be converted to use an inter-document hyperlinking mechanism outside SGML. HyTime NAMELOCS and Text Encoding Initiative extended pointers are appropriate examples (see Question 6.11 for more on both); but in any case this will involve re-coding reference attributes, perhaps adding new intermediate elements, and perhaps adding a whole new set of element types to support the new reference mechanisms.
- **ID** uniqueness cannot be validated across **SUBDOC** entities, so if you may later want to assemble all the documents into one, you will not know in advance if there will be duplicate **ID**s around.

There are several more concerns that can prevent parsing the **SUBDOC** correctly:

- **SUBDOC** entities do not inherit inclusion exceptions that were active in their referencing context. For example, if FOOTNOTE is an inclusion exception on BOOK or BODY, any FOOTNOTE in the extracted SEC is a syntax error. There is no way around this other than modifying the DTD to add the included element types into other **ELEMENT** declarations, such as SEC and any other promoted types).

- If the promoted content uses certain kinds of minimization, such as empty start-tags ("<>", see Question 2.1), **NET** (see Questions 1.4 and 1.5), or **SHORTREF**s (see Question 3.1), it may no longer parse correctly without prior context. SGML may or may not report an error.

## SUBDOC and SGML fragments

**SUBDOC** can be used for certain applications, but it does not do everything required for supporting SGML fragments such as extracting elements and shipping them around easily on demand. Because of the long-distance and context dependencies discussed above, authors and DTD designers must be austere to use it: No **#CURRENT**, no **USEMAP**, no marked sections, no **NET**, and so on. More importantly, they must give up or change how they use **IDREF** links, inclusion exceptions, and other features. Unless they can apply the same austerity in all their uses of SGML, data management problems will eventually become intractable: documents must exist in several slightly different forms that must somehow be kept in sync as changes happen.

Because of these constraints it can be impractical to solve the general problem: promoting *any* element to be a **SUBDOC** entity on demand based on reader requirements, network speed issues, security, or other concerns. Even if this is accomplished, it becomes hard to validate each promoted element's structure (that usually requires its referencing context).

The main alternative is to send SGML portions as they are, even with the troublesome constructs. But to parse them correctly a recipient needs to be told exactly what context-dependencies apply in the particular context: for example, any **#CURRENT** attributes used in the fragment and what value was last assigned them *before* the fragment.

SGML Open's specification for packaging SGML fragments provides a way to transmit the needed context information. If an SGML Open fragment specification accompanies an element extracted from some document, a receiving system can use the information there to parse the element correctly even though the rest of the document is not included. As a brief example, here is a fragment specification with most of the possible options included (many entries will not always be needed, such as LASTOPENED which is only needed if the fragment begins with "<>" as discussed in Question 2.1):

```
(COMMENT "This fragment is subsection (4.4.1) of
  the book in galley form.")
(SOURCE SYSTEM "http://xyz.com/books/draft/b.sgm"
   (ID chap4) (TREELOC 1 5 1))
(DOCTYPE book PUBLIC "-//Acme//DTD Book//EN")
(SUBSET SYSTEM "c:\foo.ent")
(LASTCLOSED CT)
(LASTOPENED CT)
(CURRENT FIGR ent="myvalue")
(CURRENT P security="top")
```

```
(CONTEXT
 book version=draft (
  fm()
  bdy #net #map="map37" (
    chp #4 ()
    chp label="5" (
      ct() sec #3 () sec ( #fragment ) sec #5 () )
    chp () )
  bm() )
)
```

The formal syntax definition for such headers, and full documentation of each part of it, can be found in SGML Open Technical Report TR9601 (DeRose and Grosso 1996), which can be obtained at www.sgmlopen.org/sgml/docs/techpubs.htm.

# 3. For Data Conversion Specialists

Many organizations and individuals have data in formats used by particular version of particular software products, and sooner or later want to move it into an open format that will allow that data to outlive any particular piece of software. I recently had the pain of trying to recover some documents I wrote only 5 years ago, using a word processor that is still popular. But the current version can't read the old version's files, and the old version doesn't run on the current operating system (though I could still read the floppy disks). To avoid countless similar problems, people often convert data from proprietary formats into SGML.

Converting data to SGML can sometimes be done automatically, but often involves either a lot of manual editing, frequent use of "global change" commands, or some level of programming using Perl or other tools. Even automatic conversions usually involve some "tuning up" at the end to get the data just right. To do this, a data conversion specialist needs to know many more details of SGML syntax, as well as the syntax of whatever format the data started out in. It's especially important to know all the strings that might have special meanings to SGML and exactly what circumstances cause them to do so. This chapter discusses many questions about contexts and meaning in SGML, and how to avoid tripping over the rules when handling massive amounts of data that might not be *quite* in SGML.

## 3.1. How long does a USEMAP last?

**USEMAP** declarations activate **SHORTREF** maps at various points. They can do this either automatically within all instances of a given element type, or manually at any given point in the document, lasting until the current element ends.

**SHORTREF** is an SGML feature which allows DTD designers to declare that certain strings should be taken as if they were references to entities, when appearing in content. This does not take the place of normal entity references ("`&name;`"), but is used for creating special cases of shorthand. For example, **SHORTREF** would allow "`--`" to serve as shorthand for "`—`" in this way:

```
<!ENTITY   mdash        SDATA "FONT=SYMBOL CODE=151">
<!SHORTREF map1         "--"          mdash>
```

The first declaration is for the entity itself; while the second creates a table of string-to-entity conversions to be performed (named "map1"). The table is called a "**SHORTREF** map", and any number of them may be created.

**SHORTREF** strings are considered SGML delimiters, and are declared in the SGML declaration (they can be declared there even if never set up for use by **SHORTREF** declarations in the DTD). In this example, notice that even though "--" is an SGML delimiter (**COM**), that use and use as a **SHORTREF** do not collide. **COM** is *not* recognized in SGML content (**CON** mode), and **SHORTREF** delimiters are *only* recognized in content (not in attribute values, for example)

However, none of this has any effect without a **USEMAP** declaration. That declaration can go either in the DTD or in the instance, with different effects that last for different durations.

### USEMAP in the DTD

```
<!USEMAP    map1          book>
```

Placed inside the DTD, this declaration says that the table called map1 should be turned on within BOOK elements. **USEMAP** declarations in the DTD associate maps with particular element contexts. There can be any number of them, each assigning a map to any number of elements, so you can swap maps in and out as elements of various types begin and end. One common example is to make quotation marks start a QUOTE element, unless one is already open, in which case they close it:

```
<!ENTITY    q-open        "<QUOTE>">
<!ENTITY    q-close       "</QUOTE>">
<!SHORTREF qmap1          '"'         q-open>
<!SHORTREF qmap2          '"'         q-close>
<!USEMAP    qmap1         book>
<!USEMAP    qmap2         quote>
```

In this case, anywhere inside of a BOOK element a double quote starts a QUOTE because qmap1 is in effect. But QUOTE turns off qmap1 and replaces it with qmap2, so a double quote inside a QUOTE closes that QUOTE via qmap2. Two cases to remember are:

- Map qmap2 goes into effect whether QUOTE is started via qmap1 or via any explicit or omitted tag.
- The fact that qmap2 is in effect does not mean that the markup *must* make use of it to end the QUOTE element; it can be done just as well with an explicit end-tag or with tag-omission.

**SHORTREF** maps that the DTD designer associates with particular element types (by using **USEMAP** in the DTD), end when the element that caused them ends. So in the QUOTE example, once the QUOTE ends qmap1 goes back into effect (which, typically, is what you want so it works the next time around). If no **SHORTREF** is in effect, no **SHORTREF** delimiters get mapped to entities. For example, qmap1 could be set up only to apply within ABSTRACT or LIST elements, with no mapping done within BOOK elements in general.

### **USEMAP** in the document instance

**USEMAP** declarations in the DTD always result in maps taking effect at element boundaries, and so fit perfectly with the hierarchical element structure of the document. SGML does, however, permit authors to insert **USEMAP** declarations anywhere in content to turn on a particular map unconditionally:

```
<P>Just for this phrase, map7 will be in effect:
<!USEMAP map7>4 20 +
</P>
```

Note that in the instance, a **USEMAP** declaration only includes a map name, and no element types. A map that gets turned on this way replaces any map otherwise in effect (such as qmap1 for BOOK), but it does not stay on forever. Rather:

- It can be suspended when some other element starts, which assigns a different map via its own **USEMAP** declaration in the DTD. For example, given the declarations shown earlier a QUOTE element would suspend any **USEMAP** in effect before it started. In that case, the suspended map resumes when that element ends.
- It can be replaced by a new map if another **USEMAP** declaration appears later in the same element.
- It ends whenever the element that it started in ends. There is no way to turn on a map and keep it in effect beyond the element in which it started, or to have multiple simultaneous maps.

The ability to turn on a map at any point can lead to long-distance effects that show up after later editing. Since such a map remains in effect for the rest of that element (until overridden by another one, or suspended in a subelement), it may be overridden by large subelements yet re-activate far later. The worst case would be where the author accidentally moves a **USEMAP** declaration just within the beginning of an entire CHAPTER or BOOK element (perhaps by moving a large block of data that the author didn't realize contained a **USEMAP** declaration). The **USEMAP** will then hang on for the rest of that element except where overridden. Authors may be mystified when the map applies in unexpected places, especially because the places are discontiguous: The map re-appears whenever you happen *not* to be in a sub-element that applies its own map.

## 3.2. Does a NOTATION attribute let me use delimiters in content?

No. Although setting a **NOTATION** attribute on some element means conceptually that the element's content is in that **NOTATION**, it has no effect on how the content is parsed. The SGML parser will still look for delimiters as usual.

Thus you cannot generally put in a GIF image, a piece of program code, or a $\TeX$ equation literally, without first replacing "<" and "&" with entities as described in Question 1.1. It may happen that such strings do not occur (or do not occur in contexts where SGML would mistake them for delimiters), but that would just be a lucky break.

The better practice is to leave such data in separate external entities, named on attributes of a special element type created for the purpose. This is described in Question 1.16. For more details on **NOTATION** attributes, see Question 5.14.

## 3.3 Can I have an end-tag for an EMPTY element?

No. SGML allows declaring an element to be **EMPTY** as shown below, so it can never have any subelements or text content. In that case the end-tag is not merely unnecessary, but is prohibited.

```
<!ELEMENT  REF           - O EMPTY>
```

In declarations not involving declared content **EMPTY**, the "O" flag means that (context permitting) the end-tag of an instance of the element type *may* be omitted. In this case, however, the end-tag *must* be omitted regardless of what flag appears. Thus the following is illegal given the declaration above:

```
<!-- WRONG -->
<REF></REF>
```

Authoring systems take care of this (though it requires them to know a little extra about the DTD during their "Save" operation). Authors without SGML-aware authoring systems, and especially anyone doing data conversion, must know which element types are **EMPTY** and tag accordingly. Start- and end-tags cannot just be put in universally.

This rule slightly complicates software's support for SGML export: it must know for every element whether the DTD declares it **EMPTY** or not, so that (unlike all other elements) it doesn't write out an end-tag. It is not enough to know that the element *is* empty, since many elements are typically permitted to be empty but not required to be. This leads to DTD-specific code in conversion and export utilities.

> **Note:** It also makes it hard to set up non-SGML-aware utility software to do simple but useful manipulations on SGML files. SGML files that totally avoid complex features, minimization, and so on, can often be usefully processed with software that knows very little about SGML; however, such software has no way of telling that it should consider "<P>" open until "</P>", but not consider "<HR>" open at all. To learn that automatically requires implementing most of an SGML parser, not just a few simple pattern-matching rules.

The effect on conversion software is actually more subtle for two reasons:

First, it is not enough to know about the **ELEMENT** declaration saying "**EMPTY**". An element instance (not element type) also counts as **EMPTY** if it specifies a value for one or more attributes that have default value **#CONREF** (see Question 5.17 for more on **#CONREF** and declared content **EMPTY**). For example, given the declaration below any instance of X that gives a value for C1 may not have an end-tag, though any instance that does not, may.

```
<!ELEMENT  WARN         - O (#PCDATA)>
<!ATTLIST  WARN
   C1      IDREF        #CONREF>
...
<WARN>Ground filter capacitor before servicing.</WARN>
...
<WARN C1=warning37> <!-- end-tag prohibited here -->
```

> **Note**: Element types may define any number of **#CONREF** attributes, and they need not be **IDREF**s:
>
> ```
> <!ATTLIST  QUOTE
>    C1       IDREF        #CONREF
>    C2       NAME         #CONREF>
> ```

Second, ESIS-based applications (see glossary) are by definition not told what element types or instances are declared-**EMPTY** as opposed to **#CONREF**-empty as opposed to merely-empty. So any ESIS-based conversion application only knows when the elements begin and end, and cannot correctly support such elements. Of course programs can exchange the information in some other way.

For the same reason an ESIS-based "normalizer" is quite difficult to build for SGML. No exclusively ESIS-based application can know enough to create an SGML file with the same ESIS as its input.

> **Note**: There are other issues with normalization such as what to do with entities, marked sections, comments, and some **RE**s. If there were a normative definition it would make SGML system testing nearly trivial: the first run would convert to the normalized form and *all* further runs would have to produce output identical to their input. Computer Scientists call this useful characteristic "idempotence".

**EMPTY** elements thus complicate use of generic software to process SGML files. Many useful things can be done to SGML entities using generic tools using regular expressions (like awk, sed, and Perl). However, such tools don't know the level of detail about SGML and about particular DTDs that would be needed to manipulate **EMPTY** elements correctly, even if integrated with an ESIS-style parser.

> **Note**: This rule is one of the very few reasons that a parser needs a DTD to get the right ESIS from minimal SGML documents. Except for a very few things, a parser could get the right ESIS *even if* for any reason the DTD were unavailable, which is a very useful characteristic especially with networked information.

## Avoiding EMPTY problems

You can avoid these issues by avoiding **EMPTY** elements as far as possible. You can always get the effect of a content-prohibited element in SGML by convention, or by a content model that happens to permit only empty instances. One such content model is shown below: the exclusion exception prevents having any instances of the one-and-only (and optional) subelement type allowed by the content model. In this case the end tag is permitted, although it is never required (unless **OMITTAG** is turned off completely):

```
<!ELEMENT  XREF          - O (XREF?) -(XREF)>
```

C. M. Sperberg-McQueen pointed out a similar method, which is to allow the element to contain only some undeclared element (referring to an undeclared element is permitted in SGML, though the referenced element cannot later occur in a valid document — see Question 5.7):

```
<!ELEMENT  XREF          - O (UNDECL?)>
```

XML prevents any problem with recognizing **EMPTY** elements because it uses distinct syntax for them. This way a human or a parser can instantly tell that such an element is in fact empty, just from the instance:

```
<XREF/>
```

This example is valid SGML even though it looks unfamiliar at first glance. The key is that it is valid SGML *given the right SGML declaration*. SGML compatibility is maintained by setting SGML's **NET** delimiter to "/>" instead of the usual "/". This makes "<XREF/>" just a **NET**-enabling start-tag (see Questions 1.4 and 1.5). Since SGML does not prohibit **EMPTY** elements from starting with **NET**-enabling start-tags, this is valid. XML states a convention that all **EMPTY** elements must be represented this way.

The SGML review is expected to introduce new delimiter roles for "content-prohibited" elements such as **EMPTY** ones. Thus instead of just **STAGO**, **ETAGO**, and a shared **TAGC**, there would be at least a distinct close delimiter for **EMPTY** element, and hopefully the full set of six delimiters: open and close delimiters for each of start-tags, end-tags, and tags for content-prohibited elements. At that time, the XML syntax can be done just by setting the content-prohibited element close delimiter to "/>" (and forgetting about **NET**). Several four-delimiter proposals have also been voiced, but each assigns a different four roles out of the six listed here, so it seems better to provide all six and let designers choose as appropriate to their applications.

**Note**: SGML could instead allow end-tags on **EMPTY** elements with no bad consequences. If the end-tag were permitted, it could still be omitted any time desired because the next tag or text portion would be incompatible with the content declared for REF, and so would force REF closed under normal the **OMITTAG** rules.

There is one possible but unlikely case where adding this rule now could affect a document: An empty end-tag ( "</>") immediately following an **EMPTY** element's start-tag would be taken as the end-tag for the **EMPTY**, not for its parent as is now the case. Such usage is unlikely since it would look very misleading, much as would omitted start-tags for **EMPTY** elements if it were permitted (see Question 2.2).

In short, when doing SGML data conversion it is important to know whether there are any **EMPTY** or **#CONREF** elements involved and exactly what they are. Any conversion software that does not understand SGML thoroughly needs to be configured to know about those elements and to neither expect nor generate end-tags for them. The easiest way to avoid this issue is not to use declared content **EMPTY** or declared value **#CONREF**; both are used seldom enough that removing them is often feasible.

## 3.4. Why do I lose one more blank line each time I parse my document?

Because Clause 7.6.1 of SGML requires that the first and the last **RE** in each element of an SGML document be "ignored" (in effect, discarded) in certain circumstances during parsing (see Question 2.5). Because of this it is hard to create a program that parses a document and produces an exact copy. In particular, such programs are prone to lose those **RE**s, and if you parse their SGML output again, they will do so again.

For the same reason, it is not easy to create a "canonical" form: a parser output form that may differ from the input SGML stream if that stream was minimized (say, by discarding insignificant spaces within tags, inserting omitted tags, and so on), but that would never differ again if you feed it back around and go through the parser again (and again, and...).

Parsing a document, saving the result as SGML, and parsing again will not reach a state where the document stops changing (until all the **RE**s are gone). An **RE** must be *added* at every element boundary where a non-ignored **RE** had also occurred, every time the SGML is saved. For example (with **RE** shown as "¶"):

```
<P>¶¶¶Our life is frittered away by detail¶¶¶</P>
```

The paragraph element will lose the first and last **RE** when parsed, producing this:

```
<P>¶¶Our life is frittered away by detail¶¶</P>
```

If the implementation fails to insert new **RE** characters at both ends when saving it back to SGML, instead just exporting what the parser gave it, then the next parse will produce this:

```
<P>¶Our life is frittered away by detail¶</P>
```

The next parse will produce this form, which will then remain stable:

```
<P>Our life is frittered away by detail</P>
```

Most SGML exporters do not insert **RE** characters to counter this (and very few SGML books mention the problem), so it is very hard to preserve a line boundary when one is really wanted. This is no doubt part of the reason that many SGML authoring systems only support creating line breaks in content via elements or processing instructions. The four solutions usually seen are:

- Inserting no **RE**s. This solution is fine as long as none are needed; if the input SGML had non-ignored **RE**s, however, they will be successively lost as shown above. Also, many non-SGML tools cannot deal with extremely long lines, and such files can therefore be awkward to manage.
- Insert an **RE** immediately after start-tags and/or immediately before end-tags. This is safe but can look awkward.
- Inserting an **RE** before start-tags and/or after end-tags. This often looks better, but is only correct in some cases (such as in element content but not always mixed content).
- Inserting **RE**s in other places where they are guaranteed to be permitted, such as within tags (typically just before the **TAGC** delimiter), or inside comments or **IGNORE** marked sections). This takes some getting used to, though can be a good compromise.

It might be argued that potential successive loss of **RE**s is a reason SGML systems ought to preserve every byte of their source files sacrosanct, but there are some drawbacks to that as well. First, because SGML requires that certain **RE** characters be "ignored", it could be argued that any parser that passes them to an application is non-conforming. Second, the questions authors have about the **RE** rules are usually about document structures, not about string representations, and they should have as few worries about the latter as possible. Third, requiring SGML systems to represent documents as unparsed SGML strings at all times would be like requiring database systems to keep all their files in tab-delimited ASCII form, and to keep track forever of whether a number was originally entered as "`0`", "`00`", "`0.0`", or "` 0000.000 `". Such solutions are always possible but inefficient, and can create more confusion than they solve.

The better solution is to follow DSSSL and HyTime, which are both defined at the level of parsed data structures (called "groves") rather than raw SGML strings. This allows for many useful optimizations and simplifications. The **RE** rules can be managed by making them moot: don't use line-breaks in places where they get complicated.

Whitespace in most places other than between words of text is seldom information from an author's point of view. This is particularly true of whitespace in markup, such as surrounding the "=" in attribute specification lists, or inserted to break up markup visually. Preserving such whitespace is useful if the user must hand-type the markup and read it without any software assistance or formatting, but it is usually best to explicitly declare it meaningless.

Even in the manual case, keeping such whitespace can be a liability:

1. It complicates any attempt to process SGML with widespread tools that were not specifically built for it, such as Perl (all your regular expressions must account for whitespace in precisely the places SGML does).
2. Most SGML-aware applications will discard it, and might pointlessly be considered wrong when they are probably actually making the user's life easier.
3. Even applications that keep the information will have a hard time showing it to the user unless they limit themselves to primitive interfaces, such as fixed-pitch ASCII fonts rather than dialog boxes with visual representations of attributes.
4. A publisher who tries to *use* such information will be unpleasantly surprised when it goes away (say, because they applied a software product that discards it, or didn't understand one of the fine points of the **RE** rules). Fortunately, stylesheet designers rarely if ever try to condition formatting or other SGML processing on irrelevant whitespace (such as formatting a paragraph in boldface only if there were three spaces between the `TYPE` attribute's name and following equal-sign).

This problem is related to Question 2.5 on ignored **RE**s, because export should ultimately write out a line-boundary in some system's representation (such as a Line Feed, or a Carriage Return/Line Feed pair). An **RE** as such is internal to SGML, being inserted by the entity manager, and may not correspond to a character in an entity at all (for example on the CMS operating system, where line-breaks are represented via length prefixes rather than reserved characters). Some kind of "reverse entity manager" is needed to turn **RE** back into a system-specific record boundary when needed.

## 3.5. Why do some Japanese characters lead to parsing errors?

Some complexities await the author who wants to use Asian languages. Japanese, Chinese, Korean, and some other languages require far more than 256 distinct characters, and this breaks a great deal of software, that assumes all characters are one (8-bit) byte wide. SGML makes no such restriction, though some software does.

Most encodings for Asian languages save space by encoding some characters in one byte, and less common ones in two or more. This means programs cannot treat a file or document as a list of equal-sized chunks as is done for most Western languages, if such treatment were possible it would lead to certain implementation efficiencies.

Theoretically an SGML system's entity manager can take in any representation desired and produce a stream of integers that is then parsed; so this should not be a problem. However, SGML provides no way to declare what representation is used in an entity. The SGML declaration only describes the coded character set itself, not the lowest level of how it is then encoded and represented (such as UTF-8 versus UCS-2 as alternative representations of Unicode). Another specification is needed somewhere outside SGML to get the entity manager started. Encoding information may differ for different entities, so would logically be associated with the entities themselves or their declarations — any other location raises maintenance issues because fundamental information about the entity can get out of sync with the entity itself, just as happens if you have duplicate copies of the same piece of information in a database.

If encodings are not handled just right (and it is not trivial to do so), then the SGML parser may end up thinking it is receiving bytes. This error may go undetected for a long time, because most of a typical SGML stream is character content, which merely gets passed on to some higher application (for formatting, searching, transformation, or other processing). The problem waits until it is triggered by the rare case when *half* of a wide character looks like SGML markup.

> **Note**: It is possible to turn SGML markup recognition on and off frequently enough to prevent this, using the markup scan characters (see Question 3.7). However, this can be quite difficult in practice because so many switches are needed (as many as two per tag), because the switch characters remain as data, and because the loss or movement of a single such character can have far-reaching effects.

Many characters can trigger this problem, whether they represent orthographic (for writing language itself) or other symbols. For example, the Unicode code point that represents the "biohazard" symbol is a two-byte value, x2623. The first byte taken by itself is equivalent to the ASCII ampersand; the second is the ASCII value for the pound sign: the two bytes together look just like the SGML **CRO** delimiter ("`&#`"). Thus, a user could try to type in the biohazard symbol, and get an error message from the SGML parser saying they were using a character entity reference incorrectly.

This is not intrinsically an SGML issue: similar cases arise with most software that is modified to handle wide characters rather than being designed for it from the ground up. The only real workaround is to test software for such problems, and to be careful to inform software of what entities are in what character sets and encodings.

## 3.6. Is "``" the same as "`&#RE;`"?

Two ways of including a Carriage Return character in an SGML document are the numeric character reference "``", and the named character reference "`&#RE;`" (named character references such as this are declared as "added functions" in the SGML declaration).

These two forms might be thought to mean the same thing (at least in the normal circumstance when the SGML declaration sets **RE** to character code point 13), especially since they are syntactically the same construct: a character reference. However, they are quite different. The numeric one is always treated as data, and *cannot* be ignored under the rules of Clause 7.6.1 (see Question 2.5). So in this example the **RE** represented by the numeric character reference is not ignored as it would be if it were came to exist via a literal line-break interpreted by the entity manager:

```
<P>&#13;A tree falling in the forest.</P>
```

The named reference, however, is treated exactly like an **RS** that was created by the entity manager in response to finding a record boundary in the input data (however it may have been represented), and so *can* be ignored, as it would be here:

```
<P>&#RE;A tree falling in the forest.</P>
```

> **Note**: The same distinctions apply to "`
`" and "`&#RS;`"; to "`	`" and "`&#TAB;`", and so on.

One explanation given for this distinction is that by making the named character reference able to represent a delimiter, delimiters that are difficult or impossible to keyboard in some (unusual) system environment could still be entered. In contrast, a numeric character reference is to a literal code point in a character set, so should definitely represent character data (**RE** is an abstract signal from the entity manager, not really an input character in the strict sense). Another possible reason is that since **RS** and **RE** are introduced by the entity manager rather than being true source characters, the named character reference provides a way to enter them directly as a workaround if any reason arises for introducing the abstract **RS** or **RE** where the entity manager would not do so. In that case, since the distinction was motivated for **RE** versus 10, it would be symmetrical to make the distinction generally.

> **Note**: This rationale is analogous to why users once had to substitute something else for the control-S and control-Q characters if they wanted to type them literally despite being connected via a modem that treats them as flow-control characters.

SGML has many grammar rules that do not operate across entity boundaries, such as that a delimiter and its following context cannot be in different entities (see Appendix B for more on this). These are related to why you can substitute "`<`" to get a literal "<" as described in Question 1.1. However, Clause 9.5 states that the boundaries of character references do not have the same "blocking" effect as many other entity boundaries. Instead, the character that they result in is "considered to be in the same entity as its reference" and is "treated as though it were entered directly except that the replacement for a numeric *character reference* is always treated as data."

Among other things (as SGML mentions in following notes), these rules mean that the numeric and named cases are not the same, and that translating a document between different coded character sets (say, ASCII and EBCDIC) requires changing every numeric character reference.

One more special case is worthy of mention. The rule above indicates that substituting a *named* character references for an actual character never changes the meaning (this is because the exception in the rule above involves *numeric* character references). For example, you can define a named character entity `LT` and do this:

```
&#LT;!-- not a good way to comment, but it works -->
```

However, Amendment 1 adds an exception in Clause 9.6: A named reference such as just shown can only be used to enter the *first* character of a delimiter. Therefore the following example where "`!`" is replaced by "`&#BANG;`" is *not* a way to express a comment. Instead, the initial "<" is not held to be in context, and the whole thing is taken as literal data after substitution of the `BANG` reference:

```
<!-- WRONG -->
<&#BANG; not a way to comment  at all -->
```

This rule will not come up much unless you define your own named character references (which is rarely done).

## 3.7. How many ways can I suppress markup recognition?

Question 1.1 talked about when you might not be able to type certain characters. It mentioned the most common way to escape them (that is, to signal SGML that you want literal less-than and ampersand characters): "`<`" and "`&`". However, there are many more ways to include such characters and prevent the SGML parser from mistakenly taking them as markup, instead taking them as literal data. This question discusses those other ways.

In effect, each method "suppresses" recognition of strings as delimiters, although each method differs in the rule governing what ends the suppressed area. Only moving the quoted content out into a separate entity suppresses markup completely, and that only works fully with external entities, since internal entities are quoted, requiring that quotation marks be escaped in them.

The basic methods available appear in the table below.

| Technique | Description |
|---|---|
| **MSSCHAR** | Prevents the very next character from being considered markup (like backslash in many other systems). However, the **MSSCHAR** character also remains as data. This method is almost never used, and the usual SGML declaration does not assign any actual character(s) to this role. However, this method has the advantage of working anywhere (such as in comments and attribute values literals), not just in content. |
| **MSICHAR, MSOCHAR** | Works like **MSSCHAR** except that you can turn markup recognition on or off, and it stays that way. **MSOCHAR** stops delimiter recognition, and **MSICHAR** starts it again. This is mainly used in documents that mix multiple single-byte character sets, so that characters in various sets (such as "<Π") cannot be mistaken for markup. |
| `<` | The most commonly used solution. |
| `<` | This is a direct reference to the decimal character code for the less-than sign. Unlike "`<`", it may not survive character set translations of documents, since not all character sets put the less-than sign at position 60. As discussed in Question 3.6, the result of a numeric character reference is *always* treated as data rather than markup. |
| `<!ENTITY mychar SYSTEM "lt.sgm">` | Uses the fact that a delimiter's following context will not be recognized across an entity-end boundary. This method is seldom used, since "`<`" is simpler. |

| Technique | Description |
|---|---|
| **CDATA** element | Common, but see Question 2.8 on various questions about what can go inside a **CDATA** element, and Question 2.4 on the **CDATA** concept in general. In a **CDATA** element, entity references cannot be used (for example "`<`"), which often makes **RCDATA** a better choice. |
| **RCDATA** element | Similar to **CDATA** elements except that entity references are recognized. This method, unlike **CDATA**, let you escape the few recognized strings when needed, via an entity reference. |
| **CDATA** marked section | Commonly used because the string that ends it ("`]]>`") is less likely to crop up in content than the "`</`" that ends **CDATA** elements (as discussed in Question 2.9 "`]]>`" must be escaped for other reasons anyway). Especially useful in books on SGML, where there are examples with many, many pointy brackets to escape. |
| **RCDATA** marked section | Much the same, but permits using entity references, such as if the content happened to include "`]]>`" (there are other ways to avoid this case, such as a nested **CDATA** marked section and "`]]]]>>`" at the end, or using **MSSCHAR**). |
| `<!ENTITY mydata SYSTEM "examp.sgm" CDATA TEXT>` | This is a very effective way because you can escape all data in the entity with no exceptions to worry about, but it requires the overhead of putting each example or other escaped data block into a separate entity. |
| `<<!>p` | The empty comment ("`<!>`") prevents the "`p`" from fulfilling the contextual constraint for the **STAGO** delimiter, so the first "<" is taken as literal data. |
| `< p` | A blank also suppresses **STAGO** recognition because of the contextual constraints: a blank cannot be the start of a GI. |
| `<!SGML... DELIMS...>` | Changing the syntax to free up "<" and/or "&" seems fairly drastic, but works (it may be harder than it seems, because "<" is part of many delimiters — see Questions 7.1 and 7.4 for more questions about delimiter changes). On the other hand, it merely shifts the problem onto some other characters or strings. |
| `<!SHORTREF...` | A short reference string can maps, in the end, to "<". Though this is possible, it is seldom considered necessary. |

A slight variation is available by using "bracketed text entities" (see Question 5.22 and Clause 10.5.4): Such entities do not suppress or ensure markup recognition, so must be used in an **RCDATA** context anyway; but then you can avoid literally typing the delimiters into an entity's replacement text, and have fewer entity references and a somewhat more readable raw text. For example, using `p.start` here looks a bit cleaner, but you still cannot use `p.end` because it would lead to a syntax error:

```
<!ENTITY   p.start     STARTTAG "p">
<!ENTITY   p.end       ENDTAG "p">
<!ELEMENT  xmp         RCDATA>
...
<xmp>Start-tags look like &p.start;.</xmp>
```

**Note**: It is likely that the SGML revision will add a way to refer to characters by hexadecimal numbers, not just decimal as in "`<`" above. It may also add an "escape" character that would work like "\" in many other languages, to make the next character literal (like **MSSCHAR** except that the escape character itself would not count as data). If added, this last option may become the most popular method of all.

## What must you escape?

Authors are generally aware that if they are typing SGML (including HTML) by hand, they must watch out when using delimiter characters as literal data. Certainly no one takes long to learn that something must distinguish "`<P>`" as a start-tag from "`<P>`" as text content. Questions arise because the rules are subtle enough that they can be misunderstood.

Not all authors may know that delimiter recognition is subject to "contextual constraints" (the SGML standard provides them in Clause 9.6.2), and so they may just replace delimiters everywhere. But this is not required, because delimiter strings are not recognized as actual delimiters unless they are "in context", which means they are followed by a character that would make sense given their role (not necessarily more than a single following character, however).

This principle can be extremely useful when writing SGML conversion tools, because they don't have to change *all* less-than signs to entity references: only those "in context" (some feel it is better to change them all anyway, so that non-SGML-aware tools need not implement contextual constraints).

For example, "<" is not taken as **STAGO** unless it is followed by a character that could start an element type name, typically a letter. Well, almost. The additional cases in the GI contextual constraint include:

- If **CONCUR** is on, "`(`" counts because of the need to recognize start-tags that specify which DTD they are from: "`<(DISCOURSE)PARA>`".
- If **SHORTTAG** is on, ">" counts because of the possibility of empty start-tags: "<>".
- "`!`" counts, but not for the same reason. It counts because when in context "`<!`" as a unit is another delimiter, namely **MDO**. If **MDO** is changed (say, to "`$$$`"), then "`!`" after "<" would have no special meaning.
- "`?`" counts because the **PIO** delimiter is "`<?`". This delimiter has no contextual constraints, so is recognized regardless of what follows.
- "`/`" does not count, although by analogy to "<>" some anticipate being able to combine **NET** and empty start-tag, using "`</`" to start a new instance of whatever element type "<>" would have started, but also enabling that instance to be closed with a **NET**. In fact SGML does not allow that.
- "<" does not count, although some anticipate being able to combine empty start-tag with omitted **TAGC**, using "`<<P>`" to start a new instance of whatever element type "<>" would have started, and also to start a `P`.
- Digits don't count, since they're *name* characters but not *name start* characters. So "`<3>`" is not a tag.

**Note:** A rule familiar to some from IBM GML does not apply, under which the whole tag would be taken as data if the GI is not known. This is a very good thing for two reasons. First, with the GML rule a parser could not discover or report the error of using an undefined GI: it would not be an error at all, but just data. Second, with the GML rule parsing SGML without a DTD would be hopeless, but in fact it is doable for SGML if you rule out only a small number of constructs (such as declared content), as XML has shown.

Similar SGML rules apply to "&" because it is used to mark entity references (as the "**ERO** delimiter"). It also has contextual constraints: to be recognized **ERO** must be followed by:

- a name start character (the characters that can start entity names and element types are required to be the same, although case is typically ignored only for the latter);
- " (", but only if **CONCUR** is on;
- "#" because "&#" is the character-reference or **CRO** delimiter, that has its own slightly different contextual constraint, namely that it must be followed by a name start character or digit.

**Note:** The various contextual constraints are similar enough that the technically inclined reader has probably noticed the possibility of eliminating some or all of them by grammar adjustments. **CREF**, **NMS**, and **GI** could be merged if digit-initial GIs were allowed. **DCL** is needed only for a few special cases such as comments (see Questions 1.6 and 1.7), marked sections, and "<!>"; **MSE** only ensures that "]]" be followed by **MDC** (">") to end a marked section (see Question 7.6); **ELEM** only supports **NET**. It is debatable whether this would be a good thing, but it is certainly possible.

Many authors who operate without software that hides them from delimiters manage the issue by escaping *all* less-than signs and ampersands. For example, when converting data to SGML they might apply a global change that turns all "<" into "`<`", or at least all "<" not followed by whitespace.

It is not usually a problem to escape delimiters when you do not need to, so this simpler model is not harmful. The exception arises from constructs that suppress markup recognition of general entities: if you change all the "<" inside **CDATA** marked sections or elements, "`<`" will not be recognized or replaced there. Inside **RCDATA** they will be recognized, but in that case there was no need to escape "<"; except when part of "</",....

Finally, it is almost always forgotten that "<" and "&" are not the only characters that must be escaped, even leaving aside issues such as variant syntax where other characters take on some but not all of those character's associated delimiter roles. For example, authors commonly forget to escape quotes within attribute values, leading to very long attribute values or to syntax errors, depending on one's luck. Authors sometimes forget that "]]>" is recognized outside marked sections, and must be escaped if it is to be treated as data content. "/" must also be escaped if you happen to use **NET**-enabling start-tags (see Question 1.5). Many current Web browsers do not recognize these cases, and so will not report them as errors, but there is no harm in escaping them anyway, thus making documents correct in all environments.

> **Note**: The patterns here can change radically if your documents use a different concrete syntax. For example, nothing prevents a DTD designer from keeping start-tags opening with "<", but changing the processing instruction open delimiter from "<?" to " {". Then you would have to substitute for any open curly braces, as well as for less-than signs.

# 3.8. Can I use global changes on my SGML?

Yes, and this works great for SGML as long as you're careful about the alternative ways SGML gives for typing markup, such as minimization.

Many data transformation tools operate by changing all occurrences of particular strings to new string, or doing the same thing with described patterns, such as the formal device computer scientists call "regular expressions". It is important to write your change expressions carefully, to account for SGML features that may appear way down inside your documents.

The most challenging cases involve minimization. These cases don't generally arise when data is authored in an SGML-aware system, but often do otherwise. An SGML document that doesn't use them is often informally called "normalized SGML", and is the easiest kind to deal with using non-SGML-aware transformation tools such as Perl, awk, sed, and the like.

The main cases to watch out for are:

- **Minimized start-tags**: don't search for "`<P LEVEL="SECRET">`" if your files might represent it as "`<P LEVEL=SECRET>`", "`<P SECRET>`", "`<P>`" with a default attribute value, "`<>`", "`<P/`", or even omit the tag entirely.
- **Minimized end-tags**: a match for "`</P>`" will miss "`</>`", "`/`", and omitted end-tags, which are more common than omitted start-tags.
- **Attributes**: a simple match for "`<P>`" will miss any tag that has attributes.
- **Excess whitespace**: a simple match for "`<P>`" will miss "`<P    >`" and many other forms (some involving whitespace between or within attributes).
- **Markup-like characters in attribute values**: a simple pattern match will only match *part* of a tag like "`<ITEM MARK='>'>`".
- **Constructs that suppress markup recognition**: **CDATA** and **RCDATA** marked sections and elements allow literal content that looks like markup, and a simple pattern match won't know the difference.

Most if not all such issues can be avoided by not using the optional forms of minimization, or by constraining exactly which forms you use and making sure your transformation programs know about them.

# 4. For Authors And Editors Using External Data Or Modifying DTDs

To refer to external data such as graphics and multimedia from SGML, you have to go through several steps. Some of the steps are a little bit more complicated than those discussed in previous chapters because they involve creating declarations, which otherwise have little or no part in authors' work on individual documents. Likewise, if you need to "adjust" your DTD a little (say, to add a special element or attribute that you happen to need), you discover a new set of questions and skill requirements.

To do this kind of modification you need to learn the other two "sub-languages" of SGML, beyond the one used in document instances *per se*: the language for DTDs and the language for SGML declarations. This chapter mainly addresses questions that arise for people doing this level of customization, or occasionally looking inside DTDs for other reasons.

## 4.1. Why can't I omit a tag? I looked in the DTD and the minimization flag is "O".

Although flags after the element type name in a DTD's element declarations say whether it is permissible to omit the start- and/or end-tags for instances of the element type, these flags do not indicate whether you can really omit those tags in actual cases. They can be used to prohibit minimization altogether, but they have no relation to whether it is sometimes (or even always) possible for the parser to figure out the correct tag in the correct place. Whenever the parser could not, you can't omit the tag even if the declaration says you may (see Questions 2.2 and 2.3 for more on tag omission).

For example, assume that FOOTNOTE elements are *permitted* everywhere as inclusions or perhaps as alternatives in **OR** content models, but are not *required* at any given point. It is perfectly valid to declare them with flags like this:

```
<!ELEMENT  BOOK         - -  (CHAP*)  +(FOOTNOTE)
<!ELEMENT  FOOTNOTE     O -  (P)>
```

Nevertheless, the presence of the "O" flag does not mean you can ever omit the start-tag for a FOOTNOTE. With a DTD as just described you *never* can (setting an unfulfillable minimization flag is not considered an SGML error). On the other hand, the second flag in the declaration above prohibits omitting the end-tag for any `FOOTNOTE` even though it would often be unambiguous: for any `FOOTNOTE` whose subelement `P` has an end-tag the parser could easily place the end-tag correctly, right after the end-tag for the `P`.

The error to avoid here is to assume that these flags affect the *possibility* of omitting tags. They only affect *permissibility*. They can be used to prohibit tag omission because the DTD author does not wish it to be used in certain cases, but they can never enable it in cases where the context does not: whether any tag *can* actually be omitted depends upon the cases at hand in the document.

Although it's a bit complicated, it would be possible for a parser to test whether a given flag could ever be fulfilled. That is, a clever SGML parser could go through the possible cases for every element type, and see whether there are any possible contexts where its tags could be omitted without causing an ambiguity. For each element type, the start- and end-tag each would be put into one of three cases:

| | |
|---|---|
| Always omissable | For example, the start-tag of an element that can only occur where it is contextually required and everything else is contextually optional. `TITLE` elements are a typical case, when the only place they can appear is at the start of divisions, and they are required there. |
| Never omissable | For example, the start-tag of an element that is only permitted as an inclusion exception (and therefore is never contextually required), or the end-tag of an element whose content model is **ANY**. Many included elements are in this category, such as `FOOTNOTE`. |
| Sometimes omissable | For example, the end-tag of an element in which some other elements may occur, but not just any elements. A typical example would be `SECTION`, in which many things can occur, but which would be ended by the start of a new `SECTION` or `CHAPTER`. |

A parser that did such tests could do some extra validation of the DTD and report useful information to the DTD designer, such as noting that they had set "`O`" for a case where the tag could never be omitted. It could also warn of setting "`-`" for a case where the tag could always be omitted, though this should only be a warning because there might be non-technical reasons never to omit that tag: readability, editorial conventions, facilitating re-use in other DTDs, and so on.

Currently, however, there are few if any parsers that will provide such warnings. You can only determine the possibility of omitting a tag by examining the particular case in relation to the structure of the DTD.

## 4.2. Can I have separate sets of `ID` attribute values for different element types?

No. In SGML, **ID** values must be unique across all element instances in a document regardless of their types. It is not enough to guarantee that all your `CHAPTER` elements' **ID**s are unique among `CHAPTER` **ID**s, all your `SECTION` **ID**s unique among `SECTION` elements, and so on.

This is a question about what computer scientists call "name spaces". Processes or conventions can lay claim to a range of unique names, such as 5-digit US Zip codes, or all strings starting with "`http://`"; or such as SGML **ID**s, element types, or attribute names. Conventions within any one name space can ensure uniqueness, but two different name spaces can contain similar names. As long as you can tell when each name space applies, overlap between name spaces is not a real problem.

> Note: Potentially conflicting name spaces are very common. International Standard Book Numbers (ISBNs) are 10-digit numbers assigned to books: every book has a unique ISBN, barring errors or books published in multiple bindings or editions (there is an interesting philosophical question of what constitutes "the same book"). U.S. telephone numbers are also 10-digit numbers if you include area codes. These name spaces overlap severely, but it is not a problem because they seldom show up in the same contexts.

For **IDs**, SGML chose to have only one name space over all element types rather than one name space per element type. So the **ID** values used on one kind of element are not separate from those used on another kind, and may not re-use values.

```
<!ATTLIST  (CHP | SEC | SSEC)
  DIVID    ID          #IMPLIED>
<!ATTLIST  ANCHOR
  ANCHID   ID          #IMPLIED>
```

Given the declarations above a document cannot then contain both of the start-tags below (SGML **IDs** normally ignore case distinctions):

```
<!-- WRONG -->
<SEC DIVID="ABC379">…
<ANCHOR ANCHID="abc379">
```

> Note: SGML **IDs** differ from identifiers in the IBM GML system, which are separate for each element type (and limited to 7 characters long with extra characters ignored, and case-sensitive). Care is required in translating GML data to SGML.

SGML **IDs** have only one name-space per document. So no two elements may have the same **ID** value even if they have different GIs. For more on ways you can organize large or complex sets of **IDs**, see Question 4.7.

## Note on SGML's name spaces

SGML has many name spaces, distinguished by context. The name spaces have been listed in many places, such as the work of the POEM project, the SGML Open Catalog, and elsewhere. SGML software systems that must resolve names may provide a way to state names with an accompanying context. For example, SGML Open catalogs give a way to get from external entity names to filenames or other identifiers for stored objects. Because the names of general and parameter entities overlap, it provides a way to say which kind a given catalog entry is talking about, as SGML **ENTITY** declarations also do.

Some of the basic SGML names spaces are listed here, to help keep them straight:

| Name | Form | Scope |
|---|---|---|
| **ID** | 'name'; case ignored | Unique across all element instances that have **ID** attributes, else an error; **IDREFs** may re-use the values any number of times. |
| general entities | 'name'; case retained | Unique across general entity names (or the first declaration is used). May be |

| Name | Form | Scope |
|---|---|---|
| | | referenced any number of times (so long as they contain no **ID**s, etc.). |
| parameter entities | 'name', case retained, shorter length | Unique across parameter entity names, or the first declaration is used. May be referenced any number of times. |
| GI (element type name) | 'name', case ignored | Unique within a single DTD, but may overlap with **CONCUR** feature. |
| Attribute names | 'name', case ignored | Unique within each element type. |
| Enumerated attribute values | name tokens | Unique within each element type (though a change is being considered in the SGML review). |
| **NOTATION** | 'name', case ignored | Unique in a DTD; can be mentioned in any number of **ENTITY** declarations and **NOTATION** attributes, once each. |
| Formal Public Identifiers (or FPIs) | minimum literal, normalized | Unique worldwide if they use registered owner identifiers (many FPIs may refer to the same object). See Chapter 4. |

A **CDATA** attribute *could* by some user's convention store a value that is conceptually an **ID**, a parameter entity name, an FPI or anything else; but SGML systems don't know about such a convention. A stylesheet or an application program built on top of SGML may know, but a **CDATA** attribute value is not an **ID** in SGML syntax terms even if it is one conceptually. Mixing spaces like that requires extra care (HyTime raises a related issue due to placing some entity names unmarked in content — see Question 5.10).

## 4.3. Can I create an ID attribute that need only be unique within its chapter or other context?

No. **ID**s must be unique within an entire document.

This question typically seems unimportant until you try to build larger documents, especially by combining smaller parts that are separately maintained. In that case, it would be useful to be able to refer to "the element with `ID=SEC1` that is within the element with `ID=CHP2`", or similar, even though `SEC1` is only unique within a smaller context than the whole book (namely, within the `CHP`, which might even have been a **SUBDOC** at some time).

It is possible to get local uniqueness by promoting each chapter or other unit to become a **SUBDOC** entity, external to the rest of the document. However, that approach has other drawbacks including that you can no longer use **IDREF**s to refer between chapters (see Question 2.13).

It is also possible, and often easier, to manage regular **ID**s as longer, structured values that include their applicable context by convention. For example, you could start all your chapter **ID**s with "`chap.`", or all your **ID**s in chapter 1 with "`chap1.`", and so on. Although an SGML parser will not validate such a convention itself, such a convention can make your **ID**s clear, unique, and easily understandable, and an application on top of SGML can be set up to validate your usage if needed. For more on ways you can structured name spaces using **IDs**, see Question 4.7.

Finally, using a reference mechanism other than just **IDs**, and that is aware of the SGML document structure, can work very well in such situations. HyTime TREELOCs and Text Encoding Initiative extended pointers are two such mechanisms, that are discussed in Question 6.11.

Managing unique names across large and diverse data collections is a hard problem. SGML provides some tools and approaches, but a complete solution involves many aspects that cannot readily be standardized without careful work in each application domain. Some aspects, such as cross-references that attach correctly despite changes to the source and destination, are still research problems with unsolved aspects.

## 4.4. Can I restrict an IDREF attribute to refer only to a certain element type(s)?

No. The only semantic constraint SGML can validate for **IDREF** attributes is that their value match the value of some **ID** attribute in the same document.

HyTime provides a REFTYPE feature that permits you to restrict **IDREFs** in a similar way. However, the restrictions are in terms of architectural forms rather than SGML element types, so in HyTime a restricted reference can still be satisfied if it points to an element of a different type (so long as it is a member of the same HyTime architectural form). This may or may not be enough, depending on your application; it is discussed with examples in Section 14.8.3 of DeRose and Durand (1994).

If you organize your **IDs**, for example by starting all **IDs** in SEC elements with "sec." and so on for other elements, then you can easily use the techniques described in Question 4.7 to manage them and it will become easier to check whether your references point to the desired kind of element:

```
<REF TARGET="SEC.947.2.1.a">See that other section.</REF>
...
<REF TARGET="BIB.yank85">See Yankelovich et al. (1985)</REF>
```

## 4.5. Can I have more than one ID attribute on the same element?

No. SGML specifically prohibits this in Clause 11.3.3. You cannot declare two separate **ID** attributes, and there is no declared value "IDS".

Multiple unique identifiers seems like a contradiction at first, but as described in Question 4.2, there are many occasions when multiple independently-unique name spaces are useful. Certainly people have many unique identifiers: social security number, state name and driver's license number, and many individuals effectively have their own 9-digit zip code. There seems to be no particular reason these could not all be recorded, though clearly each one must be labeled as to just what kind of identifier it is, lest one person's zip code match a different person's social security number (both have 9 digits, after all).

Of course you can create your own cross-references that are not **ID**s: As described in Question 4.7, you can declare them to be of a more lenient type such as **NAME** or even **CDATA**, and then use as many as needed. An SGML parser *per se* will not check them for uniqueness, but most SGML software can be set up to use them for linking even though they are not **ID**s. It is better to use the SGML mechanism when possible.

## 4.6. What if I need non-name characters in my ID attributes?

The declared value **ID** not only constrains attribute values to be unique, but also to be SGML names, which can only contain certain characters and be of a certain maximum length. You can only add other characters by modifying the SGML declaration.

Because of the character restriction, your naming scheme cannot normally permit embedded blanks, special characters, or various punctuation marks. Question 4.7 discusses ways around this; in short, you can:

- design a naming scheme where all your names are **ID**s;
- use the SGML declaration to extend what **ID**s can be; or
- switch to a different declared value such as **CDATA** instead of **ID**.

One important example where more complex naming is needed is what the Text Encoding Initiative calls "canonical references" (see Section 5.2.5 of the TEI *Guidelines*). Many literary works have been assigned standard numbering schemes, which scholars use to refer to specific verses, paragraph, or similar locations even though the page divisions in various printings differ greatly. Perhaps the most familiar example is a Biblical reference such as "Matthew 23:23", which gives a book-name, a chapter number, and a verse number.

Some special step is needed in SGML to accommodate most existing naming schemes (such as to allow the colon in this example). Some canonical or structured names can be accommodated by adding characters to the list of name (or name start) characters in the SGML declaration and increasing **NAMELEN**, but such changes can sometimes lead to subtle conflicts. For example:

- adding space as a name character collides with the use of space to separate attributes from the GI in start-tags
- parentheses collide with declarations of content models (other than **ANY**) in the DTD
- "#"collides with SGML reserved names
- "?" collides with processing instructions
- "!" collides with markup declarations (including comments and marked sections)
- "/" collides with **NET**-enabled start-tags.

Changing the concrete syntax to assign other values for various delimiters usually just moves the problem around. Because the added-name-character approach can be subtle, a simpler method is more common: change all their conceptual **ID**s to have declared value **CDATA** (the one declared value that permits a wide range of strings), and manage whitespace, case folding, and validation as part of their application rather than part of the SGML parser's work.

The Text Encoding Initiative's extended pointer syntax goes one step further, and provides a way to declare the syntax and meaning of structured ("canonical") names so they can be used for linking regardless of whether they are SGML `ID`s or not (see Question 6.11 in this book, and Sections 5.3.5 and 14.2.2 of the TEI *Guidelines*). Given that declaration, structured names can be unambiguously interpreted as pointers to specific data, and software can use them for linking without having to worry about SGML's limitations on names.

# 4.7. How can I organize large, complicated sets of `ID` values?

You may need to structure a set of names, especially in larger documents. For example, you may have a set of chapter names or numbers, a different but overlapping set of glossary item names, and a set of index terms. It is more convenient if you can think of each as being a separate space of name (see Question 4.2 on this idea of name spaces).

> Note: Hypertext links done via HyTime commonly contain many **`ID`s** in order to construct "ladders" or sequences of pointers. This is another conceptual name space and must not collide with **`ID`s** assigned for other reasons.

Since `ID`s in an SGML document must be unique over the entire document and elements of all types in it, the easiest way to separate your own conceptual name spaces is to establish a convention within that space. One good way to do this is to reserve the punctuation characters allowed in `ID`s (normally hyphen and period) to serve as dividers.

You can then use one or both of those characters like slashes or other directory-separator characters in computer file names, to separate parts of your structured ID value. For example, you could start every `ID` on a `CHP`, `SEC`, or `SSEC` element with "`div.`"; every `ID` on an `ANCHOR` element with "`anch.`"; and other `ID`s with "`gloss.`", "`index.`", "`rung.`", and so on.

This is very easy for authors to do if the prefixes make sense to them. It is also easy to automate and to validate, though that must be done by an application on top of SGML and not by the SGML parser *per se* (it would likely be "the same program" from the user's point of view, but technically speaking it would not be the parser's job internally). Such a prefix convention is also a useful memory or readability device at the **`IDREF`** end: each **`IDREF`** expresses some information about its destination.

> Note: Such schemes can be extended to multiple levels if appropriate: "`index.seealso.`", "`index.defs.`" and so on. Prefixes usually require setting **`NAMELEN`** higher than the default -character limit.

Structured names are often longer than the default 8-character limit on SGML `ID`s; this can be handled by increasing the **`NAMELEN`** setting in your SGML declaration.

Structured names are commonly used for ancient or important texts, and for large-scale industrial documents such as technical manuals. For example, Biblical references consist of a book name, a chapter number, and a verse number, such as "John 3:16" (labels of this general kind are called "expressive notation" in some circles, and "canonical references" in some others). Pre-existing structured names commonly use additional punctuation marks. The need for characters not normally allowed within SGML IDs can be handled in two basic ways:

- Stick with declared value **ID**, change any different punctuation to be hyphen or period. For example, "JOHN.3.16". This has the advantage that validation is free in a validating SGML parser, but it may also reduce readability in some cases.
- Stick with **ID**, but change the SGML declaration to add other punctuation as name or name-start characters. Adding to name and name start characters has some limitations, however, as discussed under Question 4.6.
- Don't use **ID**, but rather **CDATA**, **NAMES**, or another declared value type. This reduces the length, readability, and permitted-characters limitations (except for "&" — see Questions 1.2 and 1.9), but gives up validation by the SGML parser. **CDATA** values also regard case, unlike **ID**, and whitespace is handled differently; there is no declared value that normalizes case and spacing without imposing name length restrictions.

Most SGML software is quite happy searching for elements based on any attribute value, not just **ID**s, so these workarounds work just fine in practice for creating hyperlinks into structured objects. Some software will even perform link-testing if you tell it any rule for how to find a destination given a link origin, in which case validation is available even if not through the SGML parser itself.

## 4.8. Can I add ID or other attributes to element types that are already in the DTD?

Unlike **ENTITY** declarations but like **ELEMENT** declarations, a second **ATTLIST** declaration naming the same GI is an error (see Clause 11.3). It does *not* add the new attributes to any set previously defined for the named GI(s). Because of this rule, adding such an **ATTLIST** declaration may or may not be an error:

- If there are no attributes already defined for the element type, it works fine.
- If there are, an error is reported.

This question arises most often because of **ID** attributes: sometimes a DTD does not declare **ID** attributes for all of its element types, and authors later discover they cannot create needed links to some kinds of elements because the elements do not permit **ID**s. The logical thing to try is adding an **ATTLIST** declaration in the internal subset for one or more documents:

```
<!DOCTYPE  BOOK SYSTEM "Dogcow:SGML:DTDs:mybook.dtd" [
<!ATTLIST  BIBITEM
   ID      ID          #REQUIRED>
]>
```

This only works, however, if there is no attribute list *already* declared for the element type(s) involved. In practice, it is usually a good idea to declare an **ID** attribute for every element type, which prevents this problem. However, many DTDs do not do this, and there are occasions for adding other attributes than just **ID**s so the same syntax issue comes up there too.

DTD designers concerned for extensibility may wish to go a step further. By inserting a parameter entity reference at the end of every **ATTLIST** declaration, they can make it possible for the declaration subset to add attributes late by redefining that entity:

```
<!ATTLIST  P
   ID         ID             #IMPLIED
   %global.attrs;>
```

This is similar to using exceptions to extend element declarations as described in Question 7.14. It is also more usable, because referencing an empty parameter entity inside this context is permitted, unlike within a name group as would be needed for certain kinds of **ELEMENT** declaration extensibility.

> **Note**: Liam Quin has pointed out that this is not always enough. To do this for element types that initially have *no* attributes you would have to add an **ATTLIST** that was empty except for the (initially null) parameter entity reference. Empty **ATTLIST** declarations are not allowed in SGML, and there are some restrictions on where empty parameter entities can be referenced. The SGML review is said to be considering allowing them, but a workaround in the meantime is to declare at least one attribute for every element; providing **ID** everywhere is a useful choice.

The SGML review is expected to add the ability to extend attribute lists. Obviously it would not make sense to allow declaring the same attribute name more than once for the same GI, but there is no ambiguity in having additional **ATTLIST** declarations in general: the new attributes would be added just like multiple attributes within a single **ATTLIST** declaration. Duplicate names would remain errors in exactly the same conditions as they would in a single **ATTLIST** declaration in present SGML.

In the meantime, modifying the pre-existing **ATTLIST** declarations is the only way to go. This can be done by inserting the new attributes in them directly, or by inserting a parameter entity there which can then be set in the internal declaration subset. If your DTDs already provides a parameter entity in every **ATTLIST** to make such customization easy. So much the better.

## 4.9. How do PUBLIC and SYSTEM identifiers for entities relate?

SGML permits declaring two identifiers (one **PUBLIC** and one **SYSTEM**) rather than just one for external entities. There is a saying that all numbers but 0, 1, and infinity are suspect, and so the possibility of two identifiers immediately raises the question of how they relate. If both identifiers are present as in the final case below, SGML gives no guidance regarding which one to use:

```
<!ENTITY    chap1
            SYSTEM "c:\sgml\chap1.sgm">
<!ENTITY    chap2
            PUBLIC "-//XYZZY//TEXT My second chapter">
<!ENTITY    chap3
            PUBLIC "-//XYZZY//TEXT My third chapter"
                   "c:\sgml\chap3.sgm">
```

A convention has been settled on by the many vendors in the SGML Open Consortium, though the end result was a draw: systems must support a setting whereby users can choose which identifier takes priority. This convention is supported by many SGML systems.

The basic arguments on both sides are:

1. That the system identifier is more specific, and if specified its literal value must override any other identifier or process. For data intended to be portable, authors should never use system identifiers.
2. A **PUBLIC** identifier is by definition not system-specific, and therefore is the only portable form. Since a **SYSTEM** identifier is almost always wrong after any change in environment (moving files to other directories or other systems, mailing them, renaming, and so on), the **PUBLIC** identifier is the only reliable source. When a local override is required, this can still be accomplished by changing the (necessary) mapping of the **PUBLIC** identifier (such as in a catalog).

I strongly favor the second position. **PUBLIC** identifiers are less prone to catastrophically misleading, silent failures, because a public identifier is guaranteed to be unique to the desired data (at least, a formal one with a registered owner identifier should be). The guarantee can be defeated by someone breaking the rules (intentionally or accidentally), but at least the rules are explicit so they *can* be followed. In contrast, a **SYSTEM** identifier not only *can* be non-unique, but is highly likely to be, and even more likely to become non-unique or unresolvable after a little while.

A third option is to never use both types of identifier in the same declaration. SGML cannot enforce this convention, but it can be a useful way to avoid any ambiguity about which identifier will be used in any given case.

## 4.10. How can an SGML system find a file if all it has is a Formal Public Identifier?

Nearly every SGML system provides a way to specify an external list to help with this task. Each entry in that list gives an FPI and the corresponding file name or other identifier where the data for the entity can be found.

For some time, each product had its own format for this file, and they all differed slightly. For example, some systems required the FPI first and some had the filename first. This led to the annoying problem that anyone using multiple SGML software systems had to maintain multiple files that were doing the same thing in ever-so-slightly different ways.

The SGML Open Consortium got together and settled on a common file format for these tables, which are now called "SGML Open Entity Catalogs". Most SGML software supports that standard format, and you can now use the same catalog with many different products. These catalogs are fully described under "Entity management" at www.sgmlopen.org/sgml/docs/techpubs.htm. The simplest case involves pairs consisting of a **PUBLIC** identifier and a filename or other storage object identifier, as shown here, though much more can also be done:

```
PUBLIC "-//USA/AAP//DTD BK-1//EN" "aapbook.dtd"
PUBLIC "-//ACME DTD Writers//DTD General Report//EN"
       "report.dtd"
```

Lacking some kind of a lookup table, the best a system can probably do is to make reasonable guesses. For example, on finding a declaration for entity `CHAP1` that has only an FPI, and finding no catalog (or no matching entry in a catalog), a system might look for a file named `CHAP1.SGM`. This is helpful, but obviously no guarantee.

# 4.11. What characters can I use in a Formal Public Identifier (FPI)?

Formal Public Identifiers are used to refer to external data objects in a way that can be assured unique in the sense that a given FPI string only identifies one particular conceptual data object. In order to maximize their portability, SGML strictly limits the range of characters permitted in them.

SGML defines FPIs to be "minimum literals," in Clause 10.1.7. This has several effects.

First, a minimum literal must be quoted (using either **LIT** or **LITA**), and is normalized in much the same way as attribute values: **RS** is ignored; **RE** and **SPACE** sequences are collapsed to a single **SPACE** internally, and deleted entirely at the start or end.

Second, as discussed in Question 4.12, FPIs are limited in length regardless of changes to the SGML Declaration.

Third, minimum literals can use only a very restricted set of characters called "minimum data characters", as defined below. Clause 5.4 of ISO 9070 limits the characters in owner identifiers in the same way (though it seems to lack a definition for its "SPACE" character).

[78] minimum data character = **RS** | **RE** | **SPACE** | **LC Letter** | **UC Letter** | **Digit** | **Special**

"Special" is a character class defined in Clause 9.2.1 that contains

```
' ( ) + , - . / : = ?
```

This set of characters lacks some punctuation, as well as accented or wide characters of any kind. Thus it is difficult to create native FPIs in many human languages, or to represent some identifier syntaxes. On the other hand, there is the advantage that an FPI can be sent to any computer system with very little chance of becoming unusable because of character-set or representation issues. Anyone using FPIs should keep these factors in mind.

> **Note:** URLs (as discussed below) do not allow spaces or quotes, so putting URLs in FPIs can pose problems. URLs can use "`%`" plus two hexadecimal digits to represent non-URL characters (the most common is "`%20`" for space) — but "`%`" is not allowed in an FPI.

It is always possible to work around character set limitations by re-coding such characters using only the permitted ones. For example, a convention could state that other characters be expressed using some "trigger" string (such as "/") followed by a character-code number (perhaps two hexadecimal digits as in URLs). In that case the title "10% R&D" would appear as something like

```
10/25 R/26D
```

This is not elegant, but it can work. The larger problem with recoding data to create minimum literals as public identifiers is that the data becomes unusable to software that doesn't know the convention, and most software does not (indeed, there isn't presently any *single* convention for them to know). A lesser problem is that there is a length limit on FPIs (see the next question), which is reached more quickly if recoding is used.

> **Note:** FPIs bear some resemblance to URLs on the Web, but are actually quite different. For example, multiple copies of the same data object have the same FPI but not the same URL. URLs are more like phone numbers, which change from time to time and generally fail after the owner moves. FPIs are more like Social Security numbers, that apply permanently regardless of address or other changes.

## Tables of character safety

FPIs use a limited character set for portability, not caprice. Other systems concerned for portability make similar restrictions.

URLs on the Web use a character set defined in IETF RFC 1738 "Uniform Resource Locators (URL)". The characters allowed are A-Z, a-z, 0-9, plus these special characters:

```
- $ _ . + ! * ' ( )
```

Some additional characters (;/?:@=&) are reserved in some particular URL schemes but may be used otherwise. Some other characters are ruled out because they are used in other places in HTML files, even though they should not pose a conflict in URLs (for example, "<" and ">" pose no conflict so long as URLs are quoted as they should be). Other characters need to be expressed using a mechanism similar to SGML character references: "%" plus the hexadecimal code for the desired character.

The Text Encoding Initiative did extensive testing of what characters survive transfer through the many kinds of machines on the Internet, and established a set of "safe" characters that is documented in the TEI *Guidelines*, Section 4.3. That set, called the ISO 646 subset, includes a-z, A-Z, 0-9, and these special characters:

```
" % & ' ( ) * + , - . / : ; < = > ? _
```

A comparison of these sets is shown below. None of these sets permits characters outside of the printable 7-bit range of characters defined in ISO 646. "✓" indicates permissible characters; "~" indicates characters that are only reserved in some URL schemes, and may otherwise be usable in URLs.

| Character(s) | ISO 646 code | FPI | URL | TEI subset |
|---|---|---|---|---|
| TAB | 9 | | | |
| RS or LF | 10 | ✓ | | |
| RE or CR | 13 | ✓ | | |
| SPACE | 32 | ✓ | | |
| ! | 33 | | ✓ | |
| " | 34 | | | ✓ |
| # | 35 | | | |
| $ | 36 | | ✓ | |
| % | 37 | | (for escape) | ✓ |
| & | 38 | | ~ | ✓ |
| ' | 39 | ✓ | ✓ | ✓ |
| ( | 40 | ✓ | ✓ | ✓ |

| Character(s) | ISO 646 code | FPI | URL | TEI subset |
|---|---|---|---|---|
| ) | 41 | ✓ | ✓ | ✓ |
| * | 42 | | ✓ | ✓ |
| + | 43 | ✓ | ✓ | ✓ |
| , | 44 | ✓ | | ✓ |
| - | 45 | ✓ | ✓ | ✓ |
| . | 46 | ✓ | ✓ | ✓ |
| / | 47 | ✓ | ~ | ✓ |
| `0-9` | 48-57 | ✓ | ✓ | ✓ |
| : | 58 | ✓ | ~ | ✓ |
| ; | 59 | | ~ | ✓ |
| < | 60 | | | ✓ |
| = | 61 | ✓ | ~ | ✓ |
| > | 62 | | | ✓ |
| ? | 63 | ✓ | ~ | ✓ |
| @ | 64 | | ~ | |
| `A-Z` | 65-90 | ✓ | ✓ | ✓ |
| [ | 91 | | | |
| \ | 92 | | | |
| ] | 93 | | | |
| ^ | 94 | | | |
| _ | 95 | | ✓ | |
| ` | 96 | | | |
| `a-z` | 97-122 | ✓ | ✓ | ✓ |
| { | 123 | | | |
| \| | 124 | | | |
| } | 125 | | | |
| ~ | 126 | | | |

## Syntax of FPIs

The internal syntax of an FPI has many parts, as defined in part by the rules below (see also Appendix A and Clause 10.2). The main two parts are the owner identifier (see Question 4.13) and the text identifier:

[79] formal public identifier = *owner identifier*, "//", text identifier

[80] owner identifier = *ISO owner identifier* | *registered owner identifier* | *unregistered owner identifier*

[81] ISO owner identifier = *minimum data*

[82] registered owner identifier = "+//" , *minimum data*

[83] unregistered owner identifier = "-//" , *minimum data*

[84] text identifier = *public text class*, SPACE, *unavailable text indicator?*, *public text description*, "//" , ( *public text language* | *public text designating sequence*), ("//", *public text display version*)?

For example, an FPI that wished to identify the SGML standard as its owner would use an ISO owner identifier "`ISO 8879-1986`" (note that no particular translation of the standard is specified; that would go in the text identifier under *public text language*).

A note later in the Clause may imply that one cannot declare two different entities that map to the same FPI; that if they have the same owner and public text description, "they must be of different classes, versions, etc." This makes sense for consistency if the entities are intended to access different content. However, it would also seem to prevent giving multiple entity names to the very same data object for organizational, mnemonic, or parsing purposes such as declaring it once as **CDATA**, once as SGML text, once as **SUBDOC**, and once as **NDATA** SGML (as mentioned in Question 1.12, such distinctions can be useful). However, the Clause is probably better taken to mean that if two FPIs are the same, they must refer to "the same" text conceptually, which seems a better result.

The public text class is chosen from a list of terms defined in Clause 10.2.2.1, although technically the SGML standard states the requirement as being that the "name must be one that identifies an SGML construct in the following list". Also, unlike other parts of the FPI the public text class must be "entered with upper-case letters". The terms provided are: **CAPACITY, CHARSET, DOCUMENT, DTD, ELEMENTS, ENTITIES, LPD, NONSGML, NOTATION, SHORTREF, SUBDOC, SYNTAX, TEXT**. The most commonly used are probably **TEXT** and **DTD**.

## 4.12. How long can a Formal Public Identifier be?

SGML limits FPIs to at most 240 characters long. DTD designers might attempt to extend this limit by increasing **LITLEN** in their SGML declaration, but SGML says in Clause 10.1.7.1 that for a "minimum literal" such as an FPI, **LITLEN** is applied from "the reference quantity set, regardless of the concrete syntax used".

The reference quantity set is defined in Figure 6 found in Clause 13.4.8, and shows **LITLEN** 240. Length is counted after normalization (so extra whitespace doesn't count), and does not include the **LIT** or **LITA** delimiters (quotes) that surround the literal.

Formal Public Identifiers are defined in the SGML standard (ISO 8879), but relate closely to definitions in a separate standard, ISO 9070. ISO 9070 discusses mainly the owner identifier portion of FPIs (see the next question for more on that). It does specify in Clause 5 that an owner name shall not exceed 120 characters, and an object name, 100 characters. These portions would be separated by "//". Owner names are defined in much detail; object names are simply strings of components (each separated by "::").

## 4.13. What does the "owner identifier" part of a Formal Public Identifier actually identify?

Formal public identifiers (FPIs) include a section known as the "owner identifier" (see Question 4.10 for the syntax details). For example, "-//LC" in the FPI below:

```
<!NOTATION GIF          PUBLIC
   "-//LC//NOTATION Graphics Interchange//EN">
```

Some believe that this part of an FPI identifies the owner of the *data* in the entity being declared, but it actually identifies something quite different: the owner (or even "originator") of the FPI itself.

Thus, this FPI does not claim that the Library of Congress (LC) owns the specification of the popular GIF graphics format. The clearest explanation is in the more recent ISO 9070 (1990, amended 1991) standard, which is listed as a normative (binding) reference in the SGML standard. It states clearly and unambiguously that the owner identifier involves origination of the *identifier* itself, not the *identified*:

> **Introduction**: an "owner name", which identifies the originator of the public identifier.
>
> **3.10 note 13**: The owner of a public identifier is not necessarily the owner of the object that it identifies.

Thus the example merely claims that LC "originates" or "owns" the quoted string above, and not the GIF specification that it refers to. This is really how it must be, because if it were otherwise no one could create formal public identifiers to point to data they do not own (unless the actual owner provided them with an owner identifier); they would be forced either to use system identifiers, turn the **FORMAL** option off and use "informal" public identifiers, or persuade every individual data owner to provide an FPI (all of which seem inappropriate or implausible).

> **Note:** The SGML standard says nothing about owner identifiers except in Clause 10.2 on FPIs and in the definitions (Clause 4). Clause 4.223 phrasing things more loosely when it says that an owner identifier "identifies the owner or originator of public text" (it does not actually say *what* public text).

The definitions in ISO 9070 are less ambiguous and are given twice in very specific terms. Since 9070 is normative for SGML, since it was balloted and published later, and since doing otherwise would hamstring creators of FPIs, it seems reasonable that the 9070 definition should hold. For *registered* owner identifiers this choice seems absolutely required, because Clause 4.262 of SGML specifically defines a registered owner identifier as being one "that was constructed in accordance with ISO 9070".

Confusion about what owner identifiers identify is so common that a few readers of the book *Making Hypermedia Work* wrote letters to the authors, complaining that they were claiming to own numerous graphics formats because they provide a set of FPIs for various graphics notations with the book's ISBN as the owner identifier. One such letter even came from a member of the SGML committee (who, in fairness, acknowledged the difference immediately once the relevant Clauses were pointed out). According to ISO 9070, what the maker of an FPI claims is nothing more than ownership of the FPI itself, not the thing it identifies.

Because SGML does not provide a requirement or a way for authors to specify a normative identifier for the entities they *do* own (see Question 4.16), everyone must be able to make up FPIs for each other's data. This is why FPIs must not constitute claims to ownership. If it were not so, no one could refer to documents they do not own unless the actual owners provided FPIs for them. By analogy, consider what the Web would be like if creating a link to some URL meant that the linker was attempting to claim ownership of the data they're linking to.

# 4.14. What is the "language" for an FPI that points to data that isn't in a normal language?

Many Formal Public Identifiers end with the string "//EN" to encode the "public text language" field. This means that the data in the entity is in English (EN). However, some data is not in a natural human language, and analogous 2-letter language codes may not be readily available for such data. In such cases the best option is to create a new code that does not conflict with existing standard codes for natural languages, and which expresses the actual situation clearly.

*The SGML Handbook* (p. 387) states that this code "is simply an indicator of which natural language was used in the public text. It is usually a two-character ISO standardized code for the language". Such codes are defined by ISO 639, and cover most languages widely spoken in the world today (though linguists find the set inadequate). It then suggests that 2-letter language codes are recommended rather than required since it "frees validating parsers from the burden of checking conformance" and because it "permits extensibility in an area where it cannot compromise the integrity of SGML".

The issue remains of what to do when an entity's content is not in *any* natural language at all, but is instead in what SGML would call a **NOTATION**. For example, programs in a computer language such as C++ or Scheme, or graphics in some particular notation (which may or may not contain natural language captions). It is not clear what value to put in the language field for such entities.

DTDs are one important case of this: it seems a bit odd to say that a DTD is in English rather than in a special formal language (perhaps best called "DTD"). The tag names and the comments *in* a DTD might well be in one or more languages, but that is quite a different thing. The DTD is actually expressed in a **NOTATION** defined in the SGML standard, not in English.

> **Note**: Old Irish literature is customarily tagged in SGML using Old Irish GIs, since that is the one language certain to be common to all scholars of Old Irish. But in many cases tags and content are in different languages, raising another question of what to put in this field of FPIs.

There is sometimes a subtle interaction between the **NOTATION** and the language of the data: a digital photograph may be in no language at all, although it certainly has some representational notation; a text may be in English regardless of whether it is SGML or RTF. Some data is even more ambiguous: a computer program in C that contains comments in French; or a CAD drawing with captions in 9 different languages among which the viewer can select. Even SGML documents often contain parts in various human languages, so assigning a single language to the entire document can at times be problematic.

There is also a potential interaction between the language field and the "public text display version" (see the next question): There can be multiple versions of an entity that differ only in what natural language is used; this is an everyday situation when publishing in Europe, Canada, and many other places. Many government documents are required to be published in all the official EEC languages.

Since there is only one place to put a code, authors generally choose one language as primary. Common practice is to use a 2- or 3-letter natural language code when an appropriate one is available, and just to use "EN" when no appropriate code is available;

it would be better to create and document a new (non-conflicting) code when one is needed. One reasonable convention (though it is only that), is always to use a declared **NOTATION** name for data not in a natural language. This solves the problem nicely for **NDATA** entities: you can say accurately that they are in C, Pascal, TIFF, or whatever other representation applies.

## 4.15. What does the "version" part of an FPI mean?

Some Formal Public Identifiers use a field after the language field, which is called the "public text display version". It is defined in Clause 4.244 as being meant to distinguish different data objects that share the same public text description (and, presumably, owner identifier as well), "by describing the devices supported or coding scheme used. If omitted, the public text is not device-dependent".

In other words, this field is used to distinguish data objects that are conceptually "the same" data, but differ in being set up for different encodings or devices (perhaps such as computer screens with varying characteristics). Clause 10.2.2.5 gives the corresponding syntax rule, and adds that for "device-dependent" data, the public text display version must be included. Then, on accessing the data, an SGML system "must substitute the best available device-dependent version for the display device in use. If there is none, no substitution occurs".

The question arises whether these requirements are from the point of view of entity declarations, or of entity-managers that actually resolve FPIs to physical data objects. From the entity declaration's point of view, a document might declare an entity using an FPI that includes this field. That should probably be taken either to require that particular version (what should happen if it is incompatible with the actual physical display device is an interesting question), or at least to make that one the first choice if available, but allow fallback if it is not.

From the other point of view, a data object might identify itself as having a certain FPI, and include this field to say what version its data actually is. Omitting the field could mean either that the data is generic (not "device dependent"), or that the data is simply not identified as to its display version (this is nearly always the meaning in current practice, though the other meaning is usually more desirable).

The final question with this field is just what "device dependent" means. It seems as if color graphics must depend on having a color display, but in practice you can display them in black-and-white with passable results: are they device-dependent or not? Is the distinction between 16-color and 256-color images a device dependency? Like many questions, this seems silly until it hits you in the face. Here's one thing that could happen if a system lacks a sophisticated notion of just what device-dependency means in particular cases:

- If color depth is *not* a device-dependency, then a system has no reason to prefer a 256-color image over a 16-color one when the better display device is available. This seems bad.
- But if color depth *is* a device-dependency, a system would not use a 16-color image when the display is 256-color. It might end up choosing a black-and-white (device-independent) version. This also seems bad.

Similar conflicts come up with other distinctions such as the pixels-per-inch of displays, the overall size of images, the sound quality and frames-per-second of multimedia data, and with larger distinctions such as whether to display a movie or a still photo. A very common issue involves alternative graphic representations such as PNG versus JPEG, where one may have the advantage in resolution, and the other in size or speed.

The net effect is that all these requirements are subjective in practice; it is probably impossible to enumerate all the possibilities. To determine the "best" version of an entity, a system should examine current conditions (and user preferences), and then makes its best choice among all the data objects that have the same FPI *except for* the public text display version portion. "Best" could involve a combination of high resolution, fast display, most recent, and other characteristics. The way the choice is made is beyond SGML, which is probably as it should be even though it can lead to surprising results sometimes.

Despite these (perhaps insoluble) questions, the notion of variant forms of "the same" entity is useful and important. A similar notion of variant editions of entities as they are maintained through time is important for at least as many reasons; it is important to keep those two kinds of "versions" separate.

The functionality of display versions, where a particular version of the entity is chosen based on conditions at the time, would be very useful for switching displays between languages as well (see Question 4.14 for more on the language portion of an FPI). However, authors are generally better off representing language alternatives with SGML element structures:

```
<TITLE>
   <EN>The United States of America</EN>
   <SP>Los Estados Unidos</SP>
</TITLE>
```

By promoting this distinction into the element structure the structure can accommodate both language and content, and can be easily set up to manage them on the fly with no re-parsing (such as would be needed if you attempt this using alternative marked sections or alternative copies of entities).

## 4.16. How do I specify the FPI for a document in the document itself?

The short answer is that you can't because there is no such thing as "the" FPI. Any number of FPIs (even registered ones) may be created for the same data object. This is necessary so that you can create an identifier that points to some document even when the publisher or author didn't. However, there is no normative way in SGML for an author or publisher to specify an FPI for people to use for some particular data object.

Authors can communicate a preferred FPI in many ways, even though none of them is currently specified by an ISO standard. For example, the authors of *Making Hypermedia Work* simply provided an FPI for that book in the printed edition, namely:

```
+//ISBN 0-7923-9432-1//TEXT Making Hypermedia Work//EN
```

The intention was that people wishing to cite the work or link to it should use this FPI rather than having to invent their own. This would ease access, just as using a common cataloging scheme such as Dewey or LC catalog numbers helps different libraries share information. However, the lack of a single standard place to put the FPI means that one cannot write generic processing software that uses it. That is, even if many or all documents were to include such self-identification, each might express it in a different place and so software could not find it or reliably report whether or not it existed.

> **Note:** HTML has a `BASE` element that can be used to give the document's own URL, but there has been debate over whether it should be used for that or just for "factoring out" the common part of the URLs for many links. Shortly before `BASE` was added, SGML Open and the Web Consortium discussed the need for both concepts, but current HTML allows only one `BASE` element. In any case, many documents do not use it. Without a reliable self-id a client browser or a user may save a document locally with no URL attached. If the same URL is requested later, a browser cannot tell that there is already a copy on the local hard disk and so may re-request the whole document from some (perhaps distant or even defunct) server.

Many conventions have been proposed for putting self-identification into SGML documents (several are illustrated below), and they all work reasonably well. However, the lack of any single standard reduces the usefulness of each variant proposal.

```
<?FPI +//ISBN 0-688-01388-0//TEXT
   A History of the End of the World//EN>

<!-- FPI: +//ISBN 0123456789//TEXT
   Not The Globe and Mail//EN -->

<SELF-ID FPI="+//ISBN 0-88984-150-0//TEXT
   Christopher Columbus Answers All Charges//EN">

<!ENTITY self PUBLIC "+// ISBN 0135199840//TEXT
   Beyond HTML: SGML Publishing on the World Wide Web//EN">
<SELF-ID ENT="self">

<BASE HREF="http://www.sq.com//SGML/TheMovie.mpg">
```

SGML could address this issue by standardizing one method. I rather like the idea of a conventional entity name such as `self` or `#self` (by analogy to **#DEFAULT**), since it lets one use the full generality of external identifiers and lets the parser know what's going on. Such an entity would typically be declared in the internal declaration subset, not the DTD, since it would differ for each data object. A similar convention would be immensely useful for non-SGML data types too, such as raster graphics, but it would have to be added in those standards themselves.

The usefulness of such an identifier is great enough that it is worth including in your documents even before a standard method is settled. The best approach for now is to include them in a clear way, to be consistent at least among all your own documents, and to document clearly and explicitly exactly how you have included the identifier and where.

# 5. For Builders of SGML DTDs

Those who build SGML DTDs are often called "document analysts" or "designers", because they decide on the constraints of what document structures are allowed in some given situation. Obviously the kinds of elements they choose vary enormously (POEM versus PARTS-LIST, for example), but the same basic structures recur in many DTDs. Two especially common issues of the many that come up are:

- When the order of content in the document must differ from the "conceptual" order. The most common case is footnotes and floatable figures, whose conceptual position may be hard to pin down. Hypertext links (the links themselves, not their endpoints or anchors) and other structures also reveal this issue. In some cases, there is no single sensible order.
- When to use containers. Documents that have only titles and no containers for large structured objects like chapters, dictionary entries, and bibliography entries are generally agreed to show bad structural design. But there are gray cases, such as lists of term/definition pairs, where experts vary widely on whether the pairs ought to be grouped.

There are many options and decisions, and each one affects authors who actually use the DTD. A key thing for DTD designers to remember is that an author probably won't know the details of the DTD. An author should usually not be required to learn the language of DTDs, or to read them and all their documentation; it is about as interesting to authors as the RTF manual is to MS Word users. Thus, while the DTD designer ends up determining just what kinds of SGML minimization is allowed when typing, a more important thing to minimize is the number and complexity of rules that authors must learn in order to work. In many cases, that means giving fewer options, so that 20 different cases all fall under one general rule rather than requiring the user to learn 20 special case rules (even though those rules might be more efficient for each case, once learned).

This chapter deals with many questions that DTD designers encounter. The particular questions are gather into three groups: first those that are generally about elements, then about attributes, then about entities.

## On Elements

## 5.1. Can I set up a DTD so as to infer a container from only its title's start-tag?

No, there is no practical way to do this in SGML.

Designers commonly want to set up their DTD so they can leave the start-tags of *containers* (such as CHAPTER or SECTION) out, and have the parser infer them when it sees corresponding *titles* (such as HEAD1 or HEAD2). This is not so common when authors work natively in SGML, but is very common when dealing with "legacy" data: Documents coming from word processors, conversion programs, and old or overly-simple DTDs. Such data commonly marks the *titles* of large-scale containers but fails to mark the scope of the containers themselves. For example:

```
<H1>Introduction</H1>
<H2>How the world began</H2>
<P>Loudly</P>
<H2>How the world ended</H2>
<P>Softly</P>
<H1>Conclusions</H1>
```

This contrasts with the more hierarchical representation shown below (in a real document there would probably be more content):

```
<DIV1><H1>Introduction</H1>
   <DIV2>
      <H2>How the world began</H2>
      <P>Loudly</P>
   </DIV2>
   <DIV2>
      <H2>How the world ended</H2>
      <P>Softly</P>
   </DIV2>
</DIV1>
<DIV1><H1>Conclusions</H1>
```

In such DTDs typically H1 can *only* occur as the first child of DIV1; it may even be required there:

```
<!ELEMENT  DIV1        O O (H1, (P | DIV2)*)>
<!ELEMENT  DIV2        O O (H2, P*)>
```

Beginning DTD designers very often try to set up the DTD so that DIV start-tags of various levels can be inferred from the corresponding H start-tags, thus making data that lacks DIV tags usable anyway (experienced ones try it sometimes, too). However, there is no way to set up such a DTD in SGML. The semantic rules SGML chose to govern when start-tags may be omitted do not allow for this case. This is not much of a problem for native SGML authoring because authors can be told to insert the DIV1 instead of the H1 and because it is trivial to get an SGML parser to infer the H1 as needed. The difficulty arises in the reverse case, and is most common for those who must convert existing data.

One common proposal for a workaround within SGML is to re-interpret H1, H2, and other element types originally meant as headings, to actually *be* the container element types, and introduce required `H1TITLE`, `H2TITLE`, and so on to serve as headings (these are *always* inferred despite the absence of any start- or end-tags for them):

```
<!ELEMENT  H1          - O (H1TITLE, %stuff;)>
<!ELEMENT  H1TITLE     O O (#PCDATA)>
```

This is an especially common approach when dealing with IBM GML documents (where, many think, the `H` tags originated). But it only works in case *every* end-tag for `H1`, `H2`, etc. is omitted. Otherwise, the divisions would end after only one line each, not at all the intended effect. Since SGML provides no way to require omitting end-tags, this cannot be assured.

An unpleasant but possible alternative might be to make a **SHORTREF** delimiter reading "`<H1>`" that maps to an entity that inserts the two needed tags, something like:

```
<!ENTITY   ent1         "<DIV1><HEAD1>">
<!SHORTREF divMap       "<H1>" ent1...>
<!USEMAP   divMap       BODY>
```

Subtle map-switching might be used to apply maps only in certain contexts as well. But anything along this line would be a misleading hack, in part because the string "`<H1>`" appearing in the source would not in fact be a tag, although it looks just like one.

At present, the best workaround is to do a global change on the data to physically insert the container start-tags, or to use a specialized conversion program that does the same thing. A typical change using a regular expression tool such as sed or Perl might change "`<h1>`" to "`<div1><h1>`" and so on:

```
s/<H\([1-9]\)/<DIV\1><H\1/g
```

In short, there is no way to accomplish this particular inference just using the DTD and **OMITTAG** rules. The workarounds are not great, so the best solution is to transform the data ahead of time. Fortunately this need only be done once, and the transformation is easy to express with simple mechanisms like regular expressions (though see Question 3.8 on some cases to watch out for with any such tools).

## Technophile's note on how tags are inferred

When an SGML parser sees a start-tag for an element that can't occur in the present context (such as `H1` or `H2`), it tries to apply the **OMITTAG** rules (unless that feature is turned off). It tries inferring start-tags for "contextually required" elements and/or end-tags for open elements, in hopes of achieving a state where the tag it has actually seen would be permitted.

Difficulty inferring a container arises from details of how tag inference is defined. The set of things a parser tries to infer has nothing to do with the particular seen tag (such as `H1`). That is, the tag-inferring part of the parser may not consider what start-tag triggered it to begin with. Rather, it can only try inferring forward: creating start-tags that are absolutely, uniquely required given the prior context regardless of the following context that has just been scanned (such as a title's start-tag).

For example, in the example below the SGML rules for omitted tags cannot detect that the only way to make the `H2` start-tag valid is to start a `DIV2` first. A `DIV2` is the only element permitted to start after the `H1` (unless you close the `DIV1` first), but a `DIV2` is not *contextually required*, so SGML will not infer it:

```
<!ELEMENT  DIV1         O O (H1, DIV2*)>
<!ELEMENT  DIV2         O O (H2, DIV3*)>
<!ELEMENT  DIV3         O O (H3, P*)>
...
<DIV1>
   <H1>Introduction</H1>
   <H2>Early history</H2>
```

It would be technically feasible to define tag omission so this worked. Since the H1 start-tag has already been seen in order to trigger the **OMITTAG** rules in the first place, a language could require parsers to do one more thing after trying all the SGML tag-inference procedures. Specifically, a parser could go through all *contextually optional* elements, and see if inferring one of them would make the seen tag valid. In this example, on seeing H2 such a parser would realize that H2 cannot occur within a DIV1. After failing to find any contextually required elements, it would go through any contextually optional elements. Among them would be DIV2, and it would be the only contextually optional element that permits an initial H2, so would be inferred.

Since **OMITTAG** does not do this, however, the other approaches described above must be used. Again, the easiest is typically to insert the needed container start-tags with some kind of global-change process.

## 5.2. When was it I could use mixed content?

"Mixed content" is the term used to describe the content of elements whose models permit **#PCDATA** (they may also permit subelements of various types, which is the reason they are "mixed"). Every instance of such an element type has mixed content, whether or not the particular content actual has more than zero **#PCDATA** characters in it, or more than zero subelements.

Mixed content of any kind *can* be declared, in the sense that you can put **#PCDATA** anywhere you put any GI when writing content models. However, it is universally considered bad practice to do so except in a very limited set of cases. This section explains why.

The main reason this distinction matters is to support the rules for when **RE** characters are ignored (discarded) by an SGML parser (see Question 2.5). **RE**, or Record End, is an internal SGML construct involved with representing source file line breaks. In element content, they and whitespace characters are entirely ignored. Because of this, an **RE** between two elements in element content does not count as **#PCDATA**: it does not try to match against a **#PCDATA** token in the parent element's content model at all.

For example, the whitespace around the SEC elements here does not count as **#PCDATA** trying to occur in the CHP element — if it did this would be a syntax error, but because whitespace is ignored in element content there is no error. This can be useful for laying out SGML for greater legibility when typing it by hand:

```
<!ELEMENT  CHP          - -  (SEC*)>
<!ELEMENT  SEC          - -  (P*)>
...
<CHP>
   <SEC>...</SEC>
   <SEC>...</SEC>
</CHP>
```

In mixed content more complicated rules apply, and only some whitespace characters are ignored. **#PCDATA** can still appear anywhere inside of content models without being technically ambiguous: an SGML parser always knows what to do (computer software always knows what it *will* do — it just may not be what you *want* it to do).

One tricky case comes up when **#PCDATA** is only allowed in *some* places within an element, such as here:

```
<!ELEMENT  QUOTE         - O (AUTHOR, PAGE, #PCDATA)>
<!ELEMENT  SEC           - O (TITLE, (#PCDATA|B|I)*, SUMMARY>
```

An author typing in such an element commonly assumes that the areas of the element that don't allow **#PCDATA** must be treated like element content: after all, they don't allow **#PCDATA**, so they don't seem like mixed content from an author's point of view. But SGML determines that:

- Mixed-ness is a characteristic of entire element types, not of specific places in them.
- Thus the elements just shown always have mixed content.
- Thus whitespace in them is not ignored (except for particular cases such as the very first **RE** in an element, as discussed earlier).
- Thus a line break where **#PCDATA** is not allowed still tries to match a **#PCDATA** token in the content model. Examples would be a line break between AUTHOR and PAGE, or multiple ones just within the outermost boundaries of the QUOTE or SEC.
- Such line-breaks do not match up with any **#PCDATA** token in the right place in the content model.
- The content model does not match the content.

Since the (mixed) content model cannot account for character data at the point where it is found, the SGML parser either reports an error, or (if **OMITTAG** is **YES**) tries to recover by inferring omitted tags. It is possible that by closing some of the open elements, the parser can get to an ancestor that allows for whitespace. In that case the parser will report no error and will continue as if some end-tags had occurred and it is now parsing the continuation of that ancestor. On the other hand, if **OMITTAG** is **NO** then the error will be detected and reported immediately.

Since inferring an omitted end-tag was not the intention, an error has occurred from the author's point of view even if SGML finds none because of **OMITTAG**. Whether the SGML parser finds a syntax error some time later depends on various details, for example whether it sees an explicit end-tag for the element(s) it already inferred them for. If it does, it will report an attempt to close an element type that is not open (a few parsers will tell you where the last such end-tag was inferred, to help trace down the problem). If it never sees such an end-tag (perhaps because it was intentionally omitted), it is possible that no syntax error will ever be reported; the parser will just end up producing unintended structures.

A second tricky case was pointed out by C. M. Sperberg-McQueen. If a content model has two completely separate alternatives, and only one allows **#PCDATA**, the whole content model is considered mixed:

```
<!ENTITY   % paraCont  "#PCDATA | EMPH | FN">
<!ENTITY   % chunks    "P | NOTE | LIST">
<!ELEMENT  ITEM        ((%paraCont;)* | (%chunks;)*)>
```

Given such declarations, you cannot have whitespace even in the chunk-style `ITEM`s. Thus, the following is incorrect because of the line-breaks:

```
<ITEM>
<P>Hammer</P>
<P>Chisel</P>
<P>Granite</P>
</ITEM>
```

The reasoning is subtle enough, the rules complicated enough, and typical error-reporting limited enough, that DTD designers are best off avoiding similar situations entirely. One way to do this is to turn off **OMITTAG** so any whitespace usage errors are caught. But even when using **OMITTAG** it is possible to prevent the problem. Just allow **#PCDATA** only when it is allowed *anywhere* within its parent.

This is generally easy to accomplish; always make sure **#PCDATA** appears in content models either alone, or in a repeatable **OR** group with GIs.

```
<!ELEMENT  P            - -  (#PCDATA)>
<!ELEMENT  ITEM         - -  (#PCDATA | B | I | FOOTNOTE)*>
```

**Note**: Inclusion exceptions that may be in effect do not pose a problem, because they do not restrict the placement of **#PCDATA** within the element type(s) they apply to):

XML elevates this design principle to a rule: **#PCDATA** may only be used in this way in XML documents. It also makes a minor simplification for parsers and a minor readability enhancement for humans, by requiring that **#PCDATA** be listed first in such a group. This is always acceptable in SGML, so does not make XML incompatible. Content models of this form should be the only place **#PCDATA** is used; this will greatly reduce the potential for problems.

## 5.3. Which content models need parentheses?

The only element declarations which do not need parentheses are those that have a reserved keyword where the content model group would go. The only reserved keywords are the three declared content types **CDATA**, **RCDATA**, and **EMPTY**, plus **ANY** (which unlike the other three, is technically called a content model).

For example:

```
<!ELEMENT  SEC          - -  (ST, (SSEC | FIG)+, SUM)>
<!ELEMENT  P            - -  (ITEM)*>
<!ELEMENT  XMP          - -  CDATA>
<!ELEMENT  REV          - -  ANY>
<!ELEMENT  MILESTONE    - -  EMPTY>
```

The parentheses are used in content models to gather element type names into "groups" for which you then specify repeatability and relationships. Any single group must have only a single kind of connector (**AND**, **OR**, or **SEQ** — see Clauses 10.1.3 and 11.2.4), though nested groups can have their own. For SEC above, the outer set is a **SEQ** group that requires a sequence of three things; the second of which is an **OR** group.

Each group may be followed by an "occurrence indicator" that indicates whether it is optional ("?"), optional and able to be repeated ("*"), or required and able to be repeated ("+"). If no occurrence indicator is given the group must occur exactly once.

All content models have this form except one: the reserved word **ANY** counts as a content model. It means that the element being declared may contain any combination of other elements and/or **#PCDATA** content. **ANY** must not be parenthesized, because "(ANY)" would mean something different: that the element must contain exactly one occurrence of another element, whose element type is ANY.

The only other things that can show up without parentheses in this place are not called content models. The keywords **CDATA**, **RCDATA**, and **EMPTY** are used *instead* of content models, and are called "declared content". They are special because they have special effects on parsing such as suppressing recognition of various delimiters in content or prohibiting content (and end-tags) entirely. Declared content is mentioned in several other questions (see the Index).

Just as with **ANY**, the declared content keywords must be used without parentheses so they cannot be confused with content models that use elements with element types named CDATA, RCDATA, and EMPTY. It would not be wise to create element types with those names, but it would be even more confusing to prohibit those particular names and have declared content keywords appear in parentheses!

The only special word *inside* content models is **#PCDATA**. It is always written with "#" (the reserved name indicator or **RNI** delimiter) on the front (otherwise it would conflict with an element whose GI was PCDATA).

## 5.4. When should I create an element type to group other elements?

In general, you are better off having such containers than not, because at worst you can still ignore them. A good general guideline (pointed out to me by C.M. Sperberg-McQueen, who credits the notion to Lynne Price) is that any time you find yourself writing a parenthesized group inside a content model, and putting an occurrence indicator ("*", "+", or "?") on that group, it is a good sign that there is a conceptual unit that deserves to be named and tagged to make it a full-fledged SGML element.

For example, someone could design an (over-) simplified bibliography that just consisted of AUTHOR, TITLE, and DATE, repeated any number of times (if this were a complete bibliography DTD, of course a whole lot of other data would need to be handled as well):

```
<!ELEMENT  BIBLIO      - - (AUTHOR, TITLE, DATE)*>
...
<BIBLIO>
   <AUTHOR>Andr&eacute;, J., R. Furuta, and V. Quint</AUTHOR>
   <TITLE>Structured Documents</TITLE>
   <DATE>1989</DATE>
   <AUTHOR>Hall, W., H. Davis, and G. Hutchings</AUTHOR>
   <TITLE>Rethinking Hypermedia</TITLE>
   <DATE>1996</DATE>
</BIBLIO>
```

This will work well enough for many purposes, despite the lack of a container for each bibliography entry. However, it violates the guideline above and has the potential to pose problems later on. For example:

- If some other subelements need to be added they will likely be optional ones, and when they are absent it becomes more difficult to tell where one entry stops and another starts. Additions are the norm over time, so providing for them is wise.
- In the same way, once optional elements are added, if an element (optional or not) is accidentally omitted it can be much harder to catch the error, since it may turn out that the document still comes out valid, just different. This is even truer with **AND** models than with **OR** or **SEQ**.
- If you need to attach any information to an entry *as a whole*, there is no convenient way to do it, such as by adding an attribute to the entry element.
- Many kinds of formatting, retrieval, and other processing engines can do more with units if the units are tagged explicitly.

But the most important reason to define a container element for each individual entry is simpler: it is a way of telling the truth. There really is a conceptual unit there, and it is that unit that is being repeated. Representing the unit in the structure lets SGML in on the secret, which inevitably leads to easier processing down the road, though the exact way it helps will vary from case to case. Adding ENTRY to surround each entry is a good idea.

A similar principle can be applied when you find yourself creating parameter entities that contain parts of content models. If you find yourself re-using a sub-model often enough that you're inclined to make an entity for it, that often means it is a real conceptual unit and deserves its own element type. For example, some DTDs have a parameter entity for date, which is a handy way to include "MON, DAY, YEAR" or a similar string in various content models. But anyplace that sequence occurs, it would likely be useful to let SGML a DATE is also occurring. Typical SGML applications have no knowledge of what parameter entities were used to express content models, so if you don't introduce the element the SGML structure doesn't know it's there.

Many other examples could be raised, but the general rule is enough: whenever you find yourself writing a repeatable group within a content model, and especially if the model is getting at all complex, consider whether there is a real conceptual unit it corresponds to (often there will be a familiar name for that unit as well). When in doubt, err on the side of adding containers.

## 5.5. When should I use inclusion exceptions?

An inclusion exception is a way to say that some element type is allowed anywhere within another type — either directly, or indirectly within any descendant (unless overridden later). The most obvious application is for elements like footnotes and quotations, that can appear almost anywhere.

```
<!ELEMENT  BOOK          - -  (CHP*)  +(FOOTNOTE | QUOTE)>
```

There are several reasons for making an element an inclusion exception:

- If it is allowed in many places, then declaring it as an inclusion exception in one place is far easier than working it into many content models.
- Even if it only occurs in one element type, modifying that content model to list it everywhere can be difficult (except for the easy case of **OR** models).
- It is harder to make mistakes such as forgetting to allow it in just one place, which are hard to find and check for in the DTD. If not caught, such mistakes usually don't cause any invalidity; they just frustrate the user who wonders why they can put a footnote on any word except one inside a book title (or whatever element type was missed).
- Often the idea of an inclusion more clearly expresses the conceptual reality: it says to the DTD reader that the element is generally applicable rather having a special relationship to particular container element types.

These are the criteria most DTD designers used when considering whether to make some element be an inclusion exception.

> **Note**: Clause 11.2.5.1 of the SGML standard suggests that inclusion exceptions "should not be used for contextual subelements", but for elements that are "not logically part of the content at the point they occur..., such as index entries or floating figures". SGML does not explicitly define "contextual subelement" or what it means to be "logically part of the content", though Clause 4.53 defines "content" as "Characters that occur between the start-tag and end-tag of an element in a document instance...".

*The SGML Handbook* (p. 419) says that because of the difference in whether an **RE** after the element is ignored, "Inclusions should therefore be used only for 'floating' elements, such as sidebars, that are not part of the element structure at the point where they occur in the content". It then suggests that this implies "that the distinction between a floating figure and a stationary ('inline') one should be made by defining two element types, not by defining a 'float/nofloat' attribute".

It is not entirely clear why **RE**-ignoring (see Question 2.5) relates to this issue unless you make certain assumptions about how (and whether) authors type and minimize markup and just how a particular formatting tool does layout. It is also not necessarily true in SGML that an **RE** after an included element will be ignored; the actual rules are a bit more subtle than that.

It seems clear that at least two cases could be separated:

1. Some elements may be conceptually or structurally appropriate anywhere within certain others, while others have highly restricted placement. For example, `EMPHASIS` and `FOOTNOTE` both have almost unrestricted placement, while `CHAPTER-TITLE` is usually quite highly restricted.

2. In some DTDs and some processing scenarios, some elements are to be displayed contiguous with surrounding elements, and others are not. For example, a formatter may (or may not) move a `FOOTNOTE` or `NOTE`, but not `EMPHASIS` or `CHAPTER-TITLE` (formatters commonly *reuse* title data in the table of contents, page header, and other locations; but "the" title generally stays put).

The second case is not quite the way inclusions have come to be used in practice, perhaps for these and similar reasons:

1. Footnotes, as one example, seem clearly to be *logically* at the point they occur even though they may move *physically* during formatting. The only point at which they can be part of the content seems to be their reference point.
2. Determining markup based on formatting choices contradicts one of SGML's main principles, namely the use of descriptive markup.
3. An author may not *know* how the document is to be formatted (if at all!). For example, `FOOTNOTE` objects may be collected at the end of each page or chapter, or kept inline (as has become common for reference footnotes). In online presentation footnotes are usually suppressed except for an icon or other symbol, and displayed on demand; sometimes they are displayed inline as a special kind of block quotation. Thus a DTD designer or author cannot know whether a given kind of object is "floatable", and sometimes floatability will even differ in different presentations of the same document.
4. While the character sequence of SGML content corresponds very simply to the character order in formatted display for some common SGML cases, this cannot be assumed in general. There are cases where such a rule cannot make sense, such as documents that are by nature indexes, concordances, analytical or linguistic tools, and even documents that do not correspond to "readable text" at all, but are more like databases. See Simons (1990) on this point.
5. What characters are "logically part of the content" is a semantic question and thus falls outside the domain of SGML. In some cases it would be nonsensical or even impossible to make that distinction, although there are also many cases where it seems obvious.
6. SGML provides no other practical way to accommodate elements such as `EMPHASIS` that can occur very freely yet must not be moved by a formatter. The offert of listing them in numerous models can be substantial, especially as a DTD is maintained and enhanced over time.

It seems best to simplify the issue and use inclusions on a purely structural basis that they support very well: providing a simpler way to specify elements that would otherwise have to be listed in many, many content models. The formatting concerns need not enter in (and in some DTDs, cannot).

**Note:** Using inclusions at all affects how you must handle fragments of documents. To promote elements for use as separate documents (or as **SUBDOC** entities), you must somehow provide information about just what inclusions applied in the (no longer present) context. For example, if `FOOTNOTE` is just an inclusion exception on `BOOK`, all `FOOTNOTE` elements become invalid when you promote a `CHAPTER` to be a **SUBDOC** entity. See Question 2.13 for more on this.

# 5.6. How can I tell where spaces make a difference in elements?

Questions 1.8 and 5.2 discuss some of the parsing effects of whitespace in content. Whitespace raises a formatting issue as well. Suppose that the author has avoided all the cases discussed there, and knows exactly which whitespace will get through the parser and not be ignored. There is still the question of what happens to whitespace during formatting. Authors usually have one of two intents, depending on what kind of element they are making:

- **Preformatted or verbatim**: Code samples, ASCII artwork, tables done with box-drawing characters, and a few other things should be copied exactly as they were typed in: every line break should start a new display line, multiple spaces stay multiple, and everything is set in a fixed-pitch font (I have seen a few authors try to set this kind of data using a proportional font — it is not fun). The HTML PRE element is intended for this use.

```
         o . .
   o o o          ____  __________________    ___________T___
   o      ___^___/    | |       _         | |           o  |
 .]B____r__| [   i 1  | |  ...  | |  ...  | |  0  0  0 | | |
>(________|__|____/_____|nn|______|_|_______|)(|__________|_|_|)
_/oo 0---0        ooo   ooa   o^o^o            o^o^o   o^o          d^d
-+-+-+-+-+-+-+-+-+-+-+-+-+-+-+-+-+-+-+-+-+-+-+-+-+-+-+-+-+-+-+-+-+-+-
```

- **Normalized**: Whitespace is there only because the markup-handler or author liked to line things up while editing. It should be collapsed in just the same way as whitespace in most attribute values: multiple adjacent whitespace characters collapse to a single space, while whitespace at the beginning and end of formatted blocks (such as paragraphs) is deleted. In this case a line break formats just like a space. The most common case is internal indentation of typed list items:

```
<LIST>
    <ITEM>An em space is the width of the 'm'
          character in whatever font is currently
          in use for displaying text.</ITEM>
    <ITEM>An en space is like an em space except
          that it is the width of an 'n'.</ITEM>
    <ITEM>A thin space is usually used to separate
          adjacent punctuation just slightly.</ITEM>
</LIST>
```

Other intents are possible, but less common in practice. A few authors have data conversion or word processing software that writes out data in which record boundaries have absolutely no meaning, so the formatter is expected to utterly discard them. In that case, an individual word can be broken by a line boundary but should be rejoined in formatting unless there is *also* a space at the end of one line or the beginning of the next:

```
<P>This data might have been con
verted from RTF.
```

This case does pose some practical problems. The main ones are (1) many file storage and manipulation tools discard spaces at the end of lines, making words join up when they shouldn't; (2) many formatters do not support this discarding; and (3) many search tools, SGML-aware or not, do not know to join up words in such cases.

All these rules generally apply only to "real" whitespace: **RE**, **RS**, **SPACE**, and **TAB**. Characters like hard, em, en, thin, and non-breaking spaces are not whitespace to an SGML parser (unless you add them to the **SEPCHAR** class via the SGML declaration), so they are always real data. A formatter may do anything it likes with them, so long as it satisfies users' requirements.

To be able to support any verbatim element types, an SGML system must not do space normalization in content until it is actually formatting (presumably based on some style sheet). The HTML PRE element is a verbatim element, and supporting it requires being able to leave whitespace un-normalized.

Assuming you have such a system, it should provide some setting in its stylesheets or other processing tools, that you can use to state which elements should retain their original line-breaking. If your software does not support this, the only viable option is to tag every line (explicitly, or perhaps implicitly via **SHORTREF**), or to insert some other markup for each line, such as a line-break processing instruction.

## 5.7. I forgot to declare an element type, but named it in a content model. Why no error?

A little known fact is that SGML permits mentioning any element type name in a content model regardless of whether it has a definition elsewhere in the DTD. No instance of such an element may occur, but so long as none does there is not an error. Likewise, declaring unused elements is not a syntax error.

These cases can complicate DTD development. Although there are times when these forms are handy (especially for DTDs that support extensive customization), it is rare to want undeclared or unused elements around. The permissiveness can make it hard to test a DTD in isolation from any given document. If the DTD author forgets to declare some element or forgets to add some element to others' content models, or (most likely of all) makes a typographical error in a GI somewhere, no error arises until some document appears which happens to use that element.

An option to declare such cases unused would save DTD writers time. Indeed, several parser authors have added an option to issue a warning for this. In other cases the DTD author should simply be careful not to leave unintended elements in, or intended ones out. On the other hand, it can be very useful is certain cases and so software should not rule it out unconditionally.

## 5.8. What's the difference between a title and a container?

Several questions (such as 5.1) have mentioned the distinctions between actual containers such as entire chapters or lists, versus titles of them such as chapter titles, and term-list headers. Containers are large objects that commonly start with a title and then have much other content. Titles are small objects that somehow label or introduce following content at the same level (or, in the same container).

Most word processors have a very flat structure, with titles but little or no support for containers: documents consist of paragraphs, some of which happen to look like titles. In that world readers infer containers by comparing font sizes and layout: "everything from this big type up to the next thing with equally big type at the top of a page, is a chapter".

This works because humans are clever. Computers are not so clever, and for a long time this limited view of document structure prevented software from being able to manipulate larger objects. A few of the common examples are:

- Outliners don't always move the right amount of material when dragged, or promote and demote levels correctly, especially after repeated editing.
- Tables of contents don't always include the right objects, or display them at the correct levels.
- You can "keep" a title paragraph on the same page with the following text paragraph, but can't insist on keeping any sequence of more than two paragraphs or other objects together (such as a list or a poetry stanza).
- Numbered lists do not stay numbered correctly if you add an item (because the word processor doesn't know about the list itself, only about a series of indented paragraphs, which may happen to have been numbered once). Problems are especially common with nested lists and with multi-paragraph list items.
- Non-trivial lists usually can't be numbered correctly at all, such as ones with multi-paragraph items, or nested lists. Nested lists are usually the first concession word processors make to supporting hierarchical container structures.

Many other examples can also be raised (see André, Furuta, and Quint (1989) and DeRose, Durand, Mylonas, and Renear (1990) for more details). In short, for computers to process structured information well they need to be told about the structure somehow. As mentioned in Question 5.1, SGML start-tag minimization can't infer containers well, so it requires effort to convert flat word processor data into hierarchically structured SGML by adding those containers. When designing a DTD and an authoring or conversion process, it is important to keep in mind that using containers will buy you a lot of extra capability down the line.

## 5.9. Can I make an element that crosses element boundaries (in the rare case when I need to)?

No. In SGML, elements must nest properly making a tree or hierarchy. Put another way, any element that starts inside another one must also end there. This is illegal:

```
<!-- WRONG -->
<P>This is not the <EMPH>way</P> back.</EMPH>
```

Technically, that string (like almost any other) could be legal under a carefully constructed (and rather weird) DTD. But even in that artificial case it would not mean anything like what it appears to mean: a `P` that overlaps by three letters with an `EMPH`.

Markup like this is almost always an unintentional authoring error, and an SGML parser rightly reports it as a problem to be fixed. However, there are occasional times when elements should cross each other's boundaries.

One classic case is when more than one structure applies to a document. For example, the Bible and other ancient documents typically need to be represented in terms of several structures with different purposes:

- **Discourse**: books, pericopes, paragraphs and speeches, and sentences.
- **Reference**: books, chapters, verses.
- **Layout**: manuscript page, column, and line.
- **Prosody**: metrical units of poetry.

Each of these structures is a hierarchy if examined by itself, but each can cross the others. As Barnard et. al 1995 and 1996 show, there are times when one structure may constrain another, or when only certain types of overlap are allowed; but for the most part the structures are independent. Note also that some structures may not apply to the whole content: prosody may only apply to poetic portions, for example.

SGML provides a solution for some particular kinds of cases: The CONCUR feature. With it, each tag can contain a parenthesized DTD name and tags for any given DTD only "count" in relation to others from the same DTD:

```
<(REF)VERSE N="3.16">
```

In effect, an SGML parser can be told to ignore all tags that are not part of a particular DTD (as specified by the DTD name prefix). Very few parsers support CONCUR (I only have heard of one). Coordinating the parsed data across those multiple DTDs and providing processing capabilities that can integrate the multiple resulting document structures is even harder.

CONCUR is actually the SGML feature that adds the most to the range of document structures SGML can represent (most of the other SGML features relate to minimization, which provides alternative ways of representing structures but no new structures). For this reason I think it is one of the most important features and should be more widely available.

However, CONCUR does not really solve the overlap problem in general. This is because there are important cases where elements from a single DTD must overlap others from the same DTD, or even other instances of the same element type. The most important case is hypertext links: two different strings can be hypertext link origins even if they overlap. Authors or commentators may very well select a range and make a link from it, then later select another range that overlaps it and make a link from it as well. CONCUR does not help for this, because the links are from the same DTD as each other:

```
<!-- WRONG -->
<P>For the <XREF TGT="note1">snark was a
<XREF TGT="note2">boojum,
</XREF><!-- meant to end scope for note1 -->
you see.</XREF><!-- meant to end scope for note2 -->
</P>
```

In this example, the link anchors are intended to be "`snark was a boojum`" and "`boojum, you see.`" But this cannot be expressed with SGML element structures. The only workaround that CONCUR enables is putting the two links in different DTDs, but then you need as many DTDs as the depth of the deepest multiple overlap, which quickly gets absurd. Also, in that case which DTD you assign each link to depends purely on how much it overlaps with other links, and has nothing to do with its conceptual purpose or significance.

Links are not the only case of self-overlap. Technical manuals run into the same issue with marking revisions to the text (see Question 6.1 for more on this). Literary analysts runs into it when marking the scope of fuzzy phenomena such as allusions or themes.

It would be possible to solve these problems by using a language that could put an `ID` in both the start-tag and the end-tag of an element:

```
<P>For the <XREF TGT="note1" ID="link1">snark was a
<XREF TGT="note2" ID="link2">boojum,
</XREF ID="link1">
you see.</XREF ID="link2">
</P>
```

> **Note:** A somewhat similar mechanism is used in the Wittgenstein archives, where overlapping structures are crucial. Even that mechanism, however, cannot readily handle self-overlapping element types. See Huitfeldt (1995) for a discussion of these issues.

Within SGML, only workarounds are available for dealing with such structures. One is to insert **`EMPTY`** elements such as `LINK.START` and `LINK.END`, which are connected by **`ID`** and **`IDREF`** as shown below. Clever application software on top of SGML can make good use of this, but SGML *itself* does not know that the scope between corresponding ends is a meaningful unit at all: it cannot even validate that the ends occur in the right order, that there is exactly one end for each start, and so on. So far as SGML is concerned there is no "element" created by this convention, and general SGML software will not give much help with this approach. It can be useful, but it remains a workaround.

```
<!ELEMENT  (LINK.START | LINK.END) - - EMPTY>
<!ATTLIST  LINK.START
   UNTIL   IDREF       #REQUIRED
   TGT     IDREF       #REQUIRED>
<!ATTLIST  LINK.END
   ID      ID          #REQUIRED>
...
<P>For the <LINK.START TGT="note1" UNTIL="end1">
snark was a
<LINK.START TGT="note2" UNTIL="end2">boojum,
<LINK.END ID="end1">
you see.<LINK.END ID="end2">
</P>
```

Hypermedia systems that support out-of-line links solve this problem somewhat better. Such links would live elsewhere in a list, and each would point to exactly the anchor scope it needs, without any cross-interference. Links that reside elsewhere than directly at one of their endpoints (or anchors) were introduced by the Brown University InterMedia system, and exist in a few commercial systems now, such as MicroCosm. Out-of-line links do not run into the overlap problem, since the links themselves are not mixed in with the data they point to. HyTime includes a construct for expressing such links, called "ilink". The Text Encoding Initiative *Guidelines* (Section 14.7) define a similar construct and a way to aggregate instances of it into link databases.

Out-of-line links are not part of the Web, although there are a few specialty servers that store links out-of-line to gain the various functional benefits and then copy them into documents on the fly while serving them out to browsers. Such systems can store overlapping links but still cannot send them to a client all at once, or the client would be confused by overlapping markup. XML is presently working on a mechanism for managing such links on the Web, and will likely base it on existing standards such as HyTime and the Text Encoding Initiative (on which see Question 6.11).

# On Attributes

## 5.10. When do I use an attribute versus an element?

This is a subjective decision. A good basic principle is that attributes are used to represent short, constrained statements that associate properties or characteristics with whole elements, where subelements represent longer, more fluid or internally structured objects that constitute sub-parts of elements. However, there are numerous cases where such simple guidelines is not enough. This section discusses some of the ways you can move information between attributes and subelements or content and some of the criteria you can use in deciding which way to go.

Formally speaking, attributes *can* always be avoided in favor of subelements. That is, they don't increase the range of structures that can be represented in SGML. This is because a subelement can always be declared instead of an attribute to hold the same information. For example, instead of

```
<!ELEMENT  X             - - (A, B, C)>
<!ATTLIST  X
  TYPE     (SECRET | FREE)          "SECRET">
```

the attribute TYPE *could* become a subelement and the **ATTLIST** declaration could be discarded:

```
<!ELEMENT  X             - - (TYPE, A, B, C)>
<!ELEMENT  TYPE          - - (#PCDATA)>
```

With an enumerated name token group, creating a subelement corresponding to each name token even enables some kinds of validation (though other attribute declared values cannot readily do the same thing):

```
<!ELEMENT  X             - - (TYPE, A, B, C)>
<!ELEMENT  TYPE          - - (TYPE.SECRET | TYPE.FREE)>
<!ELEMENT  (TYPE.SECRET | TYPE.FREE) - O EMPTY>
```

Name conflicts can always be avoided: name all the new subelements starting with "ATTR-", or introduce an initial sub-element such as ATTRS and put all the former attributes inside there.

Thus, one way or another you can always choose whether any particular piece of data goes in an attribute or not. There are cases where this is not very intuitive, however. Also, there are a few constraints and differences that go along with the choice:

- Attributes have length restrictions.
- Attributes have no provision for internal sub-structure beyond flat lists of tokens, so moving data up from content into attributes can be harder.
- There is a difference in *validation* capabilities: in the example above SGML cannot check that the **#PCDATA** content of `TYPE` is one of the desired name tokens (`SECRET` or `FREE`), or even syntactically an SGML name.
- Default values, whitespace normalization, and upper-casing behavior are not available for content as they are for attributes.

> **Note**: Such capabilities could be implemented on top of SGML. Regular expressions could be used to specify attribute or content constraints, as can HyTime's "HyLex" feature.

Some have argued that attributes are unnecessary, and at one level they are right because a language that had no such notion could be simpler (in formal terms, and perhaps to implement), yet could represent the same data. However, documents done that way might not be simpler to understand and use and for that reason the avoidance of attributes seems undesirable. It is entirely appropriate to use attributes in DTD design. A good rule is to examine your data and structure it into elements and attributes keeping general criteria such as these in mind:

| **Criterion** | **Attributes** | **Elements** |
|---|---|---|
| Size | Small | Large |
| Structure | Simple or flat | Complex or hierarchical |
| Relationship | Property or characteristic of | Sub-part of |
| Scope | Applies to whole element | Is a part of an element |
| Repeatability | One or only a few tokens; can require a token | Any number of repetitions (not always: consider titles); cannot require text content. |
| Ordering | No particular order to attributes | Order is part of meaning |
| Validation | Individual token types and enumerated types | Content model structures organizing subelement types |
| Semantics | **ID, NOTATION, ENTITY** | No real SGML semantics |
| Defaulting | Several kinds | None |
| Normalization | Case-folding and whitespace | **RE** rules |
| Markup suppression | Only entity references are recognized; can't be suppressed | Various types via declared content, marked sections, etc. |

There are no hard-and-fast rules for these decisions, but intuition is usually an adequate guide. That is why markup like that shown below seems bizarre (arranging a DTD so that a `FOOTNOTE`'s reference number is its content and its text is an attribute), even though it is perfectly valid SGML:

```
<!ELEMENT  FOOTNOTE     - - (NUMBER)>
<!ATTLIST  FOOTNOTE
   TEXT    CDATA       #IMPLIED>
...
<footnote text="See Smith (1995), p. 40.">1</>
```

There are examples where intuition fails and it is impossible to decide which information is content and which is description of content. One such example arises when marking up editorial corrections. If a manuscript has an apparent error and the editor corrects it, it is often best to keep both forms around. In that case, which version belongs in content? The Text Encoding Initiative *Guidelines* (see their Section 6.5) provide a way to represent such cases using the SIC element type. The intended correction goes on the CORR attribute as shown here:

```
<SIC CORR="affect">effect</SIC>
```

The inevitable question is which spelling of the word is really "in" the text. Certainly it isn't true that one is a property and one is content, so that basic principle doesn't help; the other criteria above don't help either. The general notion that content is the "real" document while markup is not is only true in some particular situations, and also doesn't help here. Solutions differ and in some cases both forms might be needed to express slightly different interpretations; the Text Encoding Initiative *Guidelines* thus provide the opposite structure as well:

```
<CORR SIC="effect">affect</CORR>
```

Some authors would instead treat the alternatives as examples of "variant reading" apparatus, and put both in content (an option the TEI also provides for):

```
<APP>
<RDG WIT="orig">effect</RDG>
<RDG WIT="ed">affect</RDG>
</APP>
```

The problem is not that SGML lacks a principled way to decide whether something "should" be an attribute or content. Creating such a principle would involve deep issues of philosophy. Rather, the difficulty is that this *semantic* choice interacts in complex ways with *syntactic* issues such as imposing constraints on the data portions (in the example above a user might want to constraint the SIC or CORR attribute to be a single word, which can only be done by SGML if it is an attribute).

If attributes and content had more syntactic capabilities in common the choice could be made more freely, based on meaning rather than what a parser can do in one case or the other. An internal structure for attribute could be declared and validated with at least the same power as SGML provides for elements via content models. Conversely, it would be easy to provide a way to constrain **#PCDATA** with at least the power of attribute declared values. Erik Naggum is said to have designed such mechanisms once; HyTime's HyLex feature also provides some similar capabilities.

SGML has interesting relationship to object-orientation in databases and computer programming, involving just this issue of syntax versus semantics. SGML differs from most object models in at least two key ways:

- All of its "leaf" data is from the single domain "character string" (other data such as graphics can be referenced, but not included unless reduced to a character string); Simons (1990) discusses this issue.
- SGML provides no "methods" on its objects: processing is specified outside of the system. SGML "processing instructions" are not a real exception, because they are merely additional character string data, that accesses methods defined in some application context outside of SGML.

On the other hand SGML differs even more greatly from most pre-object models, on very fundamental issues such as the significance of field ordering, flat versus hierarchical data models, normal form issues, and much more. For example, in the relational model it is odd although possible to speak of "sub-records" (in a sense analogous to sub-elements) as opposed to merely data-typed "fields" (in a sense analogous to attributes).

The SGML model provides a useful distinction for its domain, between content and properties. Attributes can be used to good advantage to make document structures clearer and more intuitive, and to achieve certain kinds of syntax constraints when needed. The principles described above, as well as generally accepted principles drawn from the field of object oriented systems design, can help you to make effective use of attribute versus subelements in your DTDs.

## Related HyTime issues

HyTime provides help in constraining complex attribute values and content through a regular-expression-like feature called HyLex. HyLex can be used to check attributes or content for certain syntactic string patterns. This works by associating an expression with the attribute, against which the value is checked by HyTime, in addition to whatever checking SGML does because of the declared value.

However, HyTime also introduces cases where **IDREF** and **ENTITY** names can appear in **#PCDATA** without being marked up. Entity names and **ID** values can be placed in the content of NAMELOC elements where an SGML parser will not recognize them. HyTime can tell whether the content is an entity name or an **ID** if the NAMETYPE attribute of the element is set or if you enforce a convention guaranteeing that your particular use of the entity and **ID** name spaces do not overlap. Thus, you can have two quite different references such as:

```
<NAMELOC><NMLIST NAMETYPE="ELEMENT">chap1</NAMELOC>
<NAMELOC><NMLIST NAMETYPE="ENTITY">chap1</NAMELOC>
```

This brings the issue of semantically constraining content rather than attributes into sharp focus: Although a HyTime system could recognize and validate such values, an SGML system will not. This also means that a HyTime system must be more closely coupled to a parser than many other applications. Structure-based SGML parsers do not generally pass enough information back to an application for the application to know that certain tokens are the names of entities or **ID**s.

The usual explanation for the HyTime construct is that it adds power because you can place an **IDREFS** or **ENTITIES** list of unlimited length in content, but would be limited to **LITLEN** in an attribute. This seems a better argument against **LITLEN** than for putting bare entity names in content. Fortunately, HyTime gives you the alternative of using multiple NMLIST elements in a single NAMELOC, so **LITLEN** need not be an issue.

A second reason sometimes given for this construct is that **ID**s from another document could use added name characters, so could not be put in an attribute of type **NAME**, **IDREFS**, or similar. This is true, but giving up validation of *local* **IDREFS** and **ENTITIES** because of that is not necessary: the constructs could instead be separated, placing any non-local **IDREF** values in attributes of type **CDATA** should the need arise, and then referencing character entities within those attributes.

You can make your use of HyTime more closely reflect SGML's **IDREF** versus entity name distinction by creating two different element types both based on HyTime's NAMELOC architectural form, but each restricted to only one NAMETYPE:

```
<!ATTLIST  ELEMLOC
  HYTIME   NAME          #FIXED "NAMELOC"
  NAMETYPE NAME          #FIXED "ELEMENT">
<!ATTLIST  ENTLOC
  HYTIME   NAME          #FIXED "NAMELOC"
  NAMETYPE NAME          #FIXED "ENTITY">
```

### Summary

In general, whether information should be expressed in an attribute or in content is a semantic distinction that may get very complex. Often the distinction is very intuitive, but occasionally there is no right answer and because of that it is very important for software to handle tasks such as copying attributes into the content display, hiding certain content, or making formatting depend on characteristics of content, attributes, or both. This demands a stylesheet system with a powerful data-access and calculation language that can be used to control formatting, linking, and other processing, such as DSSSL.

## 5.11. What do people mean by "element structure" and "document trees"?

An SGML document can be viewed in two very different ways: As a stream of characters to be parsed; and as the elements, attributes, and other items that result from parsing and represent information structures more directly. The "element structure" or "document tree" is that parsed information. In practice, these terms are used when someone wants to refer to the structure and content information in an SGML document, while abstracting away from the details of how it may have been expressed in terms of markup, minimization, whitespace, and so on.

For example, you can look at the same information in these two ways. First, as the unparsed SGML character stream:

```
<CHAP ID="Chap3">
  <LIST TYPE="BULLET" ID="List37">
     <ITEM TYPE="NOVICE"><P>Remove CPU.</P></ITEM>
     <ITEM TYPE = "EXPERT"><P>Fix the thing.</></ITEM>
     <ITEM TYPE="NOVICE"><P>Insert CPU.</P></ITEM>
  </LIST>
  ...
  <XREF TARGET="List37">See procedure 37.</XREF>
</CHAP>
```

The figure below represents the same element structure using round-cornered boxes for elements and square-corner boxes for text content. It also uses arrows for element → subelement relationships, but "being in the bubble" to represent element → attribute relationships:

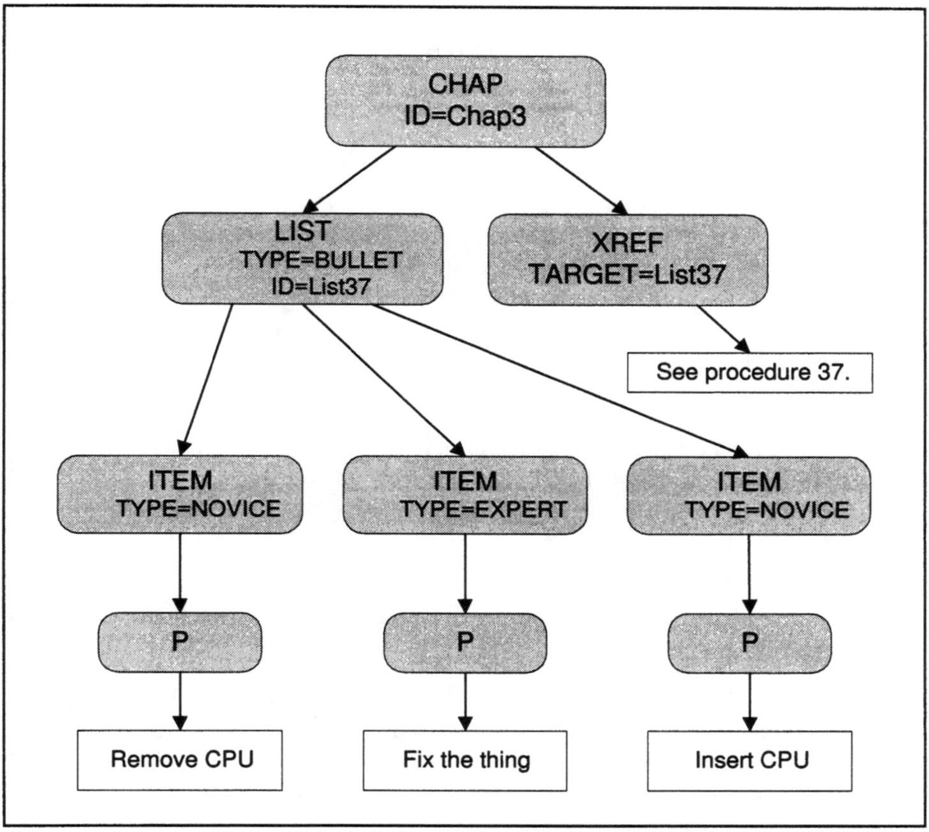


These two forms represent the same structural information in the sense that most authors mean the term. The SGML stream form also represents many details such as where whitespace occurs inside or outside of tags, where tags were abbreviated or omitted, and so on, that are not commonly part of a structural representation. For most applications such information is defined to not be meaningful (as discussed in Questions 2.5 and 3.4).

**Note:** A structural representation may or may not include other information such as processing instructions, marked section and entity boundaries, or comments; information about attribute declared values; and/or information corresponding to the DTD itself. The HyTime and DSSSL committees developed a way to declare what goes in a particular structural view of an SGML document, via a "grove plan". That specification is now part of the DSSSL standard. The two most common grove plans are the default ones given in the DSSSL and HyTime standards.

You can equally well draw a structural representation with attributes shown as full-fledged nodes, perhaps distinguished by the type of box or by having a different kind of line pointing to them as shown below. This is still equivalent (in technical terms, "isomorphic"), and is still a tree because none of these nodes ever contains any of its own containers (for example, a `P` can never contain the `LIST` node above it, or an attribute contain any element):

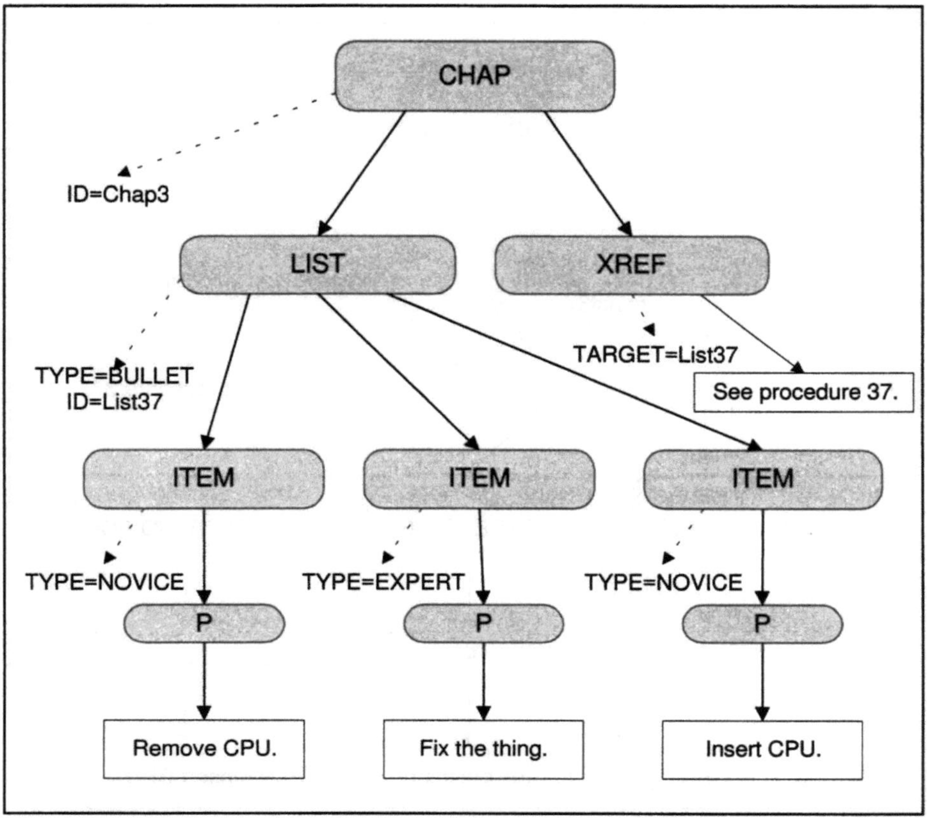


Trees of this general kind can also represent more detail: individual tokens within attribute values, which attributes are **IDs** or **NOTATIONs**, and so on. Trees are a very effective way of representing an SGML document's basic structure and are very widely used because they afford great performance benefits.

An SGML document instance includes some other information, however, which if included in just the same way could add circular paths. The most important such information is the relationship between **IDREF** attributes and the **ID** attributes they reference. If you add arrows to represent these, then any element with an **ID** ends up with more than one arrow pointing to it: one from its containing element, and any number from cross-references. In the example above, the `LIST` element or its `ID` attribute would have a second arrow into it, originating at the `XREF` element or its `TARGET` attribute.

In technical terms, if you didn't distinguish those two kinds of arrows it would mean the diagram is no longer a proper tree. However, since they are fundamentally different kinds of arrow it is appropriate to consider them separately, and the structure excluding the cross-reference arrows remains a tree. Computer scientists often draw some arrows in a different color as a conventional way of representing such distinctions (for example to distinguish "structural" versus "attributive" information in databases). Each kind of information is far too important to discard or omit, but each can be stored distinctly.

**Note:** If you include information from the DTD such as declarations, then additional cases arise because many elements may refer to a given entity or **NOTATION** name.

Because of these cases DSSSL calls its formal document structures "groves" rather than "trees". If you consider all kinds of relations at once it is clear that the combination is not a tree (the technical term is "directed graph"). It is worth remembering, however, that the *containment* structure, even if you include attributes, is a tree. Basically, **IDREFS** are like strings tied from branch to branch rather than like branches themselves.

## 5.12. I turned off minimization. Why are all my attributes wrong?

A DTD can specify default values for attributes; however, many authors do not know that using them is considered minimization. Thus, if **SHORTTAG** is **NO** a value must be given for every attribute except those that are permitted to have *no* value — namely those with default values **#IMPLIED** and **#CONREF**. Without **SHORTTAG** even **#FIXED** attributes must be specified.

### Impliable attributes

Clause 7.9 of the SGML standard states that when minimization is not in use, all attributes must be given explicit specifications "other than an impliable attribute". "Impliable" occurs in a few other Clauses:

- Clause 4.154 defines an impliable attribute as one "for which there need not be an *attribute specification...*";
- Clause 11.3.4 defines the keyword **#IMPLIED** as meaning that "the attribute is an impliable attribute";
- Clause 4.57 defines content reference (**#CONREF**) attributes as impliable.

In short, it boils down to saying that without **SHORTTAG**, only **#IMPLIED** and **#CONREF** attributes can be omitted. All others must be explicitly given on all element instances to which they apply.

### Unquoted attributes

Omitting quotes for attribute values that only contain name characters is considered minimization as well, and so turning off minimization makes any unquoted attribute values into syntax errors. Clause 7.9.3.1 states that you can express an attribute as a value rather than a (quoted) literal only with **SHORTTAG**, except for an attribute value that "occurs in an *attribute definition list*". Amendment 1 added this for values from an enumerated name token group (that is, when the **ATTLIST** declaration gives a set of specific values for the attribute rather than a data-type such as **NAME** or **ID**).

**Note:** A parser would not need extra code to handle unquoted attributes more generally (the code is already there because of enumerated types).

Many have suggested that unquoted attribute values should accept anything in a token other than whitespace and ">". This seems to be the model authors often assume at first, and seems to be the appropriate error recovery if such a character is found. Many HTML parsers also implement a rule along this line (though each differs in details).

Such a rule would pose no backward compatibility conflict, except for the case that **SHORTTAG** allows "<P<Q>", and "<P/". These are rarely seen, but the design would have to exclude **STAGO** and **NET** as well, except when **SHORTTAG** is set to **NO**.

> Note: The delimiters recognized inside a tag ("**TAG** mode", see Clause 9.6.1 and Appendix B) include **LIT** and **LITA** (to mark attribute value literals), **TAGC** (to end the tag), and when **SHORTTAG** is **YES**, **ETAGO**, **NET**, and **STAGO** (see Clause 7.4). Whitespace is also recognized to separate tokens.

The SGML review appears likely to sub-divide **SHORTTAG** and provide switches to turn individual parts of it on or off via the SGML declaration. At present the best way to avoid attribute defaulting questions is to use software that hides the quoting and defaulting. Short of that it is safest always to either use quotes or set **SHORTTAG YES**.

## 5.13. Why can't I have duplicate enumerated ("name token group") attribute values?

SGML currently prohibits defining multiple attributes of the same element type that all permit a given enumerated value. However, this is likely to be changed in the SGML review going on now.

An example of the prohibited kind of declaration is shown below. In this example, the enumerated values "T" and "F" each appear twice.

```
<!-- WRONG -->
<!ATTLIST  P
   SECRET   (T | F)      #IMPLIED
   EXPERT   (T | F)      #IMPLIED>
```

Because this is prohibited, DTD designers must work around it by choosing different values. For example they could re-cast the previous declarations as shown below:

```
<!ATTLIST  P
   SECRET   (SECRET.T | SECRET.F)   #IMPLIED
   EXPERT   (EXPERT.T | EXPERT.F)   #IMPLIED>
```

The prohibition against duplicate enumerated attribute values is one of the least popular features of SGML. DTD designers very often find it in their interest to create multiple attributes with overlapping values. The most common example is truth-valued attributes such as shown above, but there are countless other examples too. It is very common to need several of these. The good news is that the restriction is very likely to be removed.

The restriction has been supported on the ground that without it minimization by leaving out the attribute name for an enumerated attribute is impossible. However, a less drastic restriction would be enough: merely rule out *using that particular form of minimization when* such duplicates arise. This would let DTD designers choose for themselves whether to have their cake or to eat it.

Another less drastic solution would be to define what the minimization shall mean. SGML did not state what "<P T>" would mean, and instead ruled it out. *The SGML*

*Handbook* says on p. 424 that "some unambiguous rule could no doubt be created", and indeed this is trivial to do. The basic candidates for such a rule are:

- *all* attributes permitting the value shall be set if the value is given without a name;
- all those not otherwise explicitly specified on the start-tag shall be set;
- the first one declared in the **ATTLIST** shall be set.

It appears that the SGML review will repeal the restriction, probably by ruling out the minimization in case of ambiguity rather than by choosing a specific meaning for the (currently-) ambiguous case. The change cannot cause backward incompatibility, since no valid documents now use duplicates. Designers seem overwhelmingly to feel that the benefits of having the names they want outweigh a possible slight cost to parser developers, or another clause in the SGML standard to rule out conflicts.

## 5.14. Which attribute declared values mean something special, beyond restricting the character form of their values?

The declared values with special meanings include **NOTATION**, **ID**, **IDREF**, **IDREFS**, **ENTITY**, and **ENTITIES**. They don't just constrain the permissible sequences of characters in the value (on which see also Question 6.9), but also assert that the value has a special meaning. **CDATA** is also special, but only for syntax reasons, for example how it handles whitespace.

First, an attribute of type **NOTATION** must have a declared notation name as value. The declaration below requires that the FORM attribute always be given as EQN or TEX, each of which must have been declared as a **NOTATION**:

```
<!ATTLIST  EQUATION
   FORM      NOTATION (EQN | TEX)     #REQUIRED>
```

But it does not *just* mean that. The value such an attribute is given on each element instance also makes a claim about that element's content: that it conforms to the **NOTATION**. This is not mentioned in Clause 7.9.4.4 on **NOTATION** attributes, but in Clause 4.21, where a **NOTATION** attribute is defined as one that "identifies the data content notation of the element's *content*".

This is apparently why only a single **NOTATION** attribute is allowed per element type, why no **NOTATION** attribute is allowed on an **EMPTY** element type, and why there is no NOTATIONS declared value defined in Clause 11.3.3.

Achieving either of these ends (restricting the value to be a declared **NOTATION** name, versus associating that name with the content) is impossible without simultaneously doing the other. For example, a **NOTATION** cannot be named on an attribute without making the perhaps undesired claim about content. A **NOTATION** attribute cannot be used to express that the element at the *other end of an* **IDREF** should be treated as being in some notation, or to satisfy other application-specific reasons to mention a notation name, such as creating links that refer to multiple objects and constraining their respective notations.

This is not a big problem, because there is not necessarily any bad consequence to making the claim falsely. Perhaps surprisingly, a **NOTATION** attribute does not affect the parsing of the content, and so setting it when the content is actually not in the specified **NOTATION** will not result in an SGML error. The content is still parsed and SGML delimiters are still recognized in the normal way for the element type (which would typically allow character content).

So bytes within the "TIFF" element that look like "&", "<" or other markup can result in a syntax error (or possibly create valid but erroneous content). For example, if 4 bytes of the graphic file's data happen to be hexadecimal 3C212D2D, a parser will (assuming a typical character set) take those bytes as "< ! - - ", and think a comment has started.

Because of such potential conflicts, the data must be scrubbed for any unintended markup, which must then be replaced as discussed in Question 3.7.

It is implementation-dependent whether the content of an element with a given **NOTATION** attribute is passed to a special processor, even assuming it is modified so as to parse without error.

The second declared value with a special meaning is **ID**: its value must be unique. This is very useful for creating unambiguous labels, but it can be inconvenient because **ID** values are also constrained to be SGML names (Question 4.6). Under the normal settings, **ID** values longer than 8 characters or containing characters other than letters, digits, period, and hyphen are not allowed; they may not start with period or hyphen.

Third, **IDREF** and **IDREFS** have meanings mirroring that of **ID** that make them useful as pointers: they must have values whose token(s) also appear as some **ID** attribute(s) in the same document, as shown here:

```
<!ATTLIST  P
   ID      ID           #IMPLIED>
<!ATTLIST  XREF
   TARGET  IDREF        #REQUIRED>
...
<P ID="
```

Fourth, **ENTITY** and **ENTITIES** attributes are constrained to take the names of declared data or **SUBDOC** entities, as discussed in Question 1.12. Since entity names normally regard case distinctions, these attribute declared values do too.

Finally, there is declared value **CDATA**. This is somewhat different because it does not express a claim about the meaning of its value; however, it is worth mentioning because of its effects on parsing: **CDATA** attributes do not have whitespace or case normalized like most others, and delimiter recognition is not suppressed in **CDATA** attributes (although it is in other SGML constructs named **CDATA** — see Question 2.4).

## 5.15. Do I need attribute default value #FIXED?

**#FIXED** means that the attribute's value must always be the same. This can be a useful thing to validate, and **#FIXED** is a clear way to express that requirement when needed, although the effect can often be achieved in other ways, too.

If **SHORTTAG** is used a **#FIXED** attribute can be omitted and its value will default correctly; otherwise it must be specified on every applicable element instance (see Question 5.12).

Although the attribute's final *value* must be consistent wherever it is specified, the means of specifying it need not be. So given the declarations shown below, all the following tags would be valid:

```
<!ATTLIST  X
  A        NAME           #FIXED "JOHN">
<!ENTITY   who            CDATA 'john'>
...
<x a="john">
<x a="&who;">
<X A="JOHN">
<X A="      JOHN      ">
```

This is reasonable and even intuitive given an understanding of SGML's basic case and whitespace rules.

**Note**: although a general entity that returns "`john`" is fine, the unusual case of an **SDATA** entity that did so is not. **SDATA** entities can "return data", so one could conceivably return "`john`" but that would not satisfy the **#FIXED** constraint. Data returned from a processing instruction or **SDATA** entity is not parsed by the SGML parser, but handled by the implementation running on top of the parser. So when the SGML parser checks **#FIXED** attributes it would not see the "`john`" returned from the **SDATA** entity.

For the very common case where a **#FIXED** value is a name token, you can much get the same effect as **#FIXED** in this way as well:

```
<!ATTLIST  X
  A        (JOHN)        "JOHN">
```

Since only one value is permitted, that is the only value that may be specified; since it is also the default value, it may be omitted. There is a slight difference from **#FIXED**: This mechanism doesn't work for any value that is not a name, such as "`hello, world`"; and the same value cannot be used more than once in a given **ATTLIST** (on which see Question 5.13).

**Note**: Liam Quin points out a rather different use for **#FIXED** attributes. Say you want an error to be reported if you change a DTD without checking already-created documents. To achieve this, declare a **#FIXED** attribute for the document element type (such as BOOK), whose value is a version number you assign to your DTD. Set the attribute explicitly on the root element in your documents. Then, if you later update the DTD and its version number, the document will become invalid since it contains the wrong (obsolete) value for the **#FIXED** attribute.

HyTime makes extensive use of **#FIXED** attributes. Whether they only impose trivial cost because their values need not be stored on each element instance depends on implementation methods; for many current implementations they cost the same as a default that is given any other way. The number of **#FIXED** attributes on some HyTime constructs is daunting, so potential performance costs should be considered.

## 5.16. What about attribute default value #CURRENT?

**#CURRENT** attributes default to the value set on the most recent instance of the "same" attribute. "Most recent" is counted without regard to the document's hierarchical structure: it need not be an ancestor, or nearby. Questions 1.14 and 1.15 discuss some ways that document editing can cause hard-to-anticipate changes in distant attribute defaults when **#CURRENT** is involved.

Not only authors, but also designers raise questions involving **#CURRENT** because it complicates certain aspects of SGML parser construction and because it prevents shipping part of an SGML document in isolation from the rest. For example, if you extract a `P` or `SEC` from an SGML document, the parser may get wrong values for **#CURRENT** attributes, which is not true for most other aspects of a document's structure. This can happen in several circumstances:

- you paste the element somewhere else in the same or a different document;
- you turn it into a full-fledged document with the appropriate DTD, SGML declaration, and so on;
- you turn it into a **SUBDOC** entity (this is really the same as a full-fledged document, since SGML subdocument entities must be entire documents under some DTD).

In any of these cases a receiving SGML parser could infer unintended values for **#CURRENT** attributes. They would still be "valid" — unless the first instance in the resulting document has no value assigned at all — so no error would be reported. The change can happen quite mysteriously, because the "most recent" element from which a **#CURRENT** attribute needs to get its value may be arbitrarily far away, and so can easily be forgotten when an element or portion is moved later.

Other SGML structures survive such movements and promotions with no problems; but **#CURRENT** attributes and a very few other things do not. These pose problems with shipping SGML fragments around, such as by turning them into **SUBDOC** entities (see Question 2.13). The SGML Open guidelines for fragment transfer (SGML Open 1996) provide a way to package up the necessary information so that a parser receiving such a fragment can parse out the correct element structure from it anyway; the current values pending for all **#CURRENT** attributes are part of that information.

> **Note**: The other pieces include the last element type opened or closed (needed only in case of empty start-tag minimization); some details to support the **RE**-ignoring rules; and for each ancestor of the fragment, its element type (for knowing about inclusion exceptions), whether it used **NET** minimization, and whether it had a **USEMAP** in the instance. This is enough for a parser to get the right element structure for an element out of its document context, although not enough to validate (for example, the parser obviously could not check **ID** uniqueness unless given a list of all **ID**s in the document).

The easiest way to avoid any of these questions about **#CURRENT** is not to use it. Most DTDs have no more than one or two **#CURRENT** attributes at most; many have none. If no attributes have this default value in the DTD, none of the **#CURRENT** questions can arise. XML rules out **#CURRENT** attributes completely, thus preventing any such ambiguities from arising.

> **Note:** HyTime's "bitskip" attribute cannot readily help a parser optimize access to SGML documents because it could yield wrong **#CURRENT** attributes unless elements that set it somehow track **#CURRENT** attributes (plus **NET**-enabling start-tags, marked sections, **USEMAP** declarations, and so on). See Question 2.13 for a discussion of long-distance dependencies involved in such processing.

## 5.17. What does default value #CONREF mean?

**CONREF** is short for "content reference attribute". Syntactically, it means only that when the attribute has an explicit value on some element instance, that element instance must be **EMPTY**, and not have an end-tag. Semantically, SGML says that its value "is referenced by the application to generate content data". The relevant definitions are in Clauses 4.57, 7.3, and 11.3.4. The syntactic meaning is straightforward, but the semantic implications are far more subtle.

First, how the "reference" mentioned in Clause 4.57 is expressed is not defined. There is no requirement that the attribute be an **IDREF** or any particular kind of reference that an SGML parser understands. These are equally valid, though clearly an SGML system can support the first in a way it cannot do for the second:

```
<!ATTLIST  SECREF
   CAPTION IDREF          #CONREF>
<!ATTLIST  HOTQUOTE
   SOURCE  CDATA          #CONREF>
...
<SECREF CAPTION="chaptitle.37">
...
<HOTQUOTE SOURCE="the data I want">
```

Second, what an application does with the content data is not specified: it definitely does not go into the parser (for example, no delimiter recognition or content-model validation applies to whatever data may be generated); since it is not read by the parser, it is not "content data" in quite the same sense as actual SGML content is. There is no requirement that the referenced data satisfy the content model of the element that referred to it, or even that the referenced data be in SGML.

The main thing designers try to achieve with **CONREF** is to create an option for whether to put an element's conceptual content in the element itself, or to put it elsewhere and include it by reference, as illustrated under Question 3.3. This is very useful functionality, especially for sharing data. If the referenced data is retrieved and displayed dynamically just as if it had occurred there, it is a standard hypermedia technique called "transclusion" (a term coined by Ted Nelson in the 60's, along with "hypertext"), or "data mirroring" as in the Pinnacles DTD used in the semiconductor industry.

If some instances of an element type specify their content locally, but some include it by reference, **CONREF** is a construct that fits the bill. For example, if many warnings in a manual are re-uses of standard ones but a few are unique, **CONREF** provides one way to share the former from some kind of warning-library, without having to put all the latter type there too:

```
<!ATTLIST  WARN
   SOURCE  IDREF      #CONREF>
...
<WARNLIB>
   <W ID="WARN.1">Disconnect power first.</W>
   <W ID="WARN.2">Ground self before touching CPU.</W>
   <W ID="WARN.3">Check air tanks.</W>
</WARNLIB>
...
<PROC ID="REPAIR.COMPUTER">
   <WARN SOURCE="WARN.1"><WARN SOURCE="WARN.2">
   Pull board out sharply, reverse, and reinsert.
</PROC>
...
<PROC ID="REPAIR.LEM">
   <WARN SOURCE="WARN.3">
   <WARN><P>Do not trip when taking a small step for a man
   or a giant leap for mankind.</P></WARN>
   Fill LOX tank. Check oil. Wash heatshield.
</PROC>
```

In such a scenario, the rule that when the **CONREF** attribute is set the element must be **EMPTY** makes sense: Referenced content and local content are considered mutually exclusive. The rules could have been set up to permit both at once but there would be complications since the rules would then have to specify which content should be processed first, or how the two content sources are to be combined.

Although some systems support content references for content of limited complexity or amount, very few support a full-fledged dynamic content reference capability. This is probably because it is quite hard to achieve three requirements at the same time: seamless treatment of content that has gone through the parser, and that has not; adequate display performance; and *not* pre-processing the data ahead of time to resolve the references.

Since a content reference may point very far backward to data that has been processed and discarded, or may even point *forward* to data that comes far later in the document, **CONREF** semantics pose some implementation problems. Unless the software has instant access to every part of the document, the reference cannot be resolved. There are really only three ways to achieve this, and the results you will get with **CONREF** depend in part on which method your system applies:

- Compile the book's raw SGML form into a corresponding data structure that can be accessed quickly. Such a structure is now called a "grove" (a term and model defined in DSSSL; see Question 5.11).
- Make two or three separate passes over the book; the simplest model being (1) collect the references; (2) collect the referenced data for each reference; and (3) fill in the referenced data as if it had been where the **CONREF** attributes were.
- Make one main pass over the book, but every time a **CONREF** attribute is found start up a second parser that goes off and finds the referenced content. If there are many references this is prohibitively expensive even in batch formatters.

Inter-book **CONREF** references raise similar issues. Each method has different complexity and performance tradeoffs.

Many incorrect beliefs have grown up around **CONREF**, such as these:

- Some believe that the declared value of a **CONREF** attribute must be an **IDREF**, or perhaps **IDREFS**. There is no such rule, and the way to find the "referenced data" given the attribute is completely unspecified.
- Some believe that the commonly-desired display effect, where the referenced data is transcluded and formatted in place of the referencing element, is part of the meaning of **CONREF**. In fact that is a formatting convention at the stylesheet level, and there are applications (such as information retrieval) where it does not make sense.
- Some believe that a **CONREF** attribute must point to SGML data, which in turn must conform to the content model of the referencing element. For example, a BIBENTRY element's **CONREF** attribute would have to point to data that fulfills the content model of BIBENTRY such that if it were literally copied and pasted into the BIBENTRY and the **CONREF** attribute were cleared, the result would be valid. There is no such rule.

> **Note**: HyTime defines a **CONREF** attribute whose (architectural form) name is CONLOC, with almost this property. However, equivalence is tested first by counting the root of the referenced data, then by omitting it and just counting its children; and testing is done against HyTime meta-content models, not the SGML content models, which is not the same thing.

- Some believe that there must be at most one **CONREF** attribute per element, much as there can be only one **ID** or **NOTATION** attribute (see Questions 4.5 and 5.14). In fact there can be any number, although it is not clear what it means if they can all be "content references" at the same time. If any one has a value then the element must be empty (for which the latest term is "content prohibited"). HyTime provides five different **CONREF** attributes.
- Some believe that it is possible to have this "content is elsewhere" semantics as a requirement for an element type. But SGML does not provide for an element type where the **CONREF** effect is required (or where the element has declared content **EMPTY** so it will be empty whether or not its **CONREF** attribute(s) is specified). If an element allows content reference, it must *also* allow local content.
- Some believe that end-tag minimization for elements with **CONREF** attributes cannot be specified, to apply to those instance that do not set the **CONREF** attribute (and so don't amount to **EMPTY**). It is true that Clause 11.2.2 recommends specifying "O": "if the element has a content reference attribute or a declared value [content] of "EMPTY"". However, the rationale there only applies when the **CONREF** attribute is specified: when it is not, the element is not **EMPTY** (indeed, SGML rules prohibit it being **EMPTY** then), and so it might be desirable to require the end-tag.
- Although not so much a belief as a common slip, designers or authors may not be aware that Clause 7.9.4.4 prohibits specifying a **NOTATION** on an attribute if a **CONREF** attribute is also specified. If a **CONREF** is of type **ENTITY**, its **NOTATION** can be expressed through in the entity declaration; otherwise it cannot.

You can get the semantic effect usually desired for **CONREF** in other ways, but not the syntactic validation SGML provides for the empty-when-attribute-is-set constraint. The easiest way is to set up your content model to be whatever it is for local data, *or* empty.

The easiest way to do this is parenthesize the content model and add "?". This does not guarantee that if an instance has empty content the SOURCE attribute will be set or vice versa, as **CONREF** would. Such a strategy would mainly be useful if you encounter a system that just doesn't understand **CONREF**:

```
<!ELEMENT  WARN          - - (ICON?,P+)?
<!ATTLIST  WARN
   SOURCE  IDREF         #IMPLIED>
```

In practice, **CONREF** attributes are extremely rare. Most DTDs never use them and simply leave the semantics of quotation and transclusion to stylesheets and display engines. The most important exception is the Pinnacles DTD used in the semiconductor industry, which uses them heavily because so much specification data would otherwise need to be duplicated in so many places. Except in such extraordinary cases, DTD designers may want to keep things simple and just avoid **CONREF**.

## 5.18. Why did setting a #CURRENT attribute on one kind of element affect an attribute on a different kind of element far later?

An attribute with default value **#CURRENT** can be shared among several element types, causing this effect. If several element types share a single **ATTLIST** declaration, that declares the **#CURRENT** attribute, then the "most recent" value for the attribute is shared, so an instance of any of the element types can receive its default value from any of the other types: whichever most recently occurred.

**#CURRENT** is conceptually a special case of **#IMPLIED**, in which the way the actual default value is calculated is defined by SGML rather than by an application *of* SGML. The value applied by default for a **#CURRENT** attribute is the value the attribute had on the *most recent* element instance that specified the same attribute. The "last" element is reckoned without regard to the hierarchical document structure: it could be a distant 27th cousin that was closed megabytes earlier (this is one of the very few reasons SGML must be parsed serially, and that a portion of an SGML document cannot always be parsed correctly in isolation from its entire document).

**#CURRENT** raises many issues. This section focuses on a question that **#CURRENT** raises entirely apart from its relation to the larger SGML document model. SGML allows declaring a set of attributes for several element types at once (limited by SGML quantity settings such as **GRPCNT**), and a **#CURRENT** default value is shared across the types:

```
<!ATTLIST  (X | Y | Z)
   C       NUMBER        #CURRENT>
```

Given that declaration, the following markup leads to a default value of "3" on the second X element:

```
<X C="1">
   <Y C="2">
      <Z C="3">some text</Z>
   </Y>
   <Z>
</X>
<X>This element defaults to having c=3.</X>
```

As with other SGML constructs that don't mesh directly with the elements' containment relationships, this leads to particular dangers when editing. This is because seemingly minor cuts and pastes can have unexpected consequences at very distant, seemingly unrelated points.

If long-distance attribute copying like this is needed at all, it seems as if the *most* useful cases have been missed:

- Situations where the value desired is not the last value, but the last value *plus 1*. For example, to automatically number figures or tables throughout a document, regardless of where they occur in relation to sections, chapters, and the like (perhaps with some notion of periodic "resets"). SGML does not provide this, although attributes can be declared to be **NUMBERS** (by which SGML means nonnegative decimal integers except that leading zeros matter).
- Inherited attributes are much more manageable and more commonly useful in practice, but are not supported in SGML (see Question 6.8).

Few recent DTDs use **#CURRENT** attributes at all, and XML rules them out completely in its SGML subset.

## 5.19. How can I let SGML know that parts of my content are in certain (human) languages?

A great deal of processing that must be done with documents depends crucially on what natural language the text portions are in. This is true at many levels of the system. For example, without knowing the language a processor cannot reliably

- divide the text into words, whether for searching, spell-checking, hyphenation, or any other purpose;
- divide lines correctly for display; or
- choose a correct font. Even in Unicode, duplicate numbers ("code points") are assigned to characters that have different appearances (and thus require different fonts or glyphs) in Japanese, Chinese, and Korean.

Because of this an SGML system that does not integrate a mechanism for identifying what parts of documents are in what languages and processing them differently is inevitably handicapped. For this reason a great many DTDs provide a strict convention for labeling the language of elements.

Usually this is done by defining a single attribute applicable to all element types, whose value is a code identifying the applicable language. The identifier typically comes from a standardized set like that of ISO 639 or ANSI Z39.53, although it is often useful to add finer distinctions, such as the country or era. For example:

```
<QUOTE LANG="GR">Ωνθρωπε, μη κτεινε Κροισον</QUOTE>
```

Note that this is very different from a **NOTATION** attribute, though it may sound like a similar application. The attribute is typically declared for all element types and expected to inherit its value when unspecified (this expectation must be fulfilled outside SGML, as there is no #INHERITED attribute default value; see Question 6.8).

Another element almost always becomes necessary, to be used when a foreign phrase has no semantic or structural role but still must be marked up to have a place to hang the LANG attribute:

```
<P LANG="EN">The word <FOREIGN LANG="GR">λογοσ</FOREIGN> is
self-referential.</P>
```

The Text Encoding Initiative provides specific mechanisms for this kind of task, as well as ways to describe the particular writing systems in use and their characteristics, via "Writing System Declarations" or "WSDs". Some languages are written with multiple different writing systems, and those in turn may be represented by multiple coded character sets and multiple fonts. Chapter 25 of the TEI *Guidelines* deals with these issues.

Formatters, indexers, and other tools must all be made aware of the convention in order to work well for multilingual documents. This solution works reasonably well using existing SGML constructs, except for the pain of declaring the attribute for so many element types, and the difficulty of updating the DTD consistently (such as when elements are added or **ATTLIST** declarations are changed). SGML could gain further benefits by standardizing the notion that text content is "in" some language (not necessarily limited to current human languages), and by standardizing a way for representing this all-important aspect of textual information. It is much like the advantage of databases and retrieval software knowing whether a field is an integer or a date, or knowing what units a quantity is in.

At the present time, careful use of conventions for representing information about the language applicable in each part of your documents can be of great benefit.

# On Entities

## 5.20. Why don't my special character entities work?

This usually means that you are using declarations for **SDATA** entities, which are not the correct or current ones for the particular software system you are using. This can happen if you move from one system to another without updating these definition files. Unlike most SGML data, **SDATA** entities need to be changed for each system; in effect, they are the place where system-dependent data is isolated in SGML, so that many other things do *not* need to change.

**SDATA** or "specific character data" entities permit including non-portable characters in SGML documents. Authors may be surprised that the declarations cannot be used as-is in many implementations. The SGML standard is actually quite clear in Clauses D.4.1.1-2 that the entity declarations shown are merely "definitional" rather than normative. They give a name and an English description, but are not intended to provide a formal definition sufficient for a computer to find the right image to display:

```
<!ENTITY   agr     SDATA "[agr   ]"--=small alpha, Greek-->
```

Because of this, each system "will need to provide corresponding display entity sets for the output devices it supports". The Annex indicates that those system-specific versions would replace the quoted text in the samples with "processing instructions or character sequences that will produce the desired visual depiction".

The set of such characters in Annex D is large but necessarily incomplete: many characters used by linguists, typographers, mathematicians, or others are not included. People using or especially setting up SGML systems are sometimes surprised when they discover that Annex D is also not normative. That is, it is not a binding part of the SGML standard. It is therefore not a violation of SGML to re-use any of these entity names to mean something else, or to create new entity sets that add or delete entities as compared to Annex D. This can be especially important in international settings or other in disciplines such as mathematics where specialized symbols are necessary.

It is also worth noting that some of the entity sets in Annex D have been officially withdrawn, in favor of sets defined in parts 12-16 of ISO 9573. The entity sets in ISO 9573 provide something like 1200 special characters. Many of these are important for high-quality typesetting (most especially for mathematics), and the set defined there is a more nearly complete than even the extensive Unicode standard, which lacks about half of them.

**Note**: Part 13 of ISO 9573 includes these entity sets: Added Math Symbols: Arrow Relations, Added Math Symbols: Binary Operators, Added Math Symbols: Delimiters, Added Math Symbols: Negated Relations, Added Math Symbols: Ordinary, Added Math Symbols: Relations, Greek Symbols, Alternative Greek Symbols, Latin Letters and Digits, Math Alphabets: Fraktur, Math Alphabets: Open Face, Math Alphabets: Script, General Technical. The SGML Annex D entity sets that have thus not be superseded are: Publishing, Numeric and Special Graphic, Diacritical Marks, Box and Line Drawing, Added Latin 1, Added Latin 2, Russian Cyrillic, Non-Russian Cyrillic, Greek Letters, and Monotoniko Greek

A close look at Annex D makes it clear why the entity sets must be redefined for use in applications: they give replacement text (what a parser tells an application program) that has the same information that the entity name provided to begin with:

```
<!ENTITY   xgr          SDATA "[xgr    ]"
                        --=small xi, Greek-->
<!ENTITY   khgr         SDATA "[khgr   ]"
                        --=small chi, Greek-->
```

If these were intended to be the actual values there would be little point in having the declarations, or they could just as easily have no replacement text (few programmers would have difficulty creating "`[xgr    ]`" from "`xgr`"!):

```
<!ENTITY   xgr          SDATA>
```

SGML acknowledges this in Clause 10.5.3, where it notes that **SDATA** is appropriate for entities that "would be redefined for different applications, systems, or output devices". Clause 4.304 defines them accordingly as being "dependent on a specific system, device, or application process" and says they "would normally be redefined for different applications, systems, or output devices".

SGML vendors have been struggling with the **SDATA** portability issue for some time. In general, they provide some way to associate a font and a numeric code point with each character. There are two main kinds of solutions:

The first solution involves listing every **SDATA** entity name in a file in a proprietary format. The SGML system looks up entries in that file based on either the **SDATA** entity's name or the square-bracketed text of Annex D (which amounts to the same thing). For example, the entry below says to obtain the character represented by the `xgr` entity (this is customarily the Greek letter xi) from the Symbol font, position 99:

```
xgr Symbol 99
```

> **Note:** In this case the SDATA entity declarations provide no real additional information except that the entity is in fact of type SDATA: the rest of the information (excluding the prose comment) is redundant with the entity name. If a system defaulted to considering undeclared entities to be SDATA, it could get successful resolution by accessing this kind of lookup table directly via the entity name, as when it sees "`&xgr;`".

The second kind of solution instead adds the information right in the **SDATA** entities' replacement text, as shown here:

```
<!ENTITY   xgr        SDATA "name=xgr font=Symbol code=99">
```

Both methods work fairly well, though the second is more efficient because it eliminates a redundant step. However, neither solution is portable because neither typically abstracts away from *fonts* to actual *character sets* (a character set may have many applicable fonts). Many have suggested that SGML itself provide a standard expression for this information. This is harder than it looks, but could provide a way around the non-portability problems.

> **Note:** As mentioned in Question 1.17, **SDATA** entities must also be used for processing instructions "that return data", even though there is also such a thing as a **PI** entity.

Another common suggestion is for SGML to provide separate syntax for referring to special characters, somewhat like named character references ("`&#RE;`" and so on). Such a system could use standard sets of character names so no declarations would be needed, and SGML would gain a formal distinction between entities for characters and those that serve as inclusions or abbreviations. For example, SGML could state that any name between certain delimiters must be the name of a special character (to be defined in an implementation-dependent manner, just as in SGML):

```
Bach is pronounced /ba{xgr}/.
```

Character names could be drawn from a number of relevant standards. However, this syntax is not in place in SGML at this time, and there is not yet a standard form in which to express SDATA entity sets across all applications, so entity sets must be customized for each piece of software.

## Numeric characters

Authors can specify characters by their code point numbers instead of by name, for example coding "`ÿ`" as "`ÿ`" instead. This may be done in hopes of avoiding the problem of **SDATA** being non-portable, but it can actually make the problem worse. With **SDATA**, when the document is translated to a new character set you can plug in new **SDATA** definitions in one step, and it should all work. Numeric references have to be changed every place they occur, however.

Unicode is the closest thing to a universal character set now available. If the data is in Unicode there is a better chance of survival, if only because there are fewer occasions to have to translate back out. However, SGML numeric character references are awkward because Unicode and nearly all modern character-set standards specify character codes in hexadecimal (base-16), not in decimal as SGML requires. XML therefore conventionally reserves entity names for the hexadecimal codes for all Unicode characters, and the SGML review is considering adding syntax for hexadecimal character references as well.

> Note: The obvious form "`ꯍ`" would have a potential conflict, should someone define a new named character reference (analogous to #RS, #RE, and #SPACE) that starts with "x".

## Standardizing SDATA entities

What the user typically wants is to be able to read and write documents correctly regardless of platform, application, and the like. The obvious solution is to associate enough information with special character entities so that a program can find the right image (called a "glyph" or "rendered glyph") to display.

Proposals are being considered to standardize a form for the replacement text of **SDATA** entities. There are now very large, widely accepted inventories of characters available. The Unicode standard and closely related ISO 10646 provide code points for many characters (more than SGML's Annex D but less than ISO 9573), though it is still short on math-drawing characters and on some indigenous and historical languages. The AFII glyph registry provides names for an even wider range of actual character shapes (this section glosses over the distinction between glyphs and characters here, although it is very important in the larger scheme of things).

Given the availability of such inventories, schemes under consideration (for example by the SGML Open Consortium) define a convention for the **SDATA** replacement text, such that it must contain a "scheme" name such as "Unicode" or "AFII", followed by some unique identifier for a particular object (character, glyph, rendered glyph, etc.) defined by that scheme. WWW users will recognize this as being very similar to URLs. This is enough to get the right result. For example:

```
<!ENTITY   biohazard   SDATA "iso10646:x2623">
```

Had SGML standardized a solution for this issue perhaps **SDATA** would (much like **NDATA**) specify a named character set the **SDATA** conformed to:

```
<!CHARSET  iso10646     PUBLIC "+//ISO 10646…">
<!ENTITY   xgr          "&#x2623;" SDATA iso10646>
```

Until conventions for sharing the replacement text of **SDATA** entities are settled, implemented, and in common use, the user's only recourse is to use different **SDATA** entity sets with different systems. Most vendors supply at least the basic Annex D entities with their software.

## 5.21. What does the external identifier for a NOTATION identify?

Creators of DTDs may believe that in a **NOTATION** declaration, the external identifier should point to a program that can interpret the notation, such as a viewer for graphics. They commonly design their DTDs in this way:

```
<!NOTATION TIFF
  SYSTEM   "c:\windows\apps\tiffview.exe">
```

Many software products accommodate or encourage this by bringing up the specified viewer when an entity in the given **NOTATION** is to be presented. This works very well. However, SGML does not require it. Clause 4.213 says that a notation identifier can be a public identifier, or "if not", it can be "a description or other information sufficient to invoke a program to interpret the notation".

The phrase "if not" could refer either to the external identifier being **PUBLIC**, or to the **NOTATION** being public. In either case this definition could be taken to imply that the identifier should not refer to a program to interpret the notation, but to an actual specification of the notation such as its documentation. That is, a more correct example for TIFF would be:

```
<!NOTATION TIFF          PUBLIC
  "+//ISBN 0-7923-9432-1::Graphic Notation//NOTATION
  Aldus/Microsoft Tagged Interchange File Format//EN">
  "c:\docfiles\tiffspec.doc">
```

There is a sense in which any program that (perfectly) implements a processor for some notation can be thought of as a "definition" for that notation, but that is quite a broad sense, and not in harmony with the examples SGML gives.

From the end-user's standpoint a viewer for the notation is often more useful than the paper specification: most readers do not wish each graphic to appear on screen as a link to a 100-page document (which, if read and understood, will enable them to write a program to view the graphic); they just want to see the graphic. In *some* systems this can at least be specified in a stylesheet or configuration file if not in the **NOTATION** declaration.

On the other hand, if the viewer is broken or doesn't work on the user's platform, a pointer to the definition document is important so the user can find or create a solution. Ideally, there should be a way to specify *both* pieces of information. Given that, the external identifier for the *specification* would logically describe it as being in some human language, and the one for the interpreter program would describe it as being in some (non-human) language such as C or a Win95 executable.

One way to finesse this question is to provide a **PUBLIC** identifier that points to the specification, and a **SYSTEM** identifier that points to the local implementation of a processor for it. This seems inelegant, but can work fine in many situations; the main problem would be eliminating **SYSTEM** identifiers in order to make files portable across multiple system environment via catalogs or naming services.

## 5.22. How do the various kinds of entities relate, such as internal/external, NDATA, etc?

Clause 10.5 (including important changes from Amendment 1) defines the syntax for **ENTITY** declarations through a number of rules that generate many special cases. The many options for general entities are summarized here. "p" below is short for "parameter literal" (Clause 10.1.2), basically a string quoted with either **LIT** or **LITA** delimiters:

| Name | Prefix | Source | Suffix | | |
|---|---|---|---|---|---|
| parameter literal | | p | | | |
| data text | CDATA<br>SDATA<br>PI | p | | | |
| bracketed text | STARTTAG<br>ENDTAG<br>MS<br>MD | p | | | |
| SGML text | | PUBLIC p<br>SYSTEM p<br>SYSTEM<br>PUBLIC p p | | | |
| external (SUBDOC) | | PUBLIC p<br>SYSTEM p<br>SYSTEM<br>PUBLIC p p | SUBDOC | | |
| external (data) | | PUBLIC p<br>SYSTEM p<br>SYSTEM<br>PUBLIC p p | CDATA<br>SDATA<br>NDATA | notation name | data attributes |

Users commonly wonder what to call external entities other than **SUBDOC**, **NDATA**, **CDATA**. and **SDATA**. The other kind has no keyword. It is just called an "SGML text entity". It is also the only kind of external entity that can be a parameter entity. SGML text entities are the kind commonly used to split big DTDs or documents up into manageable "chunks" such as chapters, which are then included by reference in a much smaller "driver" file.

DTD designers often ask why they cannot have a very small internal **SUBDOC** or **NDATA** entity, or an external **PI** entity. Internal **SUBDOC** entities may actually become an important notion as growing numbers of smaller data fragments move onto the Internet. None of the "bracketed text" entities can be external either, but they would always be short, and are very seldom used. All they do is prefix and suffix certain delimiters onto their replacement text (their "p" above), such as **STAGO** and **TAGC** in the case of **STARTTAG** entities. They are not seen in practice.

Some of the other details to remember are:

- You cannot associate a notation or data attributes with **SDATA** or **CDATA** *internal* entities (they would probably be the most useful for **SDATA**).
- Bracketed text entities do not necessarily create the constructs they are named after: referring to an **ENDTAG** entity does not necessarily amount to creating an end-tag. The effect is purely one of inserting the *strings* that are assigned to delimiter roles,

such as "<". If you're in an **RCDATA** context, or if the bracketed text entity's replacement text starts with a blank or even " ! " or " ? ", the reference will not produce the expected construct.

- In any case where your intent *is* to use bracketed text entities for literal data (perhaps this could be useful within SGML examples, so you didn't have to escape the characters — see Question 3.7), the literal data inserted will change if you change the SGML declaration later.
- Systems vary in how they resolve external entity references to get actual data objects, depending on which of **PUBLIC** and/or **SYSTEM** identifiers are present, and in how they deal with **PUBLIC** identifiers for objects with multiple display text versions (see Question 4.15).
- The names of parameter entities, and the replacement text of bracketed text entities, have lower length limits than other similar items, because certain delimiters "count" toward the length, apparently as a concession to certain implementation approaches (see Question 5.23).
- When declaring a parameter entity the space following the **PERO** delimiter (normally "%") is required, to distinguish this from an attempt to reference the entity whose name follows (parameter entity references are allowed there, and can be useful there). The choice to use **PERO** as the signal to distinguish general from parameter entities (rather than various alternatives such as "<!GENERAL" versus "<!PARAMETER") led to a few other rules, such as a statement in Clause 10.5.1 that the contextual constraints stated in Clause 9.6.2 do not apply in this particular context.
- A processing instruction, if it returns data, must not be placed in a **PI** entity, but in an **SDATA** entity (see Clauses 8.0 and 10.5.3).
- If a **CONREF** attribute (see Question 5.17) refers to an internal entity, there is no way to specify a notation for it (allowing internal **NDATA** entities would fix this).

## 5.23. The parser says my parameter entity names are too long, but they're no longer than my other names. What's wrong?

SGML states that parameter entity names have a lower length limit than other SGML names. Other names are limited to the **NAMELEN** setting in the SGML declaration, normally 8. Parameter entity names are limited to that *minus* the length of the parameter entity reference open (**PERO**) delimiter, normally "%", hence 7.

This rule (from Clause 10.5.1.1) is generally considered to reflect an implementation method where the programmer keeps all names in fixed-length storage areas and combines two conceptual tables (one for general entities and one for parameter entities) by literally storing the **PERO** delimiter as part of the name (how else would every parameter entity name have to "take up" as many extra characters as the **PERO** delimiter is long?). Other implementations are possible.

The rule also creates a more user-visible side-effect: if you change your **PERO** delimiter and it happens to get longer, you may have to change parameter entity declarations and references to use shorter entity names.

**Note**: Prior to Amendment 1 the Clause above read "one character shorter"; this would actually be less restrictive since even in an implementation that did combine the table and use a prefix to distinguish entries, there would be no particular reason the prefix should be **PERO**.

A second, similar issue arises because SGML limits the replacement text of bracketed text entities (see Question 5.22) to be shorter than **LITLEN** by the length of the inserted delimiters. This makes sense on a certain implementation assumption: namely that a system will store the delimiters with the replacement text in fixed-size areas that are the same size for all literals. This is possible but hardly necessary.

Clause 10.5.1.2 creates a third implementation-dependent limit, because it requires that every undeclared entity count towards the entity capacity limit ("**ENTCAP**"). A similar notion about implementation appears to be at work here too: as entity references to undeclared entities are found, they are added to an entity table along with a redundant copy of the **#DEFAULT** entity's entire replacement text. Other implementations are possible, such as leaving them out of the table entirely and using **#DEFAULT** itself whenever a reference to an undeclared entity is found, or making the new entry refer to the **#DEFAULT** entry's replacement text rather than copying it.

As it is, designers must simply remember these rules and implementers must implement in those particular ways or do extra work to accommodate such rules. The SGML review is expected to make capacity and quantity validation completely optional, at which point DTD designers can simply turn it off. The other limits, however, are not reported to be under consideration.

# 6. For Builders of SGML DTDs Who Must Constrain Data In Special Ways

As an organization's document requirements grow, new areas become relevant to the SGML designer. In a small publishing operation information can be managed with traditional methods, and there is not so great a problem maintaining consistency across documents. But as the enterprise grows these problems can become very large. The SGML designer in such situation must be careful to insure that information from many differs authors and sources can be integrated smoothly, or the cost of bringing diverse formats, styles, and layouts together to make new documents, will soon far exceed the cost of creating all that information in the first place.

This chapter, therefore, addresses questions about how to use SGML to check and ensure that information fulfills various application-specific requirements. SGML is very unusual in giving *any* way to do such validation; nevertheless, it cannot do everything, and some kinds of constraints must be applied at a higher level (if at all).

This chapter also addresses several questions that frequently come up in configuring software to deal with various SGML structures. Strictly speaking these are not "SGML" questions. However, the choice of *how* you represent your information in SGML can make a big difference to what software (if any) you can use to get the formatting, retrieval, or other processing behaviors you want. Because of this relationship, I include a few related questions here.

## 6.1. Can I create inclusion exceptions that don't affect the content model context when used?

No. An included element is like any other: inside of it, its own content model governs. There is no way to make an element that is "transparent" to other elements, so that it just signals it's own meaning but leaves its parent's content model unchanged, just as if the included element's tags were not there. This is mainly an issue with special tagging such as for marking revisions to a document, as described in this section.

When an included element occurs it becomes the current element in SGML, and its content model must be satisfied for the document to be valid. This is exactly the right behavior for most uses, such as typical footnotes where the structure and content of a FOOTNOTE element is independent of where it occurs. For example,

```
<!ELEMENT  BOOK       (CHAPTER*) +(FOOTNOTE)>
<!ELEMENT  SEC        (ST, (P | LIST)*)>
<!ELEMENT  FOOTNOTE   (NUM, P, REF)>
```

SGML gets just the desired effect: FOOTNOTE can occur anywhere within a BOOK, such as within a particular SEC. But once you're inside the FOOTNOTE you can only have footnote-ish things, not the things permitted in SEC. Thus this is not allowed given the declarations above:

```
<!-- WRONG -->
<SEC><FOOTNOTE><LIST>...</FOOTNOTE>
```

The SGML rule is that the included element's content model applies while the included element is still open, and after the included element the container's model is reactivated. This is usually exactly what is needed.

However, cases arise where it would be useful if the DTD designer could state that some element does *not* take over. Instead, any subelements within the included element are treated as if they had occurred in the parent, and advance *its* content mode. In that case, once you're in the included element you still want the restrictions of the parent. This would be very useful for element types such as:

FOREIGN — to mark passages in another language, without having to change the constraints or requirements on what can occur within the parent element.

REV — to mark passages that have been revised or otherwise changed.

For example, consider a small element such as a LABEL, with required subelements such as NAME, ADDRESS, and PHONE:

```
<LABEL>
   <NAME>Bob Dobalina</NAME>
   <ADDRESS>100 Zilch Drive</ADDRESS>
   <PHONE>555-9106</PHONE>
</LABEL>
```

To modify the ADDRESS element and mark the revision, the options are limited. The DTD can be expanded to allow REV attributes on every element type, with an attribute for the revision number, and express the change like this:

```
<LABEL>
   <NAME>Bob Dobalina</NAME>
   <ADDRESS REV="1">100 Zilch Drive</ADDRESS>
   <ADDRESS REV="2">0 Century Drive</ADDRESS>
   <PHONE>555-9106</PHONE>
</LABEL>
```

With this approach it is hard to express that a single revision event affects more or less than a single element. A large change must be reflected in an attribute on each changed element individually, and a new low-level element must be introduced to surround changes that affect only a small piece of content. This solution also requires that every element (at least, every one to be revision-tagged) be repeatable in all its contexts. Otherwise (if ADDRESS were not repeatable), the modified LABEL would be invalid.

This solution also gives no way to represent changes to the markup itself, such as indicating that an attribute or GI has been modified (various sections of the Text Encoding Initiative *Guidelines* provide markup definitions relevant to enable such problems as well).

A more general solution would be to have a single element such as REV, which can go almost anywhere and hold the revision-level attributes; no other elements need to do so. Thus, a case like the present example where text content is the real location of the revision would result in markup like this:

```
<LABEL>
   <NAME>Bob Dabolina</NAME>
   <ADDRESS>
      <REV N="1">100 Zilch Drive</REV>
      <REV N="2">0 Century Drive</REV>
   </ADDRESS>
   <PHONE>555-9106</PHONE>
</LABEL>
```

REV can be made an inclusion exception at a high level and so permitted anywhere. But what content model should REV itself have? The only workable one is **ANY**, since the intent of REV is to be able to enclose any element or synchronous sequence at all. However, **ANY** means not only that anything might possibly occur within REV somewhere, but that anything may occur within any REV anywhere. In the present case, even though ADDRESS may be restricted to **#PCDATA**, REV is not, so a CHAPTER or any other defined element type can sneak inside. This is a severe loss of validation and can lead to very misleading results.

Since transparent elements do not exist in SGML, the usual workaround in SGML is indeed to make such elements high-level inclusion exceptions and to give them content model **ANY** so that whatever *would have been* permitted given whatever state their parent element was in, is still permitted within the inclusion. This solution seems too costly.

A language could provide for defining an element such that its parent's content model state remains in effect within it. This is not very difficult to implement: elements within it are simply treated as they would have been if it had *not* been opened. Such elements can impose no conditions whatsoever on their own content, and must always be synchronous with the rest of the tree (that is, anything opened within them must be closed within them and vice versa):

```
<!ELEMENT  rev          - -  #TRANSPARENT>
```

A more sophisticated system would allow transparent elements to impose their own *additional* content model restrictions, which would be imposed in addition to whatever ones their context imposes. This would achieve much of the capability needed for validating HyTime architectural forms, where an element instance must fulfill both its actual content model, and a second, typically less restrictive, meta-model for its form.

> **Note:** Revisions and other constructs have also been represented by inserting two unrelated **EMPTY** elements for the beginning and end of each span to be marked, such as the STEMPH and ENDEMPH elements in early versions of the CALS DTD. Each such tag can also go in a marked section or in an entity so they can all be ignored if desired. This can work in theory, but has many problems: SGML is unaware of any relationship between the elements that are intended to be the ends of the construct (that is, the span is not an element to SGML at all); SGML cannot verify that ends match, or that the span fits with the tree structure, or that the end comes after the beginning. Also, typical application semantics such as inheritance break down in such a model.

The usual workaround for such cases is to make the elements inclusion exceptions, usually on the document element (this allows them to appear anywhere), and to give them content model ANY (this allows them to contain whatever their parent could have contained).

## 6.2. How can I format run-in titles appropriately?

A common formatting practice is to run titles right in on the first line of whatever they are the titles of, rather than putting them on separate lines. Accomplishing this formatting goal is not really an SGML issue, but with typical stylesheet languages the way you set up your SGML can make this formatting task far easier or harder.

Sometimes such titles are constructed to fit in as part of the first sentence and sometimes not; but they are nearly always set off in boldface or other special type:

> **Buffalo herds** have been known to fly by rotating leadership extremely quickly. This looks a lot like doing "the wave" in a football stadium.

This is a formatting preference rather than an issue of document structure, so the run-in title information should in principle be marked up no differently than any other kind of title:

```
<SEC><ST>Buffalo herds</ST>
have been known to fly by rotating leadership extremely
quickly. This looks a lot like doing <Q>the wave</Q> in a
football stadium.</SEC>
```

Most SGML-based formatting tools categorize elements as inline (such as EMPHASIS, BOOK-TITLE, etc.), blocks (P, ITEM, BLOCK-QUOTE, etc.), or containers (CHAPTER, SECTION, etc.). Titles of the kind just shown don't fit well in any of those categories. This is because "blocks" as a general category have display line-breaks before and after; but in this kind of formatting the ST has a display break before but not after, and the following text has no break before, just one after (the one after might be imposed by the end of the whole SEC, depending on the particular case). So getting this effect can be difficult in some formatting tools.

Ideally, formatting tools should all be able to deal with this. However, in the current non-utopian software environment this is not the case. If your software can't achieve this effect, but you want it, the only workaround may be to change the tagging in some way. Just what is needed may depend on the particular formatting limitations you need to work around. One method that may help is to group the title and the following text into a single paragraph-level container (such as RUN-IN-PARA below), thus treating the title very much like inline markup such as for emphasis and letting the new container handle the line-breaking:

```
<SEC>
<RUN-IN-PARA><ST>Buffalo herds</ST>
have been known to fly by rotating leadership extremely
quickly. This looks a lot like doing <Q>the wave</Q> in a
football stadium.</RUN-IN-PARA></SEC>
```

This makes for a slightly odd-looking DTD structure because the title is no longer directly part of the thing it titles, but of its first sub-element. But it may be the only way to get the desired formatting with some style mechanisms.

Some stylesheet mechanisms instead have separate "break-before" and "break-after" or similar settings. They can handle this kind of formatting more easily, though they may have difficulty in some other cases. It is a trade-off with no particular "right" answer. DSSSL lets designers avoid the issue, since even in the worst possible case it can re-structure a local part of the tree before final formatting happens, creating any extra containers desired or moving data around as needed to get the right effect.

## 6.3. How can my software know which SGML element types cause word boundaries for formatting and indexing?

Any information about this is expressed outside of SGML as part of the semantics you associate with particular types. It is possible to add markup for this particular purpose, such as an `IMPLIES-WORD-BONDARIES` attribute on every element, but this is not typically done. SGML itself has no need of this information for correct parsing. Applications such as formatters and search engines that need it for other purposes must be provided with the information by some other method, such as a configuration file or stylesheet.

This question arises because end users want to be able to search, format, and do other processing that depends on word-boundaries, and these user requirement can be hard to accommodate in some special cases. Information about word boundaries, however, is outside the scope of what SGML does, and it is very difficult for a generic SGML system to determine it without knowing the particulars and conventions of DTDs and authors.

Any element that "causes a break" or is a "block" for formatting purposes, implies a word-boundary; so a system seeing this data ought not to find a hit for the word "nowHere" (assuming `ITEM` elements are to be formatted as separate blocks):

```
<LIST>
<ITEM>Hypermedia is now</ITEM>
<ITEM>here is how to use it.</ITEM>
</LIST>
```

Inline markup, however, should not usually imply a word-boundary, so a system seeing this ought to find a hit for the word "nowhere":

```
<P>The first word in <B>now</B>here is "now".</P>
```

The difficulty arises because there is no principled way to tell whether a given element boundary "counts" as a word break or not. A DTD (and SGML in general) knows little or nothing about formatting intentions such as where to insert line breaks; some DTDs are for data that is never meant to be formatted at all, which may be easiest to see from an example where the tag names don't given any intuitive clues: is this content one word or two?

```
<X>now</X><Y>here</Y>
```

Full-text indexing systems usually care quite a lot about word boundaries; some index by the word, others index characters but have way to constrain a query to match just words. Either way, the behavior desired cannot be determined without (shudder!) *semantics*: you have to know the user's intent, at least a little bit. So to get the right effects in your formatting, retrieval, or other SGML processing application, you will need to inform it of the conventions you use, such as which element types imply word boundaries.

**Note:** HyTime and DSSSL have similar issues when counting nodes in document structures (technically "groves", on which see Question 5.11). They have no way to decide where word boundaries fall, since the only evidence may be in a processing specification.

## 6.4. How can elements represent conditional text? Or do I need marked sections?

Marked sections that switch between **INCLUDE** and **IGNORE** are often used to represent revision-marking and other cases where certain parts of the document are not always applicable. The simplest case is where a phrase appears only in some versions:

```
<!ENTITY   % mac        "INCLUDE">
...
<P>When you want to start a program,
<![ %mac; [ double-click its icon, and ]]>
follow the instructions in the manual.</P>
```

More practical cases involve marking each portion of the document as to what version it belongs to; then you can switch versions by changing entities and re-parsing:

```
<!ENTITY   % v1         "INCLUDE">
<!ENTITY   % v2         "IGNORE">
...
<P>Those who like
<![%v1;[ sausage ]]> <![%v2;[ the law ]]>
or respect
<![%v2;[ sausage ]]> <![%v1;[ the law ]]>,
should not watch either being made.</P>
```

By swapping the replacement text for the entities `v1` and `v2`, a user who knows about entity declarations and marked sections can switch versions.

Many systems provide analogous ways of "including" or "excluding" data via some kind of switch. For example, many word processors have a "hidden text" feature, and most programming languages have something like C's `#ifdef...#endif` construct.

SGML elements can accomplish this effect too, though they do so after, rather than during, parsing. A DTD designer can define a special element for this purpose, perhaps calling it REV for "revision". They then tell their application to discard or hide portions based on some expression or some keywords, thus accomplishing an effect like conditional marked section, but using methods such as these:

```
<P>When you want to start a program,
<REV KEY="mac"> double-click its icon, and </REV>
follow the instructions in the manual.</P>
```

```
<P>Those who like
<REV KEY="v1"> sausage </REV>
<REV KEY="v2" the law </REV>
or respect
<REV KEY="v1"> the law </REV>,
<REV KEY="v2"> sausage </REV>
should not watch either being made.</P>
```

Both marked sections and elements can work for managing versions or other conditional content. The element-based approach has several advantages in terms of structure, and marked sections have some advantages if one wants to manipulate structure itself, from a different angle. The fundamental reason is that marked sections do not relate closely to the element structure, but can cross it in arbitrary ways. For many uses this is too powerful because you can easily do things accidentally, that might surprise you later on. Keeping the conditional structures in sync with the element structure by expressing it using elements, has these plusses:

- A conditional element, unlike a marked section, cannot cross the document structure in odd ways (such as enclosing just the end-tag of one element and the start-tag of the next). Turning a conditional *element* on and off can have only very localized effects on document structure, such as adding or subtracting an entire element or set of sibling elements. It is almost impossible for it to have long-range effects on how remote parts of the document are parsed, or create distant validation errors.

> **Note**: I have to say "almost" because a *few* other long-distance dependencies still exist: even a synchronous marked section might include a **#CURRENT** attribute (see Question 1.14), or might contain a duplicate **ID**; but the potential problem cases are very limited.

- The structure formed by elements has all the processing conveniences natural to trees, such as inheritance of formatting and other properties. Inheritance across two arbitrarily-intersecting trees is more complex.

- Probably as a consequence of the last point, software generally provides a far wider range of processing for elements than for marked sections, so using elements often makes it practical to provide more capabilities for end users.

- Interesting things can happen if a marked section switches between **CDATA** or **RCDATA** and **IGNORE**, rather than between **INCLUDE** and **IGNORE**, since the effects of conditional content and markup suppression interact. Yet that kind of alternation can be necessary: sometimes conditional content also needs markup suppression. Cases where the two effects happen to both be needed are probably best handled by using two mechanisms, such as embedding a **CDATA** marked section inside one that alternates between **INCLUDE** and **IGNORE**.

- Marked sections can change the document structure tree in other ways than mere deletion of portions; so changing their status keywords generally requires a complete re-parse of the document. On large documents this makes real-time version switching quite difficult (or slow) as compared to an element-based approach. This makes them impractical for some high-end applications such as interactive technical manuals and diagnostic systems.
- Marked sections do not support logically complex conditions, which limits their usefulness for version-management (see the next question for details). Several large companies use very sophisticated logic or expert systems to determine which information is visible when, for example in response to test connections or other inputs. In such situations the control is best left to a semantic layer long after parsing, and in that case representing conditional content using elements is preferable.

## Using elements for conditional content

Conditional content can be done very effectively using elements instead of marked sections. The DTD designer creates an element type (or types) for that purpose, perhaps called COND. The element can take whatever attributes are appropriate, and the SGML system is then set up to hide or show such elements based on those attributes (and any other applicable information, such as the user, environment, or time). For example:

```
<p>To exit,
   <COND sys="unix">press Control-D </COND>
   <COND sys="mac">select the Shutdown menu item </COND>
   and then unplug your machine.
</p>
```

Such an element would have to be allowed nearly anywhere and allow nearly anything within it (otherwise a variety of element types would be needed for different contexts). This is easily accomplished in the DTD:

```
<!ELEMENT  BOOK         - - (FM, BODY, BM) +(COND)>
<!ELEMENT  COND         - - ANY>
```

As discussed in Question 6.1, such declarations compromise validation but SGML could introduce a notion of "transparent" included elements to eliminate that drawback. Transparent elements would not modify the content model context of their parent, so content would be checked against content models as if the transparent elements did not intervene. That question discussed how such elements would be useful for managing revision or versioning markup; the situation here is almost the same because you can think of alternative content as alternative versions: the main difference is that a version is chosen by circumstances ("user is on a Macintosh") rather than by time ("user wants latest revision").

In practice, the portions that need to be switched in and out are very often elements that are already marked up, in which case control attributes can just be added to them. The markup can usually be arranged so that the portions don't run into conflicts because of having multiple (conceptually alternative) instances; this means they are repeatable elements in the context where the occur (or sometimes just **#PCDATA** portions, which is just as good). Thus, markup like the COND example above can accommodate many cases of conditional text.

In the absence of an SGML system with flexible content-hiding, or in case it is not practical to modify the DTD to allow the extra (alternative) element instances in various contexts, there is still a solution: a processor like DSSSL can be added as a pre-processor step that selects the desired conditional content portions and deletes all others. Since DSSSL typically operates on the element structure, and the element structure is never re-shaped by such deletions, this kind of filtering is very easy to do.

The situation would be even better if alternatives were accommodated at the SGML level. Then the parser would be aware of the alternatives: you could mark up any number of copies or versions of a certain element, and SGML validation would know not to complain that there are too many instances of the element type (see the next question about ensuring that conditional portions actually alternate).

## 6.5. Can I choose between marked sections based on combinations of values?

No. Although marked sections may have any number of status keywords, the actual effective one is simply the highest-priority one. From high to low priority, the status keywords are **IGNORE**, **CDATA**, **RCDATA**, and **INCLUDE**. Thus, if one of the keywords is **IGNORE**, nothing can override it.

Marked sections have several purposes in SGML. The main two are escaping markup (on which see Question 3.7) and making parts of a document conditional. Conditional marked sections can be turned on or off by changing their status keyword from **INCLUDE** to **IGNORE** or vice-versa. Usually this is done by putting the keyword in a parameter entity because (a) the entity can have a name that reminds authors of what it controls, and (b) authors can then turn a lot of marked sections on or off at once, just by changing the entity. It works like this:

```
<!ENTITY   % unix       "IGNORE">
<!ENTITY   % mac        "INCLUDE">
...
<p>To exit,
   <![ %unix; [ press Control-D ]]>
   <![ %mac; [ select the Shutdown menu item ]]>
   and then unplug your machine.
</p>
```

Parameter entities in general can take any values, but ones intended to be used for marked sections can contain only the 5 marked section status keywords (they may contain more than one of them). SGML does not define a special kind of entity for this, that is constrained like attribute declared values can be.

General entities cannot be used to control marked sections, although for the most part general entities are referenced in the document instance and parameter entities in the DTD. Presumably parameter entities are used here because marked sections start with the markup declaration open (**MDO**) delimiter and thus are technically markup declarations (see Clause 4.180).

Three other things about marked sections are especially important to remember:

1. Because they can cross element boundaries arbitrarily, they form a separate tree from the element structure. This means they require separate implementation features, interfaces, processing control, and so on. An attractive alternative is to use elements that are conditionally hidden during processing, as discussed in the previous question.
2. Although any number of status keywords can be listed on a marked section, the status is determined only by priority: if any keyword is **`IGNORE`** the marked section is ignored regardless of any other keywords that may also occur. There is no way to make the marked section be included or ignored based on a combination of conditions. This issue is discussed below.
3. There is no way to create a set of *alternative* marked sections, such that only one of them is ever included at a time. This would be a useful capability, and is discussed further below.

> **Note:** In some other computer languages address portions included by reference must be syntactic wholes (though the C preprocessor is not like that). Some also provide logical operators such as AND, OR, and NOT to express logical conditions on what should be included, and mutually-exclusive blocks such as switch statements, if...then...else, and so on. Some SGML authors use the C preprocessor as a front end to process SGML files in order to manage some of these conditions, which can work reasonably well.

### Conditional expressions

Control of marked sections in SGML is like a set of switches in series: set any one parameter entity to off ("**`IGNORE`**") and the lights go out. Authors very often need the equivalent of 3-way switches, so that the content is included or ignored based on a combination of criteria. In the world of real documents and publishing (in print, online, or otherwise) this is a very widespread requirement.

For example, maintenance manuals for cars, aircraft, and other complicated machines often contain repair procedures that apply only if certain combinations of options are installed. For example, a particular jet may have engines from one company, a certain seating configuration, but not a certain in-service upgrade. A part can't be included or ignored based on just one of these things: only a combination of them works. In the same way, an ancient work may exist in several different manuscripts that differ slightly, and each manuscript may have several scholars who have attempted to decipher its less legible parts; studying such a text requires considering both of these factors (and a lot of others!).

Another example is that for any text being formatted or displayed, layout requirements may be a factor in determining what portions are included or ignored, such as when printed dictionaries drop or add main entries for words ending in -ly or -ness in order to shorten or lengthen columns. There are many *interacting* factors that determine how inclusions actually work, seldom just one.

The standard way of combining conditions is called Boolean algebra; most people know it by it primary combining terms: AND, OR, and NOT. If marked sections could perform tests on any number of conditions and combine them, they would serve a far wider range of purpose. The SGML review will likely add at least the basic combining operators.

> **Note**: It is also useful to be able to test things other than parameter entities. The expression language could be defined as part of SGML (as ANSI C does for #if), or left as a reference to a named external **NOTATION**.

Authors should be able to specify such conditional expressions either in a declaration (say, on a declaration of the reserved element type COND), or as a software parameter at runtime. Ideally, implementations could even refer to environmental information as part of conditions: in the example above, the SGML system might check what platform it is running on, and apply unix or mac automatically.

> **Note**: User-controllable conditional text in structured documents wa first established and implemented in a structured hypermedia publishing system called FRESS, which was built in the late 1960s at Brown University and widely used for many years. In FRESS just as in SGML, elements (called "blocks") could be hierarchical and could have attributes (called "keywords"). FRESS fully integrated document structure and conditional inclusion: at any time, the user could state a rule for just what blocks were visible or invisible for display and/or printing, or followed automatically to do dynamic document assembly. The rule could specify any number of keywords (as well as mathematical comparisons and other complex conditions), and combine them arbitrarily via AND, OR, NOT, and parentheses.

Although SGML does not require that software provide any semantics for run-time conditional text, SGML implementations can let the user access such attributes and state conditions for controlling output. In the *Dyna*Text system, for example, the conditional display effect just shown is achieved by using a stylesheet that contains (or references) a condition, such as:

```
<style name="P">
   <hide> if(and(eq(attr(status),"TEMPORARY"),
                 lt(attr(expire),1995)),
              All, Off)
</style>
```

Another feature this system took over from FRESS is that following a hypertext link can apply a whole new set of conditions for what is and is not hidden (as well as a while new stylesheet). This capability is especially valuable in large collections where the user's history or path tells you a lot about what they'll need next, such as in repair manuals and customer service databases.

> **Note**: The much more recent IBMIDDOC DTD used for documentation at IBM provides markup for a similar capability called "property-based retrieval".

Another advantage of doing conditional text via elements rather than marked sections is that it occurs *after* parsing. You cannot invalidate the document by changing the environment, and you do not need to re-parse to see the effects (this is especially important when you consider SGML's constraint that parsing can only be guaranteed correct if it starts at the very beginning of the document (SGML Open fragments and XML both provide solutions to this). Thus, changes can be done far more quickly, while the end-user is reading. With marked sections it is quite easy to invalidate the document or radically change its structure by changing their status, as in these two examples:

```
<![ %switch; [ <P! foo=bar" ]]>
<![ %switch; [ </CHP> ]]>
```

### Mutually exclusive marked sections

One of the most common uses of conditional structures in many languages is not merely to turn one thing on and off, but instead to switch between various forms of the "same" thing as needed for various contexts. The C programming language's preprocessor makes this very easy, as do most programming languages:

```
#if defined(MAC) || defined(UNIX)...
   initializeToolbox();
#elif defined(WIN)
   initializeWindows();
#else
   exit();
#endif
```

```
if (mac | unix) then {
...
}
else {
...
}
```

SGML has no similar notion of alternatives. The nearest thing occurs in content models, although the **AND**, **OR**, and **SEQ** operators there do not mean quite the same thing. To get the above effect using marked sections in SGML, the best one can do is to have independent switches:

```
<![ %mac;   [ ... ]]>
<![ %unix;  [ ... ]]>
<![ %win;   [ ... ]]>
```

Under ideal circumstances this will get the effect. But it has these problems:

- There is no practical way to guarantee that only one option is chosen, and so one can easily make the error of including mutually contradictory or redundant portions.

> **Note:** In the special case that each alternative marked section contains something that is allowed only once in the context where the marked sections occur, including more than one would produce a syntax error. But the error message would not likely be very specific ("element `TITLE` is not allowed here", or some such), and this is only a special case anyway.

- There is no way to have a "default" or "else" case, so one cannot prevent or automatically detect the case where *no* option is chosen at all and the document is left incomplete.

> **Note:** If the marked sections each contain some *required* element then a syntax error would be detected. But this is uncertain, and probably unlikely because if something is required the author would likely move it outside the marked sections to save space and maintenance effort, and it could no longer help catch the case where no marked section is included.

- The user must maintain as many variables (parameter entities) as there are cases, rather than one variable (such as "platform-name") with that many values. This makes changes error-prone because multiple variables must be changed even though only one actual "fact" (in this example, the environment) is changing.

The syntax possibilities for providing alternatives are well known. Such a mechanism would be easy to add to SGML, particularly if the markup-suppression aspects of marked sections (**CDATA** and **RCDATA**) were first separated from the conditional-text aspects (**INCLUDE** and **IGNORE**). It would be more effective, however, to integrate conditional sections more smoothly with the element structure.

## 6.6. How can I require the author to have at least *some* content in an element?

There is no way to require that an author actually provide data content anywhere. That is, **#PCDATA** in a content model is satisfied even by no characters at all.

SGML does provides a way to constrain the values of attributes, but no similar mechanism that can be applied to text in content. The only content constraints at this level are **#PCDATA**, **CDATA**, and **RCDATA**, all of which permit any text or no text (except anything that would be unintentionally taken as markup, such as "</" meant as literal text content).

**#PCDATA** cannot be modified by *, +, or ? to control repetitions, as other tokens can. Likewise, it is incorrect to combine multiple **#PCDATA** tokens in a single content model in certain ways, such as adjacent (since there would be no way to tell which characters to consider as satisfying which **#PCDATA** token):

```
<!-- WRONG -->
<!ELEMENT  p              - -  (#PCDATA+)>
<!ELEMENT  p              - -  (#PCDATA, #PCDATA)>
```

A means for constraining the content of given element types would be useful, and a rudimentary one called HyLex is added in HyTime. This is similar to some aspects of "data dictionaries" in database and spreadsheet programs, where given data can be constrained to be a date, an integer or real number, a string of a given (minimum/maximum) length or pattern, a key field drawn from a specified vocabulary, or some other formal type. To get such constraints on your SGML content you must enforce them at a higher level, through HyLex or another application. See also Questions 6.9 and 6.10, which discuss the same issue in relation to attributes.

## 6.7. How can I include or exclude #PCDATA?

**#PCDATA** may not be specified in a list of inclusion or exclusion exceptions. Although element types can be allowed anywhere within others as inclusion exceptions, and exclusion exceptions can override this, the same techniques are not available to control the placement of character content.

**#PCDATA** is most often declared to be permissible anywhere within certain kinds of element. Amendment 1 and most experts strongly recommend using **#PCDATA** in content models *only* when it can occur anywhere, which usually means using it in repeatable **OR** groups (see Question 5.2). If **#PCDATA** could be specified as an inclusion exception the desired effect would have a natural expression; indeed, it might be possible to permit **#PCDATA** *only* via exception, thus simplifying the overall formal specification of the language. For example, a syntax like this could be supported:

```
<!ELEMENT  FOOTNOTE     - -  (CITE*)>
<!ELEMENT  BOOK         - -  (FRONT,BODY,BACK)  +(FOOTNOTE)>
<!ELEMENT  P            - -  (EMPH)*  +(#PCDATA)>
```

Exceptions inherit down to all descendants, and this behavior is very often what DTD designers want with **#PCDATA**: Mixed content elements (those allowing **#PCDATA**) most often occur at the lowest levels of the document tree, with only a few elements allowed within them (typically emphasis, footnotes, index entries, links, and so on). It is less common for them to have subelements with element content, but allowing **#PCDATA** as an inclusion exception would, if supported, work fine in either case: a subelement that didn't want **#PCDATA** could still exclude it.

Such exclusion would be especially useful in applications involving formal structures such as database data. For example, this declaration might go well with those above if it were supported:

```
<!ELEMENT  CITE         - -  (AUTHOR, TITLE)  -(#PCDATA)>
```

A similar rule can be expressed with a **#CONREF** attributes (see Question 5.17), but that prohibits all content including any subelements, and seems to be overkill.

At this time, SGML does not support **#PCDATA** as an inclusion or exclusion exception. To get these effects you must list **#PCDATA** explicitly in each content model where it applies. This can be done using a parameter entity to list **#PCDATA** and various other widely-distributed small elements together, making the DTD more readable; on the whole this works quite well. Still, content models cannot readily be used to get an inclusion-like effect where **#PCDATA** is allowed in a certain element type only when an instance of it is embedded within an element of a certain other type(s); but that is seldom needed.

## 6.8. How can I get attribute values to be inherited by subelements?

There is no hierarchical defaulting mechanism for attributes in SGML. That is, you cannot declare an attribute so that when unspecified, its value defaults to the value the same attribute had on the parent element, or the nearest ancestor element that specified it. Some implementations do provide tools for getting this effect through style sheets or other processing tools, but it is not part of SGML processing *per se*.

While a tree-ignoring defaulting mechanism such as **#CURRENT** may seem surprising in a basically hierarchical document model, the lack of a specifically tree-oriented default value mechanism seems even more surprising.

It is very common in DTDs to want an attribute value to "inherit" from parents. For example, a LANGUAGE attribute should in most scenarios default to the LANGUAGE value of the parent element; in this example the LANGUAGE of the SECTION should be considered KR (for "Korean") because it does not override that of its containing CHAPTER (see Question 5.19 for more on this particular usage)

```
<CHAPTER LANGUAGE="KR">...
  <SECTION>...
```

The same method is useful for revision control, security clearance settings (though Wayne Wohler has pointed out that security may also propagate upwards), and many other cases. Formatting characteristics such as fonts, margins, and the like also frequently inherit in this way, though fortunately SGML suggests (under "Background") keeping these out of documents, and expressing them outside (typically this means in formatting specifications such as stylesheets).

Such defaults cannot be specified in SGML, although they seem natural for SGML's tree-structured documents. Many DTDs make it an application requirement. For example, the Text Encoding Initiative *Guidelines* have declarations of the form:

```
<!ATTLIST  X
  LANG     IDREF        %INHERITED;>
```

"`%INHERITED;`" is defined merely as **`#IMPLIED`**; but TEI-aware applications are expected to implement inheritance as the defaulting mechanism. Unfortunately, SGML parsers do not typically inform an application that some default value was specified as "`%INHERITED;`", instead they just say that it resolved to **`#IMPLIED`**. Because of this an application may not be able to find out directly from the parser just what elements use this convention. Some software systems provide a stylesheet-accessible function that can be asked to look up through an element's ancestors until it finds a like-named attribute and return the nearest value; this allows many of the desired effects.

## 6.9. Can I require an attribute to be an integer, real number, date, truth value, or similar type?

No. There are no attribute declared values in SGML that correspond to these types. The nearest ones are **`NUMBER`** and **`NUMBERS`**, but they do not allow plus, minus, or decimal point, and they are treated lexically rather than numerically (so "`1`" is not considered the same as "`01`").

An element type can declare what attributes it permits, and which of several lexical types they can take. There is a long list of specific datatypes for attributes defined in Clause 11.3.3, called "declared values" (in computer science terminology they would be called types):

> [145] declared value = "CDATA" | "ENTITY" | "ENTITIES" | "ID" | "IDREF" | "IDREFS" | "NAME" | "NAMES" | "NMTOKEN" | "NMTOKENS" | "NUMBER" | "NUMBERS" | "NUTOKEN" | "NUTOKENS" | *notation* | *name token group*
>
> [146] notation = "NOTATION" , ps+, name group

Each declared value constrains the character strings that are allowed as values (syntax or form), and has rules about whitespace normalization and case-folding. A few add special validity constraints (semantics or meaning) as discussed in Question 5.14. Those include **`ID`**, **`IDREF`**, **`ENTITY`**, **`NOTATION`**, and related plurals. All the semantically special types are equivalent to **`NAME`** in terms of their syntax (except for case-folding, which does not normally apply to **`ENTITY`** or **`ENTITIES`**).

There is sentiment in the SGML community for separating the form and the meaning, and for modifying the set of syntax types for attributes. Question 6.10 discusses some SGML constructs that you may have occasion to place in attributes (and thus could be useful additional declared values); this question is about datatypes and characteristics typical of other systems:

- There are none of the familiar types such as character, date, signed integer, truth values, real numbers, and so on.
- The **NUMBER** and **NUMBERS** types are not really numeric, as Clause 9.3 states (after Amendment 1): "A *number* or *number token* is not a quantity but a character string". This reduces their usefulness for some applications, since authors may expect something called a **NUMBER** to support arithmetic operations, such as comparing values numerically ("2" as opposed to "02", etc.).
- Lists of values can only be separated by whitespace, not other punctuation such as commas or colons. Some software has used **CDATA** in some cases such as column-width lists separated by colons, where if **NUMBERS** could be used SGML could actually help with validation.
- Although most declared values distinguish single versus multiple values (for example, **IDREF** versus **IDREFS**), **ID** and **NOTATION** do not because only one of each is permitted (Clause 11.3.3). SGML does not provide for specifying a range of permissible numbers of occurrences, as do various regular expression languages: "[-.a-z0-9]{1,4}".

Some applications have reason to constrain attribute values to particular forms or to constrain repetitions. The obvious way is to apply regular expressions. As one example, many DTDs for tables provide a width attribute that takes integer or real number values followed by an abbreviation for some unit (such as "i" for inch or "m" for millimeter). This can easily be specified by a regular expression like "[0-9]+[im]". Currently SGML cannot express or validate such constraints; although they can be implemented on top. HyTime adds "HyLex", a regular-expression-like language for this, although it poses implementation difficulties due to an unusual definition of "shortest match" in certain cases.

DTD designers who need these and other data types must assign the attributes a more generic syntax type such as **CDATA** or **NAMES**, and handle validation at a level beyond the SGML parser. It is worth remembering that **CDATA** values do not get whitespace normalization or case-folding, so if needed, that must also be done at a higher level.

## 6.10. Are there attribute declared values for constructs like FPI and inter-document link?

No. SGML provides a limited set of attribute declared value types, as discussed in the last question, but they only include a few SGML constructs.

*The SGML Handbook* says (p. 422) that for the many declared values that have no special semantics, just **CDATA** would be enough but the other types are included in SGML "because an SGML parser must already have code for recognizing names, name tokens, numbers, and number tokens". However, number token and number token list do not appear anywhere in the SGML standard *except* as attribute declared values, so it seems no other code could need those two.

However, given that suggestion several other constructs might be expected as declared values as well: minimum literals, external identifiers, status keywords, name or model groups, specific classes of names such as GIs, attributes, entities, short reference map names; and so on. Everyday datatypes like real and negative numbers, dates, and so on might also be useful — see Question 6.9.

These types have many potential uses (especially in allowing markup to operate as a true-meta-language that could represent not only information about content, but also about other markup). They would also have the advantage of requiring no new code in an SGML parser.

A particularly important single case arises when authors need to create a link to an **ID** that lives in another document. Presumably, such an attribute would specify something like an entity name or an external identifier, plus an **IDREF** expected to be resolvable in that target entity. Many SGML applications have re-invented this construct in one way or another. This is discussed in detail in Question 6.11.

DTD designers who need particular attribute constraints that SGML does not supply can use declared value **CDATA** and validate at a higher level. This works fine in principle, but requires care about whitespace normalization and case-folding, which do not apply to **CDATA** attributes, and validation must be set up separately (if at all) in each different system. Some cases can also be managed by HyLex.

## 6.11. How do I link to an IDREF across books?

SGML does not provide any constructs for this, although it provides a mechanism for making cross-references within a single document, using **ID** and **IDREF** attributes as shown below.

One of the great strengths of SGML's intra-book linking mechanism is validation: the parser itself will sanity check a document for any non-unique **ID** values, and for any **IDREF** that points to a non-existent **ID** value (it cannot, of course, check for an **IDREF** pointing to the *wrong* **ID**). This feature works very well and is widely used:

```
<P>See all <XREF target="c4.s2">Section 4.2</P>
...
<SEC ID="c4.s2"><ST>Now that you're here,...
```

SGML also provides a way to refer to other whole documents, whether they are in SGML or not. Such inter-book or inter-document links are quite different from intra-book links (see Question 1.16 for more details on linking to entire external entities):

```
<!NOTATION SUNRASTER   PUBLIC
   "+//ISBN 0-7923-9432-1::Graphic Notation//NOTATION
   Sun Microsystems raster//EN">
<!ENTITY   fig32        SYSTEM "c:\pix\helios.sr"
                        NDATA SUNRASTER>
<!ENTITY   book5        SYSTEM "c:\books\book5.sgm"
                        SUBDOC>
...
<P>A link service could work as shown here:
<FIGREF ent="fig32">Pearl, 1987</FIGREF></P>
...
<P>This is also discussed in <XREF ent="book5">.</P>
```

What about the combination, however? Authors very frequently want to refer to a specific portion with an **ID**, that happens to be in another document. SGML does not provide any syntax for doing this in a standard way. Thus, creating links to specific locations or ranges in other documents must be done some other way. Several methods are possible, though all go beyond the SGML standard:

- Use two attributes: one for the **ENTITY**, and one for the desired **ID** in it.
- Add element location information inside **SYSTEM** or **PUBLIC** identifiers.
- Use Text Encoding Initiative extended pointers.
- Use HyTime location ladders.

Since SGML itself provides no mechanism, DTD designers must do something more or less like this or do without inter-book linking (except to whole entities, which is clearly not enough). Many DTDs include such a construct.

> **Note**: HyTime did not originally support prior methods due to certain syntax limitations. The changes being done on HyTime now are expected to accommodate each of the prior methods; this is extraordinarily important because of the many Gigabytes of data using each of them.

Each of these methods is discussed below.

### The two-attribute method

Specific inter-book links are so important that many, probably most DTDs have a way to do them (even very early DTDs). The most common method historically has been to use two attributes, one for the **ENTITY** and one for the **IDREF**:

```
<!ATTLIST  INTERBOOK
   ENT      ENTITY      #REQUIRED
   XID      NAME        #REQUIRED>
...
<XLINK ENT="book5" XID="c3s3">
See the Introduction to SGML.</XLINK>
```

This works fine since it provides exactly the needed information, and many SGML implementations provide linking capability that handles it easily. The drawbacks are mainly those common to all these methods because SGML doesn't know what's going on and so can't provide any help:

- The **IDREF** must be declared only as a **NAME** because using **IDREF** would lead to a validation error: the value would not be resolvable to any **ID** within the current document (except by chance).
- SGML will not validate the links even if the entity is available during parsing and could be opened and checked for the `xid`'s presence as an **ID**.
- SGML does not know that there is any relationship between the parts of the location specification (`ent` and `xid`).
- SGML cannot validate that only **SUBDOC** entities (that is, whole SGML documents) are specified for ENT.

There might also be performance consequences. For example, an implementation that knew to optimize **ID**s and **IDREF**s (say, by indexing them for very fast access) might *not* optimize **NAME**s since they are less obvious search targets. A better implementation indexes everything or lets the designer specify exactly what to index.

### The complex SYSTEM/PUBLIC identifier method

Another method of supporting inter-document links is to pack the target **ID** value into the entity's **SYSTEM** or **PUBLIC** identifier using a naming convention:

```
<!ENTITY   book5.c3s3  SYSTEM "c:\books\book5.sgm#c3s3"
                       SUBDOC>
<!ENTITY   book5.c3s3  PUBLIC
  "+//ISBN 0-7923-9432-1//TEXT Making Hypermedia Work::
  ID (c3s3)//EN"       SUBDOC>
```

This is also valid in SGML, since SGML says almost nothing about the content or meaning of **SYSTEM** identifiers or the descriptive portion of FPIs. However, it has some drawbacks:

- Every link to a different location must have a separate entity name, even if many of them all point to different parts of the same document.
- Those entity names end up either being non-mnemonic, or packing something like **ID** into the entity name as well (see example above), which is redundant and therefore a pain to maintain over time.
- Since entity names generally regard upper-case/lower-case distinctions but **ID**s do not, packing **ID**s into the entity names to make them readable can confuse people about just when case does and doesn't matter.
- The set of characters allowed in **PUBLIC** identifiers is extremely limited (see Question 4.11), and does not include many characters that would typically be allowed in **ID** values in non-English documents.
- Every link to a different location must have a separate external identifier, which may put extra strain on resources.
- SGML has no way of knowing those external identifiers are related, so cannot know to optimize retrieval. For example, when each location has a distinct entity declaration it is hard for a system to know that once it has retrieved `book1` to get **ID** `chap1`, getting `book1` **ID** `chap2` does not require re-fetching the whole book.
- The fact that *parts* of external identifiers are redundant leads to maintenance headaches if the common parts ever change.

It is thought that the SGML review will add some similar construct, probably related to the new HyTime changes that formalize an internal syntax for **SYSTEM** identifiers.

> **Note**: This method and the previous one could be combined by assembling the information in an attribute value instead of a **SYSTEM** or **PUBLIC** identifier. That has other drawbacks, mainly because SGML is less aware of what is going on; if SGML standardized such an attribute type it might amount to a very good solution.

It is worth noting that this is basically the solution the World Wide Web has chosen: pack the reference (called a "fragment identifier") onto the end of the URL, separated by "#". The whole thing, however, is placed in an attribute such as `HREF` rather than in an **ENTITY** declaration like an SGML external identifier (see Question 1.16 for more on this kind of situation):

```
<A HREF="http://xyz.com//books/book5.htm#c3s3">
See the Introduction to SGML.</A>
```

HTML hyperlinks do not use the SGML **ENTITY** mechanism. There is also a slight difference in meaning because the "#" field of a URL is taken to specify a location to *scroll to,* not a document portion to retrieve. Such a link retrieves the entire "entity" (typically a file) even if it is enormous, though some servers can be configured to extract a more manageable, relevant portion to send. Separate control of each operation can be useful, as addressed in the XML linking specification now under development.

## The Text Encoding Initiative extended pointer method

The Text Encoding Initiative, or TEI, was founded in 1987 and brings together scholars from a variety of fields to develop ways of representing and interchanging documents of scholarly interest. In addition to providing DTDs for literary and poetic works, philosophical papers, multilingual dictionaries, and so on, the TEI *Guidelines* provide a way to specify locations in documents, and tools for making hypertext links that have proven useful in a much wide range of applications (see below for references).

Inter-book TEI links use a method similar to the two-attributes method described earlier: an attribute typically called DOC names the destination entity, and two other attributes specify the beginning and end of the destination there (very often the beginning is enough because it specifies an element which is the whole destination).

As mentioned earlier, a non-local **ID** cannot have declared value **ID** locally in SGML, and many DTDs therefore substitute **NAME**. The TEI's attributes for specifying locations support not only remote **ID**s, but also provide extra syntax within that value that lets links point to remote elements or other data that lack **ID**s. These attributes use a syntax called "extended pointers", and have declared value **CDATA**. Each type of pointing is labeled to distinguish it from the others (**ID**s are, not surprisingly, labeled "ID"), and operates on structural representations such as DSSSL groves.

In addition to the extended pointer syntax itself, the TEI *Guidelines* (TEI 1990, 1994) provide representative element types that can use it, mainly XREF and XPTR (the "X" is for "extended"). Using those element types as an example, the inter-book link shown above would be expressed as:

```
<!ENTITY   book5       SYSTEM "c:\books\book5.sgm" SUBDOC>
...
<XREF DOC="book5" FROM="ID (c3s3)">
See the Introduction to SGML.</XREF>
```

TEI extended pointers support many other ways of locating data, that can be combined as needed. Each has a name (like "ID") and some parameters (like "(c3s3)"). For example, to:

1. find the element with **ID** A25,
2. within that element, find the second child of type CHAP (which might be the third child overall due to a TITLE element at the beginning of the CHAP),
3. within that element, find the fourth child of type SEC (fifth child overall),
4. within that element, find the fourth child of type P (fourth child overall),
5. within that element, find the 5th word-token.

The entire TEI extended pointer to locate that token is:

```
ID (a25) CHILD (2 CHAP) (4 SEC) (4 P) TOKEN (5)
```

The element type parameters (CHAP, SEC, and P) mean that, for example, the second CHAP subelement is to be found, not just the second subelement regardless of type. Using them is good for robustness and readability, but they can also be left out, giving

```
ID (a25) CHILD (3) (5) (4) TOKEN (5)
```

**Note**: The TEI extended pointer syntax will likely be amended to permit parameters to be separated by commas instead of spaces, to make it more convenient to embed them within URLs where spaces must be replaced by "%20". XML will very likely use the TEI extended pointer syntax as part of its linking support.

Extended pointers can filter elements by attributes as well as by element types, and can use regular expressions to search for content patterns or to match sets of element types or attribute values, such as "DIV[123]". The various location types are defined in Clause 14.2.2.2 of the TEI *Guidelines*. They include these absolute and relative location methods that can be chained together as needed:

| Loc. Term | Description |
|---|---|
| ROOT | Locates the root of the target document. |
| HERE | Locates the pointer itself (mainly used with other terms that locate data relative to the starting point). |
| ID | Locates an element by its ID. |
| REF | Locates an element pointed to by a 'canonical reference' in certain defined formats. |
| CHILD | Locates a direct subelement of the current location, based on GI, attributes, and/or sequence. |
| DESCENDANT | Like CHILD, but can also locate indirect subelements. |
| ANCESTOR | Locates an element among elements containing the location source. |
| PREVIOUS | Locates older siblings of the current location source (counting left, with the same filtering features as CHILD etc.). |
| NEXT | Locates younger siblings of the current location source. |
| PRECEDING | Locates any element that starts before the current location source. |
| FOLLOWING | Locates any element that starts after the current location source. |
| PATTERN | Locates content within the location source that matches a regular expression. |
| TOKEN | Locates one or more word tokens in content (by counting). |
| STR | Locates one or more characters in content (by counting). |
| SPACE | Locates a geometric region using coordinates. |
| FOREIGN | Locates data by a (named) method outside of TEI. |
| HYQ | Locates data using HyTime's HyQ query language (this will likely be obsolete shortly, and DSSSL's SDQL should be used instead). |
| DITTO | Locates whatever was indicated by another locator, so a relative range can be stated. TEI places this in a second attribute, though a way to append it onto the FROM attribute separated by the keyword "TO" will likely be added. |
| LITERAL | This proposed addition is a simple sub-case of PATTERN, that locates a fixed string rather than a match to a regular expression |

| Loc. Term | Description |
|---|---|
| ATTR | This proposed addition locates the values of particular attributes (as opposed to using attributes to locate other data). |

The TEI hypermedia features also include a JOIN element that points to any number of locations to create a composite data object from them; a LINK element analogous to HyTime's ILINK form for putting several locators together to form an actual link; and a LINKGRP element used to build link databases.

**Note**: The central source for the TEI *Guidelines* is www-tei.uic.edu/orgs/tei/. You can browse them online at dynaweb.ebt.com:8080/usrbooks/teip3 (append "/26759" to get right to the extended pointer section) and at etext.virginia.edu/TEI.html. Lou Burnard's tutorial on TEI extended pointers is at users.ox.ac.uk/~lou/wip/XR.htm, and other information can be found in Ide and Veronis (1995).

## The HyTime method

HyTime (ISO 10744:1994) provides a wide variety of structures for locating data and creating links; they operate on the "groves" formalized by DSSSL. A basic inter-book ID link (using SGML minimization) looks something like this:

```
<NAMELOC ID=PTR38 DOCORSUB=book5>
   <NMLIST NAMETYPE=ELEMENT> c2s4 </NAMELOC>
...
<CLINK LINKEND=ptr38>
See the Introduction to SGML.</CLINK>
```

HyTime can also chain together various location types to walk around trees, select tokens, invoke query languages, and so on. For example, to do a "tree-walk" similar to the one shown above using Text Encoding Initiative extended pointers, HyTime would do something like shown below (except that HyTime does not filter steps by element type or attribute value):

```
<NAMELOC ID="STEP1" HYTIME="NAMELOC" DOCORSUB="BOOK5">
   <NMLIST NAMETYPE="ELEMENT">a25</NMLIST></NAMELOC>
<TREELOC ID="STEP2" LOCSRC="STEP1"
         LEXTYPE="LOCSRC (IDREF, (s*, IDREF)+)"
         REFLEVEL="1" HYTIME="TREELOC">
   <MARKLIST HYTIME="MARKLIST">1 3 5 4</MARKLIST></TREELOC>
<DATALOC ID="STEP3" LOCSRC="STEP2"
      HYTIME="DATALOC" QUANTUM="WORD">
   <DIMLIST HYTIME="DIMLIST">5 1</DIMLIST></DATALOC>
```

With SGML minimization this can reduce to:

```
<NAMELOC ID=STEP1 DOCORSUB=BOOK5>
   <NMLIST>a25 </NAMELOC>
<TREELOC ID=STEP2 LOCSRC=STEP1>
   <MARKLIST>1 3 5 4 </TREELOC>
<DATALOC ID=STEP3 LOCSRC=STEP2>
   <DIMLIST>5 1 </DATALOC>
```

SGML could avoid the portability problem of everyone having to create their own inter-book linking convention by standardizing a syntax to use for the basic case. HyTime does standardize some solutions, but a simple way to do simple cases within SGML itself would be even easier to apply. One possibility would be a new attribute declared value that includes *both* an **ENTITY** name and an **IDREF** value (presumably separated by whitespace).

In the meantime, DTD designers who need to support inter-book linking should follow one of the commonly used and supported methods, rather than inventing yet another new way. That way there is the best chance for widespread software support.

## 6.12. What does it mean if I refer to an entity but omit the semicolon?

Entity references are ended by the **REFC** delimiter, which is normally "`;`". However, SGML adds some special exceptions where the closing delimiter can be left out; the result is still the same entity reference.

According to Clause 9.4.5 you can end an entity reference with the **REFC** delimiter, an **RE**, or any non-name character (that is, normally anything but letters, digits, hyphen, or period). But these cases differ in what happens to that character or delimiter:

- A **REFC** is part of the entity reference, and never remains as text content.
- An **RE** used in this way "has the effect of suppressing the record end", which appears to mean much the same thing as "ignoring" a record end (on which see Question 2.5). This usage can interact subtly with the **RE**-ignoring rules, for example if the suppressed **RE** that ends an entity reference is also the first **RE** in an element.
- Any other character, however, stays around as data (or possibly markup). For example, in the string "`&gt]>`" the literal bracket terminates the entity reference (since it is not an allowed character in entity names). Thus the result is a reference to the `gt` entity followed by a literal "`]>`".

Some authors leave out the **REFC** whenever they can; others try to but forget that space is not discarded, or that **RE** is. To prevent confusion and/or errors many publishers have house policies demanding the **REFC** always be used. To prevent parsers from erroneously implementing slight variations, XML has also applied this simplification.

SGML currently provides no option for enforcing the presence of the **REFC**. Omitting it is not considered minimization, as omitting **TAGC** or quotes on attribute values is. However, it is never an error to include the **REFC**, so authors who do so never get in trouble over **REFC**. If SGML were to provide a way to require the **REFC** (as the SGML review is considering), it would likely involve a new **FEATURE** that could be declared in the SGML declaration, perhaps something like this:

```
FEATURES   OMITREFC NO
```

> **Note:** SGML could instead add a new class of "characters which are suppressed if they end an entity reference"; or could allow multiple strings to be assigned to **REFC**, something like the **LIT** and **LITA** roles (see Question 7.4 for more on delimiter sets). The contemplated simplification seems better on the whole.

On the whole, the best strategy for authors and DTD designers is probably to always use the **REFC**. That way confusion is less likely, and documents become more consistent and readable.

# 7. For Builders of SGML DTDs and SGML Declarations

Some DTD designers also decide to make changes that affect the SGML declaration, and this chapter is mainly for them. The most common case is fairly simple: increasing length limits such as those on element and attribute names. Many designs do this, including HTML. Some DTDs, especially internationalized ones, use SGML declarations that add to the characters permitted in SGML names. Less common and more prone to raise questions are changes like assigning new strings to delimiters (creating a "variant concrete syntax"). As the questions here reflect, this can be a complex task with subtle side-effects; it is fairly uncommon to do it at all, and extremely uncommon to change more than one or two delimiters. This chapter discusses many of these changes and their effects, as well as a few questions relating to optional SGML features.

## 7.1. Why can't I change some delimiters without affecting others?

Some SGML delimiters have two purposes each, such as the **PLUS** and **MINUS** delimiters. Designers who start changing delimiter settings may be surprised when they realize that changing a delimiter when they are thinking about one of its uses, also necessarily affects its other uses. There is no way to change "half" a delimiter in SGML; you can only change the delimiter by name, and thus affect all its contexts.

For example, the **PLUS** delimiter is used to mark inclusion exceptions in element declarations, and to mean "required and repeatable" in content models. The **MINUS** delimiter is used for minimization flags and for exclusion exceptions:

```
<!ELEMENT  CHAP            - -  (TI,SEC+)  -(CHAP)  +(FN)>
```

Since a single abstract name is used for more than one syntactic role, the delimiters cannot be set differently for each role. Although DTD designers rarely change delimiters at all, particularly those applicable only in the DTD, this limitation can pose interesting problems in case you do choose to do that.

Internationally the combination of these two meanings may be more of a problem, because intuition that they are related is English-dependent. In the case of **PLUS** an

English speaker might find it intuitive to represent both "added repetitions of self" and "added permissible descendants" with the addition symbol ("+"). However, a Greek speaker might want separate symbols because Greek uses distinct words for "additional instances of the same kind" and "additional kinds". Another language might distinguish notions such as "additional instance" and "lessened constraint".

The **MINUS** delimiter is analogous, though for a different reason. **MINUS** is used both for exclusion exceptions and for indicating omitted tag minimization in element declarations; the two applications cannot have different delimiters assigned. The comment delimiter is normally two hyphens, but is defined separately as the **COM** delimiter and so can be set separately (see Question 7.8 for more on the hyphen's role in various delimiters).

The **PLUS** and **MINUS** limitations are far enough off the beaten track that few will trip over them. The SGML review is considering dividing up some of these delimiter roles so the strings for distinct purposes can be distinct; this could be done symmetrically across all delimiter roles, or only in some cases (see Question 7.4 for more on delimiter symmetry). Making the set fully symmetrical would not pose either backward compatibility issues or implementation complexity.

## 7.2. Why can't I set STAGO = TAGC?

This particular delimiter change cannot be done because **STAGO** is recognized inside of tags in order to support a particular **SHORTTAG** minimization: "<P<Q>" (see Clause 9.6.1 and Appendix B).

This detail rules out markup schemes that look symmetrical at the element level, such as "{p{...}p}". No problem arises in the reference concrete syntax; this is only a limitation on the range of alternate or pre-existing concrete syntaxes that SGML can accommodate. For example, TeX "groups" use much this style of syntax and so cannot be readily supported.

A language could avoid this limitation either by discarding that particular means of minimization, or by making each means of minimization a separate option that could be turned off at will. In current SGML there is no clear workaround other than not to attempt such variant delimiter settings.

## 7.3. Why don't LIT, LITA, NET, and COM distinguish Open/Close like other delimiters?

Despite the special accommodation for two kinds of quotes (**LIT** and **LITA**), it is not possible to define a variant SGML syntax that distinguishes

- open- verses close- quotes for literals:

```
<!-- WRONG -->
<SEC TYPE="SECRET">
```

- ending a NET-enabling start tag versus being a null end-tag:

```
<!-- WRONG -->
<EMPH/very\>
```

- opening versus closing a comment:

```
<!-- WRONG -->
<!/* hello, world */>
```

These and similar cases are ruled out because unlike with other syntactic constructs, SGML does not distinguish the open- and close- roles for these delimiters. For example, there is no LITO versus LITC delimiter pair.

The most common resulting question is how to use distinct open- and close-quotation marks to delimit literals in SGML, and the answer is that it cannot be done. Given how commonplace such quotes have become (they are even automatically inserted by many document systems), this question often arises when authors find themselves doing tedious repair. For example, it required great care to ensure that no software touching the files for this book would "enhance" quotation marks within SGML examples (the fact that most software can't do a change in "all but" certain element types does not help). SGML software knows to distinguish quotes around attributes from quotes in content, but generic file-processing tools do not, so that if generic software is used at any point then markup is in jeopardy. If it were possible in SGML to define distinct LITO and LITC delimiters, designers could more easily exercise options.

Along the same line, there is no NETO/NETC distinction in SGML. That is, the delimiter that closes a **NET**-enabled start-tag is forced to be the same as the delimiter that serves as the (null-) end-tag in the content of such an element. A language (for example, TEX) might instead support balanced pairs of characters or strings for this function, such as curly braces: "`\P{...}`".

The **COM** delimiter ("`--`") also lacks an open/close distinction (no COMO or COMC). This makes it impossible to create variant syntaxes for SGML comments that are symmetrical, for example "`/*...*/`" and "`(*...*)`". This distinction will likely be added by the SGML review; I hope the other cases are considered as well (see the next question for a table of possibilities).

> **Note**: In the meantime, you can achieve the delimiter distinction by a convention to follow comment opens with something (say, "`*`", to make "`--*`"), and to precede comment closes with the same thing (making "`*--`"). SGML ignores the asterisks because they are inside what SGML considers the comment; if and when SGML adds the COMO/COMC distinction, you can then use it without any documents having to change.

Many characters come in open/close or left/right pairs, such as parentheses, brackets, braces, pointy brackets, and slash/backslash. A DTD designer may want to use them as SGML delimiters to open and close SGML constructs. But SGML does not allow some cases, such as "`<P{...}`". At this time, there is no workaround for using delimiters that do not fit SGML's pattern. See Question 7.4 for more on this.

## 7.4. Why can't I change some close delimiters when I can change related open delimiters?

This happens because different start delimiters sometimes share a single end delimiter.

For example, **STAGO** is the start-tag open delimiter, normally "<". There is a distinct end-tag open delimiter, called **ETAGO**, normally "</". The fact that both these

delimiters begin with “<” is coincidence. The *opening* delimiters for start- versus end-tags can be set completely separately. For example, **STAGO** can be set to “{” and **ETAGO** to “}” so markup looks as shown below (not a particularly pretty choice, in my opinion, but easy to do):

```
{p>some text}P>
```

On the other hand, start-tags and end-tags in SGML must share the same *closing* delimiter (called **TAGC**, normally “>”). The delimiter that closes start-tags cannot be set separately from the one closing end-tags, so it is impossible to support a markup variant like:

```
<!-- WRONG -->
{P{ text of paragraph }P}
```

> **Note:** SGML experts vary in their intuitions about what makes delimiters “symmetrical”. Some think every *tag* should be internally symmetrical, so “{P}” would be fine but “{P{” unacceptable; others think whole *elements* should be symmetrical, so that end- tags should balance start-tags as in the last example. If the delimiters were all separately named, everyone could be accommodated.

Similarly, SGML distinguishes several kinds of entities, referenced using distinct open delimiters, as shown below. The three types share one close-delimiter (**REFC**, which is also optional as discussed in Question 6.12).

| Type of entity | Syntax | Open Delimiter |
|---|---|---|
| Parameter | `%p.attrs;` | **PERO** |
| General | `&chap7;` | **ERO** |
| Character-reference | `í` | **CRO** |

At this time there is no workaround if you want delimiters to form a different pattern than SGML's distinctions provide. A more completely symmetrical delimiter set might look something like this:

| Name | String | Name | String | Name | String |
|---|---|---|---|---|---|
| AND | & | ETAG-CLOSE | > | OMIT-YES | O |
| COM-OPEN | -- | EXCLUSION | - | OPT | ? |
| COM-CLOSE | -- | GRP-OPEN | ( | OR | \| |
| CPTAG-OPEN | < | GRP-CLOSE | ) | PER-OPEN | % |
| CPTAG-CLOSE | > | INCLUSION | + | PER-CLOSE | ; |
| CR-OPEN | &# | LIT-OPEN | " | PI-OPEN | <? |
| CR-CLOSE | ; | LIT-CLOSE | " | PI-CLOSE | > |
| DS-OPEN | [ | MD-OPEN | <! | REQ | + |
| DS-CLOSE | ] | MD-CLOSE | > | REP | * |
| DTG-OPEN | [ | MS-OPEN | <![ | RNI | # |
| DTG-CLOSE | ] | MS-CLOSE | ]> | SEQ | , |
| ER-OPEN | & | NET-OPEN | / | STAG-OPEN | < |
| ER-CLOSE | ; | NET-CLOSE | / | STAG-CLOSE | > |
| ETAG-OPEN | </ | OMIT-NO | - | VI | = |

In this table, the delimiters are named very similarly to the actual SGML set, and serve the same net purposes. The main possibilities illustrated are that several more delimiters distinguish open- versus close-roles; that empty (“content-prohibited” or CP) elements have their own delimiters (see Question 3.3); and that some of the dual-use delimiters are divided up, such as separating the use of ">" to close processing instructions from the use of it to close markup declarations. The existing reference concrete syntax could remain unchanged despite such restructuring. This table also omits the alternative literal delimiter **LITA** (see Question 7.7), but of course it could be kept. Some changes along these lines will likely be made in the SGML review, such as the introduction of separate delimiters for content-prohibited tags and for comment open versus close.

## 7.5. What do the delimiters between GIs mean when I declare several elements at once?

SGML allows declaring multiple elements in a single declaration. The names occur in parentheses, with separating delimiters as shown below. Which of the permitted delimiters is actually used to separate the names has no significance:

```
<!ELEMENT  (ITEM | DT | GLOSSITEM)      - -  (#PCDATA)>
<!ELEMENT  (P, WARN, FN)                - -  (#PCDATA)>
<!ELEMENT  (TITLE & AUTHOR & DATE)      - -  (#PCDATA)>
```

Any of the delimiters used as connectors in SGML content models may be used to separate the GIs. That is, the **OR**, **SEQ**, or **AND** delimiters but not just whitespace.

The explanation for this may sound a bit odd at first, but actually proves useful in practice (see Clause 10.1.3): permitting various delimiters lets DTD writers re-use parameter entities as macros, *both* for listing elements within a content model *and* as a name group in declarations. For example:

```
<!ENTITY   % para-types               "ITEM | DT | GLOSSITEM">
<!ELEMENT  (%para-types;)             - - (#PCDATA)>
<!ELEMENT  SEC                        - - (%para-types;)*>
```

The choice of delimiter obviously makes a difference when the entity is referenced within a content model. Making the delimiters allowed but irrelevant when the entity is referenced within a list of GIs means DTD designers need not create and maintain two entities for the same list of GIs just so one will have the delimiters and one not.

## 7.6. Why do some delimiters not have names?

The beginning and ending of marked sections do not have their own delimiter, but are represented using sequences of other delimiters. Marked sections are started by "<! [", which is really a markup declaration open ("**MDO**") plus a declaration subset open ("**DSO**").

Presumably the one function is accomplished by two delimiters so that the **MDO** portion ("<!") can be shared with the many kinds of markup declarations (although it is not clear in what sense a marked section declares markup).

The rules in detail are in Clause 10.4; the second open square bracket is not at the same level as the first or as its balancing close square bracket:

> [93] marked section declaration = *marked section start*, *status keyword specification*, **dso**, *marked section*, *marked section end*

[94] marked section start = **mdo**, **dso**

[95] marked section end = **msc**, **mdc**

[96] marked section = *SGML character**

The two opening square brackets are copies of the **DSO** delimiter (there is no MSO delimiter) and are in separate grammar rules. In contrast, the two closing square brackets are a single delimiter (**MSC**) and occur in a single rule. This means you can change the closing delimiters in isolation, but cannot change the open delimiters without affecting the several other uses of **DSO**, and some other details differ, such as whether whitespace is permitted between the brackets. See the previous question for more on delimiter asymmetry; the table there addresses this case as well.

It is easy but inaccurate to think of a marked section as having a start and an end marker, like tags, or to think of the status keywords as being like attributes. With tags both the start- and the end-tag have delimiters for their open and close (the beginning of the beginning, the end of the beginning, the beginning of the end, and the end of the end). SGML marked section syntax is not that way, however, and cannot easily be made so by changing delimiters in the SGML declaration, such as:

```
<!-- WRONG -->
<![ IGNORE ] content of marked section []!>
```

The easiest way to avoid any difficulty with the subtleties of marked section delimiters is not to change the delimiters used, namely **MDO**, **DSO**, **MSC**, and **MDC**.

## 7.7. Why can I have only two forms of quote delimiters, and no alternatives for others?

In exactly one case there are alternative delimiters permitted: either single quotes (**LITA**) or double quotes (**LIT**) can enclose a variety of literals, such as attribute values. This appears to be inherited from IBM GML, an early IBM document processing language, which had a similar characteristic.

The distinction is sometimes thought to exist in order to allow putting quotes within quoted literals. However, because entity references are recognized within literals this is not necessary; inserting a single or double quote would be possible anyway. Also, having only the two alternatives does not solve the case where a literal must include *both* single and double quotes.

The notion of alternative delimiters is potentially useful. SGML has similar example as well in that it allows **RE** to act just like the **REFC** delimiter to close an entity reference, as discussed in Question 6.12. A language could permit declaring any number of strings for each delimiter role; however, it seems more elegant to simplify by subtracting the notion completely rather than extending it (the SGML review is likely to provide an option to require **REFC** on all entity references, for example). At this time, SGML provides no way to set up extra alternative forms of quotations marks, or to eliminate the alternative ways to end entity references (see also Question 7.3).

# 7.8. Can name characters occur in delimiters?

Yes, but it is generally inadvisable. The SGML rules for changes to delimiter strings are in Clause 9.6.6, and determine that it is *possible* to do this; *The SGML Handbook* says on p. 364 that "it is not a good idea to do so".

SGML expresses a few exceptions to this generally good advice, since it uses the name character "-" (hyphen) as the **MINUS** delimiter (for marking inclusion exceptions in **ELEMENT** declarations and for indicating whether start- and/or end-tags may be omitted — see Question 7.1 on such dual-use delimiters), and assigns two hyphens as the **COM** delimiter. So it is possible to create cases such as these:

```
<!ELEMENT  FOO--           - - (#PCDATA)>
<!ELEMENT  FOO-            - - (#PCDATA)>
<!ELEMENT  -- remove later -- FOO-
                           - - (#PCDATA)>
<!ELEMENT  FOO             -- - - -- O O (#PCDATA)>
```

The first case declares an element type whose name is "FOO--". The second declares one whose name is "FOO-", as does the third but with a comment before the element type name. The last case declares just "FOO", but comments out the hyphens used to indicate minimization options so that the actual options are "O O", not "- -". These cases arise because both comments and names can have double hyphens, and both can appear in many places within markup declarations (as in the last case above).

Comments are not generally mentioned in upper-level grammar rules, but are instead considered a component of separators (particularly ps and ds — see below for the formal rules) as in Clause 11.2 which makes the examples above valid:

[116] element declaration =
  **mdo**, "ELEMENT", *ps+*, *element type*,
  ( *ps+*, *omitted tag minimization* )?,
  *ps+*, ( *declared content* | *content model* ),
  *ps**, **mdc**

A comment as the last part of the ps *before* an element type (as in the third case above) is not a conflict, because a GI cannot *start* with a hyphen (hyphen is a name character but not a name start character). However, a comment as the first part of the ps following the element type introduces what might appear to be a conflict:

```
<!ELEMENT  ABC-- remove later --
                           - - (#PCDATA)>
```

Is the "--" part of the GI or the start of a comment? In SGML it is part of the GI because of matching rules that apply left to right. For example, Clause 9.6.4 states: that the longest matchable delimiter applies (it could not be otherwise, or there would be no way to specify the longer delimiter at all).

As a parser collects the characters of a GI, it does not know enough to stop at ABC ("ABC--" is a perfectly valid GI, if also an inadvisable one). So in this case it will find a 5-character GI and then report that "remove" is not a valid omitted tag minimization, declared content, or content model. Thus a comment after any SGML name must be preceded by some other kind of ps portion such as whitespace, entity end, or a parameter entity reference.

> **Note:** Although a parameter entity reference only fulfills the SGML grammar rules in some respects (see Appendix C on SGML Grammar Productions), it does serve to terminate the GI in any case, because a name token is not recognized if split across an entity boundary.

Unlike ps, the ts separator does not allow comments; it is used in many smaller DTD constructs such as "name group". The element type in an element declaration can be specified as a name group instead of just an element name; name group in turn is defined in Clause 10.1.3 (p. 374) as:

[69] name group =
    **grpo**, *ts**, *name*, (*ts**, *connector*, *ts**, *name*)*, *ts**, **grpc**

Since ts supports parameter entity references but not comments, no comment can follow a name in the group at all, and so the rule about longest matching does not even come up. Question 7.3 discusses some other issues with comment delimiters.

The omnipresent hyphen leads to potential complications in SGML DTDs. However, the delimiters in which it occurs are recognized only in declarations, so the only uses (and potential complexities) in document instances are buried inside of constructs such as comment declarations, and authors seldom encounter them. Question 7.9, on SGML separators, discusses more about such interactions between whitespace and comments.

> **Note:** Most computer languages allow underscores in names, but not hyphens. This reduces confusion because the hyphen character is commonly meaningful (for subtraction) but the underscore is not. Scheme and its relatives are one exception, but the subtraction operator is just a symbol named " - " so the usage doesn't get in the way; Cobol is another exception.
>
> SGML's choice may reflect a more general reluctance to accommodate negative numbers — SGML lacks notions of numbers other than positive integers; HyTime adds positive rational numbers, and those only for scaling measurement units (such as inches to meters). Combined units such as meters per second are not supported, nor are real-number operations, such as scaling degrees to radians. A minus sign in HyTime does not indicate values less than zero, merely counting backward from the end of a range.

## 7.9. What are "separators" in SGML?

SGML defines four different kinds of "separators", which are used between tokens in various SGML constructs. They generally have no significance beyond their use to separate other tokens; they can contain whitespace, and various selections of other things such as comments.

Separators also interact with how SGML entities are managed, since the recognition of entity references, as well as the matching of the results of expanding those references, are both expressed in the grammar (on which see Appendix C). Likewise, certain constraints about what entities may contain are implemented in the SGML grammar by prohibiting the Entity-end signal from occurring within certain separators.

The four separator types are s, ps, ts, and ds (short for separator, parameter separator, token separator, and declaration separator). The ps and ts separators are involved in the rules discussed in Question 7.8, where they affect how names and comments interact.

The recognized things in each separator type's SGML grammar rule are summarized in the table below:

| Component | s | ps | ts | ds |
|---|---|---|---|---|
| **Clause where defined:** | **6.2.1** | **10.1.1** | **10.1.3** | **10.1.4** |
| **SPACE** | Y | Y | Y | Y |
| **RE** | Y | Y | Y | Y |
| **RS** | Y | Y | Y | Y |
| **SEPCHAR** | Y | Y | Y | Y |
| Ee (entity end — subject to constraints in each case) | | Y | Y | Y |
| parameter entity reference | | Y | Y | Y |
| comment | | Y | | |
| comment declaration | | | | Y |
| processing instruction | | | | Y |
| marked section declaration | | | | Y |

Comments (as in many other computer languages) function much like whitespace, which is one reason they can be used to escape markup characters as described in Question 3.7; but they may only occur in parameter separators.

Parameter entity references are listed as permissible parts of separators (other than s) to indicate where they are and are not recognized. However, the result of such a reference will typically be some tokens that are not part of the separator, but must match against higher grammar rules. Their content is also constrained by certain prose rules particular to each separator type in which a parameter entity reference can occur (the Clauses also have various other prose constraints not discussed here):

- In ps: Must contain *zero* or more complete parameters, and cannot include the end of the declaration where it started.
- In ts: Must contain *one* or more complete parameters, and cannot include the end of the parenthesized group where it started.
- In ds: Must contain *zero* or more entire markup declarations or recursive *ds* separators.

Relevant parts of SGML's separator definitions appear below; accompanying prose portions state some additional constraints:

6.2.1 **S Separator**

[5] s = SPACE | RE | RS | SEPCHAR

10.1.1 **Parameter Separator**

[65] ps = *s* | **Ee** | *parameter entity reference* | *comment*

10.1.3 **Group...**

[70] ts = *s* | **Ee** | *parameter entity reference*

10.1.4 **Declaration Separator**

[71] ds = *s* | **Ee** | *parameter entity reference* | *comment declaration* | *processing instruction* | *marked section declaration*

Clearly the four separator types are quite similar, but they differ in many details such as on whether end-of-entity or parameter entity references are allowed. One other difference is seldom-noticed but can be quite important: A parameter entity whose reference is part of a separator, may be null for ds and ps, but *must* contain at least one complete token in the case of ts. Since ts is the separator used in groups such as content models, entities cannot readily provide all the kinds of DTD extensibility desired. See Question 4.8 for further details.

Given these details, it is worth double-checking the SGML grammar to see exactly which kind of whitespace is used in any given case (see Clauses 10.1.3, 11.2.1, 11.2.4, and 11.2.4.4, though some of these uses are uncommon). Syd Bauman has pointed out at least one case that remains mysterious even then: SGML does not require a separator between the GI and a following attribute in a start-tag, even though it is clearly necessary to prevent ambiguity (other rules such as for markup declarations do require spaces after element type names in similar contexts):

**7.4 Start-tag**

[14] start-tag = ( **stago**, *document type specification*, *generic identifier specification*, *attribute specification list*, *s**, **tagc**) | *minimized start-tag*

**7.9 Attribute Specification List**

[31] attribute specification list = *attribute specification**

[32] attribute specification = *s**, (*name*, *s**, **vi**, *s**)?, *attribute value specification*

**Note**: Subtle interactions when delimiters come together is not a problem unique to SGML. For example, comments in the C programming language begin with "/*", but dividing x by whatever y points to can be expressed as "x/*y", which is a notorious trap for C programmers. Comments are an especially bad construct to have accidentally opened, because they may close much later, and if things fall just right the result may be syntactically valid but completely wrong. Programmers can spent days discovering a missing comment-close delimiter in a program, that deletes a few lines but produces no syntax errors.

## 7.10. Why can't `SHORTREF` delimiters contain the letter 'B'?

When defining short reference delimiters (see Clause 4.6.3) the delimiter to be matched must be given literally, with the possible exception that one sequence of one or more "`B`"s may occur as a wildcard. Such a sequence will match a string of literal spaces ("blanks") and/or separator characters (normally tab, but not carriage return or linefeed) containing at least as many characters as the number of `B`s.

Because of this, "`B`" cannot be used literally in a short reference. "`B`" is not itself a delimiter and cannot be changed via the SGML declaration. It is not clear what would happen in a non-English character set that does not contain the letter B — it has occasionally been suggested that such a character set is not worth supporting, but that seems wrong.

SGML specifically deprecates many kinds of short reference strings (such as any longer than 1 character except "a common keyboarding convention or coding sequence", and ones containing delimiters if they are "likely to create the impression that the delimiter was erroneously ignored" — see Clause 13.4.6). Nevertheless, it does not deprecate short references containing alphabetic characters.

Although many do not find them useful very often, **`SHORTREF`**s can be handy to accommodate common keyboarding conventions for special kinds of content, such as equations, tables, and non-Latin-based writing systems such as Greek. For example, a transliteration system called BetaCode is common for representing Classical and Biblical Greek, and is best accommodated in SGML by creating **SHORTREF**s with delimiter strings that include letters. BetaCode uses simple English analogs: s for sigma, m for mu, and so on (there is some difference in practice over xi). Vowels with accents and similar diacritical marks (of which Greek has many) are represented with punctuation marks generally following the vowels: alpha with an acute accent would be "a/". If a character set attempts to define each combination separately rather than defining accents as separate "combinable" characters, **SHORTREF** can accommodate this and similar schemes (although it requires quite a long map, listing every case individually):

```
<!SHORTREF greek-map
   "a/"      alphaacute
   "a\"      alphagrave
   "a(\,"    alpharoughgraveiota
...>
<!USEMAP   greek       greek-map>
```

Fortunately, in ancient Greek beta does not take accents, so a direct conflict with "B" does not arise. However, there are other cases to worry about: Consonants can take accents, as both Greek scholars and linguists in general can testify; and manuscript scholars have myriad special marks that look a lot like accents and can appear on any letters at all.

There are other accent-representation schemes that use letters to stand for accents when following some "join" character (which at one time was thought of as a backspace): Thus, "a+C" might mean "a combined with Circumflex accent", and "o+B" would mean "o combined with Breve accent", thus motivating a **SHORTREF** delimiter containing B.

> **Note:** Interestingly, this method is very common in SCRIPT, a mainframe formatter used with IBM GML.

SGML is unusual in using a letter as the wildcard character. Many computer users are familiar with wildcards, but always expressed as some punctuation mark (usually ".", "?", or "*"). There is also no way to "escape" the "B" so it can be used literally (many languages support this via "\" before the special character), or to redefine the wildcard character. Escaping would allow short references with all alphabetic characters, or preferably, any characters at all. Blank sequences could be handled with a general mechanism such as regular expressions, thus gaining flexibility and power while requiring no rocket science. See also Question 6.9 for a discussion of how standard regular expressions could be used to good advantage with attribute declared values.

The easiest way to avoid any issues with "B" is to avoid **SHORTREF**, or at least to avoid wildcards or "B" entirely in **SHORTREF**s.

## 7.11. How can I tell whether my delimiter change creates a conflict?

Because of the complexity of SGML's delimiter set and the many interactions and context-dependent rules, it may sometimes be hard to predict whether a given change will produce conflicts. Thus this question comes up when designers want to use variant concrete syntaxes. The best solution is not to change the delimiters, or to be very certain you consider all possible conflicts.

For example, adding "/" and ":" to the set of permissible name characters may be desired (for example, to facilitate using existing HTML documents with unquoted URL attributes as-is within SGML and HyTime systems):

```
<!-- WRONG unless you add name characters -->
<A HREF=http://reality.sgi.com/csp/ioccc/index.html>
```

However, this change has the perhaps-subtle side-effect that you can no longer use the **NET** delimiter freely: it won't work immediately following a non-quoted attribute or a GI, but will instead be taken as part of the previous name token (since it's now a name character):

```
<!-- WRONG -->
<EMPH TYPE=STRONG/wow/
<MENU/File/
```

**NET** would still work after a quoted attribute, however, should someone try it there:

```
<EMPH TYPE="STRONG"/wow/
```

There are other subtle cases as well. One is that a DTD designer may want to set **TAGC** to space or carriage return to accommodate certain older markup systems such as SCRIPT or troff. Such a delimiter change, however, would make it difficult to use attributes because they are generally set off from the GI by space, which after this change would end the tag instead:

```
.sk A new line
.pp And a following paragraph.
```

Setting **VI** (normally "=") to space would also create a conflict, since space is permissible in the same syntactic positions as **VI**, namely in attribute specification lists. Thus it is it hard to support attributes that resemble parameters in command-line operating systems, such as:

```
<MAIL USER 'sjd' SUBJECT 'Delimiters'>
```

While attribute syntax with an explicit "=" seems far preferable, older markup systems like that shown do exist and being able to accommodate them could be useful.

In practice, it is usually best to avoid this entire class of issues and the task of figuring out what delimiter changes are permissible and what side effects (if any) they have, by sticking with the reference concrete syntax.

## 7.12. What if I need to add a lot of name characters (like Kanji characters)

To permit Japanese tag names a document needs an SGML declaration that lists every permissible added name character (see Clause 13.4.5, p. 463). Unless the system accepts SGML declarations that are themselves encoded with wide characters they must be entered via character entities:

```
...
UCNMSTRT "&#257;&#258;&#259
...
&#49999;&#50000;
```

Assuming 50,000 important characters (if anything, that figure is too low), such a declaration occupies about 400K or 200 pages (and the length of the parameter literal might pose problems). It would be more efficient to specify large ranges of values instead of having to list every value in the range.

The excellent news is that the SGML committee recently amended the syntax of SGML declarations to allow such specifications. This enhancement was crucial to make SGML usable in Asian language environments.

## 7.13. Why must all my names (and all SGML's built-in ones) be limited to 8 characters?

The default SGML declaration places a limit of 8 characters on the length of SGML names such as GIs, attribute and entity names, and `ID`s. These limits are called "quantities"; there are also limits on how many `ID`s, GIs, and other objects can occur in a document, called "capacities" (they can be changed via the SGML declaration). This kind of limit was very common in older software although it has largely (not entirely) disappeared now. The setting in your SGML declaration that controls the maximum length of SGML names (such as element, attribute, and entity names) is called **NAMELEN**.

The typical arguments for such limits are based on storage and programming concerns: longer names take up too much space, or make it harder to implement tables of names. This is purely a conflict between user convenience and implementer convenience. For good reason, authors like names that are familiar descriptive words. Many words are longer than 8 characters (linguistically speaking many shorter words are also function words like "the" and "of", and are not very useful for labeling things). Since implementers must do the slight extra work to support long names only once per system while authors deal with those names millions of times, it seems a wise investment.

> **Note:** From a computer science standpoint, such memory savings are illusory. Although it seems economical that each name does not need to know how long it is, storing all the names in equal-sized areas means that *every* name takes up as much space as the longest *permissible* name. Checking lengths needn't force implementers to store names that way, but checking is relatively pointless otherwise.

A third argument is sometimes made that unless the size and quantity of all values is known in advance a program is bound to fail on large input. Any program that remembers cumulative information must fail on large enough input because every computer has limited memory. A validating SGML parser has cumulative information, mainly the list of `ID`s that have occurred (so it can test for uniqueness). However. there is no particular reason a program has to fail "just in case" before it starts, rather than reporting the error if it actually arises. Furthermore, counting sizes and quantities takes time and memory, so a program that counts will have less capacity free for its primary task, and be unable to handle documents as large as it could if it didn't count them.

The same holds for the author's time: an author who slips past an SGML limit on number-of-`IDs` does not want to stop, learn about capacity validation, count `IDs` by hand, learn SGML declaration syntax, change a number, and re-run the parser. Most would rather set a capacity limit ridiculously high so it is never hit, or do nothing at all unless and until they really have a document that can't possibly be handled. If they *do* exceed their system's capacity, they don't want to modify the SGML declaration after they buy more RAM (or merely "Quit" from another program to free up space!). Even if a need could be shown for pre-allocating everything, it is easier for a program to scan the document and figure out how many `IDs`, GIs, etc. it will need, than for an author to do so manually and tell the computer via the SGML declaration.

The fundamental problem is that this way of thinking about system capacity leads to frequent false alarms: failures that arise only because the calculation or possibly the implementation is naïve. SGML's model is that the parser must check that it really could deal with the largest document that the capacity settings theoretically permit, and fail if not. Failure is based on not having enough resources for the worst case combination: every individual capacity used to the theoretical maximum. Capacity is calculated this way even though the present document may be tiny, or may have lots of `IDs` but few GIs, short names, and so on.

> **Note**: This is similar to the way memory and disk space were assigned in many mainframe systems of the 70's: each user got a fixed space, without any sharing based on how much each program was *using* of its maximum permitted space at any given time.

It seems better to save memory by:

- deleting all the code and memory used up by counting limits,
- allocating only the space needed for each actual name (and not extra blanks), and
- using memory for `IDs`, attributes, GIs, or anything else as they actually come up, instead of reserving the theoretical maximum space to each category up front.

Such a program can use that saved space to handle larger documents, and need only fail when it's *truly* out of memory, which will be later than it would have been given the other model. Software that uses dynamic memory management instead of fixed-size table can still detect when it runs out of memory and tell the user exactly what happened and where:

> Ran out of memory processing the 3,942,167th ID attribute, on `<P ID="sec1">` at line 2419 of the entity in file `c:\documents\small\747.sgm`.

Really good software will go even further and recover gracefully. For example, it could shift the list of `IDs` to a disk file and free up all the memory space to use for other things), or stop validating `IDs` for uniqueness. The goal here is not to define or explain how a parser might work, but merely to point out that limitations on name lengths are not necessary.

In current SGML practice, many parsers do not implement capacities. For those that do, the best approach is to turn capacity and quantity validation off if possible, or to simply set high but not enormous limits on quantities and capacities in your SGML declaration. The SGML review is likely to make capacities and quantities completely optional.

# 7.14. Why does extending my DTD by changing inclusions or content models cause line breaks to appear or disappear?

As described in Question 2.5, whether a given **RE** is ignored or not can depend on whether adjacent elements are valid by virtue of being inclusion exceptions. This has the possibly surprising effect that changing a DTD slightly can change the line-breaking or other appearance of documents. For example, making `FOOTNOTE` or `FIGURE` more generally available by moving it from a content model, to an inclusion or a higher-level inclusion, can make instances of those elements "improper" where they were "proper" before (while valid in both cases); that can affect just which nearby **RE**s are ignored.

*The SGML Handbook* (p. 152) recommends exceptions as a way to allow subelements "that are not part of the element structure" and to "allow modification of 'read-only' DTDs". It is important to be aware of the difference in whitespace handling that can arise in the former case. It is also not entirely trivial to modify a "read-only" DTD in this way, since the declaration subset cannot replace an existing **ELEMENT** declaration (only an **ENTITY** declaration — see Clause 11.2.1).

To permit modification by adding exceptions from the internal declaration subset the writer of the "read-only" DTD has to provide explicitly for it ahead of time. The Text Encoding Initiative has provided a "parameterized" form of their DTD that supports this. Each declaration expands to something like:

```
<!ENTITY    % p.gi       "P">
<!ENTITY    % p.con      "#PCDATA">
<!ENTITY    % p.incl     "FOOTNOTE">
<!ENTITY    % p.excl     "CHAPTER">
<!ELEMENT   %p.gi;       - - (%p.con;) -(%p.incl;) +(%p.excl;)>
```

This provides the modification capability, but the cost is high enough that the TEI also provides a non-parameterized form (that is probably used more often). There is also one subtle limitation: parameter entity references within ts separators are required to contain at least one token (see Question 7.9). So it is illegal to put references anywhere inside content models, exceptions, or other similar places unless they always add some token(s): they cannot be inserted simply as placeholders for later extensibility. The usual workaround is to put one item in such entities that will always be desired there.

Customization could be enabled in several ways within SGML itself, and stylesheet mechanisms can be set up without defining every possible context in advance, making such changes more efficient. Among the ways to add such syntax would be defining **ELEMENT** declarations either to be overridable (like SGML **ENTITY** declarations) or additive. Additive declarations could be useful even in the simplest-to-define case, where they could only add exceptions, as shown here:

```
<!EXCEPTIONS P          -(SPEECH) +(FOOTNOTE | SIDEBAR)>
```

The SGML review is likely to add a way to extend attribute declarations (see Question 4.8), but it is not clear whether a similar enhancement will be made for element declarations. In the meantime, customization must be done by actually modifying the DTD in place, or via pre-defined parameter entity hooks.

## 7.15. What is RANK?

The **RANK** feature allows authors to omit the level number part of element type names that end in numbers, such as `DIV1`, `DIV2`, etc. The elements must also be intended to nest in numbered order, with no skipped or repeated levels. This saves a few keystrokes with manual data entry, at the cost of being unable to validate whether "`</DIV>`" is closing the desired level or not.

A more useful advantage is that if you use **RANK**, any `DIV` can be promoted or demoted (say, from `DIV2` to `DIV3`) merely by naive cutting and pasting with no need to renumber all descendants of the same type. On the other hand, editing software can easily accomplish the same thing by scanning the part to be pasted and renumbering the appropriate tags automatically before completing the "Paste" command. That's the sort of things computers are very good at.

Most parsers do not implement **RANK**, most SGML declarations do not set the **RANK** feature to **YES**, and most DTDs do not declare any ranked elements. Thus authors seldom encounter **RANK** in practice. This is probably as it should be.

## 7.16. Can I manipulate parts of elements, or only entire elements using the LINK features?

Three SGML **FEATURES** are commonly referred to together as LINK, even though there is no "LINK" feature as such (the three are **IMPLICIT**, **EXPLICIT**, and **SIMPLE**). The link-related features are sometimes proposed as a way to transform SGML documents without having to resort to separate programs like Perl scripts. It is not commonly known, however, that even when fully implemented these features cannot be used to change to add, delete, reorder, or shift the boundaries of elements in any way. The operations they can do are:

- Substitute a different GI for an element.
- Add new attributes to an existing element (but not in the same name space as pre-existing ones: for example, they may duplicate names already used).

These changes can be done on a per-element type basis: you can change `P` elements into `PARA` elements, while also changing `PARA` to `QUOTE`. It is also possible to swap in a different set of changes based on certain limited contextual information. This makes it possible to limit a change to a certain Qualified GI (QGI), such as only `FOOTNOTE` within `LIST`. However, this can get complex.

The larger question is whether you can reach down inside an element and add markup. For example, if you do not have a formatter that can create drop-initial capital letters directly but you need the effect, you may want to enclose the first letter of the first `P` in each `SECTION` in a new element, such as `DROPCAP`:

```
<SECTION><P><DROPCAP>T</DROPCAP>he quality of typography is
not strained.</P>
```

Since this is a makeshift solution for getting a formatting effect rather than a real claim about document structure, it would be best not to *actually* re-tag the document this way. LINK seems appropriate for this case because it allows certain on-the-fly markup changes during parsing. However, LINK cannot achieve this kind of effect because it provides no way to refer to (or "locate" or "address") anything that is not an element already; in this case the first character of every `SECTION`, around which a new element is to be created.

> **Note:** Of course you can create a stylesheet language that does have such an addressing mechanism, and then use LINK to add expressions in *that* language onto elements. For example you could add a "drop-cap the character 37 bytes over in my content" attribute to the `SECTION` above. Or you can create an SGML transformation language that allows you to introduce new elements wherever needed (DSSSL can do this very nicely). But since in either case you must build a more powerful tool, you can skip LINK and learn just one tool.

The DSSSL, HyTime, and Text Encoding Initiative location models can all refer to such specific locations easily (see Questions 6.11 and 5.11 for more on these). DSSSL has the additional benefit that it provides a general mechanism to transform SGML document structures and to associate formatting effects with any character or other structure once it is located.

Many similar examples are needed in high-quality typesetting: marking the first word, sentence, or even line of each block to make it bold; emphasizing the first occurrence of certain terms; replacing the author name by "--------" for all but their first work listed in a bibliography. There are also non-formatting examples, such as changing between two common ways of tagging definition lists:

```
<DEFLIST>
   <TERM>drop-cap</TERM>
   <DEFN>A letter that hangs down a few lines.</DEFN>
   <TERM>drop-cap(2)</TERM>
   <DEFN>To misplace one's hat</DEFN>
</DEFLIST>
```

versus:

```
<DEFLIST>
   <DEFITEM>
      <TERM>drop-cap</TERM>
      <DEFN>A letter that hangs down a few lines.</DEFN>
   </DEFITEM>
   <DEFITEM>
      <TERM>drop-cap(2)</TERM>
      <DEFN>To misplace one's hat</DEFN>
   </DEFITEM>
</DEFLIST>
```

When there is need to make such changes, LINK is not a viable approach. The best workaround is to insert the tagging with some kind of a global-change process (anything from an editor's "change" command on up to a DSSSL grove transformation). Depending on how meaningful the addition is, it may be wise to make the generated markup conditional. For example, insertions can go in a conditional marked section or in an entity, so they can be turned on and off at will:

```
<!ENTITY   % item-grp  "IGNORE">
...
<DEFLIST>
   <![ %item-grp;  [<DEFITEM>]]>
           <TERM>drop-cap</TERM>
           <DEFN>A letter that hangs down a few lines.</DEFN>
   <![ %item-grp;  [</DEFITEM>]]>
</DEFLIST>
```

or

```
<!ENTITY   di.start     "<DEFITEM>">
<!ENTITY   di.end       "</DEFITEM>">
...
<DEFLIST>
   &di.start;
           <TERM>drop-cap</TERM>
           <DEFN>A letter that hangs down a few lines.</DEFN>
   &di.end;
</DEFLIST>
```

**Note**: Transforming between markup alternatives like these often raises questions in relation to HyTime architectural forms. Architectural forms are templates for element types, which abstract away from specific GIs and let you define multiple GIs that share a common structure. This is extremely useful, but designers should be aware that even slight changes of structure can make different element types ineligible to be unified under a single architectural form. For example, an architectural form for lists would either have or lack a grouping construct as shown for `DEFITEM` above, and be incompatible with the other form. It could "or" the two constructs, but this must be thought of in advance, and cannot handle more complex cases.

In short, LINK offers a certain range of possibilities for element renaming and attribute addition. However, those possibilities do not cover the full range of common needs, so more powerful tools are also needed, that can do all that and more. Given that and the general lack of support for LINK, it is probably better to use other tools.

# 8. XML: A Simple, Standard Subset

Many of the questions that come up about SGML involve optional features. Most of those optional features provide alternate ways of representing essentially the same document structures. For example, all these are valid ways of starting a `P` element, given the right declarations and context:

```
<P>
<P/
<P
<>

&my.starttag.entity;
&#RE;&#RS;
```

Whichever way the markup is represented, it expresses the same concept and structure: start a `P` element. In a WYSIWYG SGML authoring system the user should probably never see any of these: instead they will see some graphical representation of the element itself. Because of all this, it is clear that a subset of SGML that omitted these options could be created.

Such a subset could still represent the full range of information structures that SGML can, but have many fewer special cases. This would save learning time for authors, and implementation time and bug-counts for implementers. For example, no one need deal with the rule that "/" after a GI has a special meaning if **NET**-enabling start-tags were never used.

Many SGML experts have pointed this out, and many have proposed formal subsets. Subsets state simplifying conventions that express structure using simpler syntax. Likewise, many SGML authors and publishers impose such constraints on their own SGML usage in order to gain consistency, efficiency, and other cost-saving benefits.

The word "subset" here can easily be misunderstood. A "subset" of SGML is not a DTD. It is a set of choices of just which SGML capabilities and alternatives are used. Because of this, once you make an actual subset,

> any document that conforms to the subset also conforms to SGML.

However, this is *completely* different from saying that every conforming SGML document also conforms to the subset. To get that property as well, you're back to exactly the full set of all SGML options, which is not a subset in the usual sense.

For example, anyone can decide they will never use **NET** in their documents. This defines an SGML subset: any SGML document that uses **NET** does not conform to the subset, but any document that conforms to the subset still conforms to SGML too; it just happens to never use **NET**. That's what it means to be a subset.

> **Note**: In mathematics, any set is an "improper" subset of itself, so SGML with all its options could be called an improper subset of SGML (though it would not usually be helpful to do so).

This chapter summarizes may of the proposals that have been advanced for creating an effective subset of SGML. The many proposals have finally come together in a formal committee sponsored by the World Wide Web Consortium. This committee has produced a complete formal definition of a subset, called the eXtensible Markup Language, or XML. The latest revision of that specification is also included here. It totals about 20 pages, which is a sign of how simplified it is. Yet it retains the flexibility and structural power originally built into the SGML standard.

I believe that XML has great potential to bring the flexibility and power of SGML to a far larger audience. The fact that major Web browser vendors and other software developers appear likely to add support for it (some have already) adds to its broad appeal and ease of use.

## 8.1. Related work

This book is far from the only place where the idea can be found that SGML can be made simpler and more elegant without loss of functionality: that the brilliance of SGML lies in its methodology and flexibility rather than in particular syntax details. The Text Encoding Initiative, Eliot Kimber, Wayne Wohler, Joe Gangemi, Dan Connolly, Tim Bray, Erik Naggum, and many computer scientists and others who use SGML have all proposed various simplifications to ease use of SGML. Perhaps the most convincing testimony is the World Wide Web itself, and its huge success using only a tiny subset of SGML's capabilities.

### Earlier efforts

Many individuals and organizations have designed subsets of SGML that are more remarkable for their similarity than for their differences:

- The SGML standard defines two subsets, "Basic SGML documents" and "Minimal SGML documents" (in clause 15). These subsets of course had to be defined before there was extensive user experience of SGML, so a few complex bits are required even in the minimal subset, and a few simple but useful features are excluded.
- Software implementers have discovered that most customers do not want all the options, and almost no parsers have implemented all of the SGML options. It is far more common to implement "Basic SGML Documents," which use very few SGML features.

> **Note**: The first version of *Dyna*Text, a general browsing and retrieval system for SGML documents up to hundreds of Megabytes in size, supported only a small subset of SGML syntax when it first appeared in 1990 (it supports far more now). It quickly became the software of choice for SGML document delivery, presumably because it did *not* omit crucial structure and flexibility capabilities: arbitrary/extensible tag sets, separation of style from content, hierarchical structure, large documents, complex hypertext, and searching that is aware of the structure.

- In 1990 the Text Encoding Initiative published the first edition of its encoding guidelines, including a subset specification for interchange. This is now known as the "TEI Interchange Subset", as part of the TEI *Guidelines* for using SGML for scholarly, literary, and similar documents (Questions 6.11, 5.19 and 4.11 discuss various aspects of the *Guidelines*). The formal grammar there defines a proper subset of SGML documents that is very easy to parse.
- Wayne Wohler and Eliot Kimber developed a subset called "Monastic SGML". It was presented in a poster session at the SGML '93 conference. Others have cut it even smaller and playfully called it "Ascetic SGML".
- C. M. Sperberg-McQueen and staff at the University of Illinois developed "Poor-Folks SGML" or PSGML. It is defined in "PSGML: Poor-Folks SGML: A Subset of SGML for Use in Distributed Applications", Document UIC CC DB92-10. This was dated October 8, 1992 (www.uic.edu/~cmsmcq/uic/db92-10.tei or www.uic.edu/ ~cmsmcq/uic/db92-10.html).
- Rick Jelliffe developed "MiniSGML". It was defined in a posting to the comp.text.sgml newsgroup on September 28, 1994.
- Eliot Kimber developed "SGML Online" (SO). It is defined in "SGML Revision, Proposal for Minimal SGML Feature Set" (a draft existed as early as June 3, 1996. It is accessible at www.textuality.com/sgml-erb/kimber/index.html). This proposes dividing up SGML's "optional feature" setting more finely, so the complex *portions* of some current features can be separately turned off.
- Dan Connolly developed "LA". It is defined in "A Lexical Analyzer for HTML and Basic SGML: W3C Working Draft", dated June 15, 1996, and is available online at www.w3.org/pub/WWW/TR/WD-sgml-lex.
- Henry Thompson, David McKelvie, and Steve Finch developed "Normalised SGML" (NSGML). It is defined in "The Normalised SGML Library (NSL)". NSL Version 1.4.4 is dated August 2, 1996 and is available from www.ltg.ed.ac.uk/corpora/ nsldoc/nsldoc.html.
- Tim Bray, Erik Naggum, C. M. Sperberg-McQueen and I started a mail group to work on a formal proposal after the SGML '95 conference, and worked out a set of design goals and basic approaches, though we never published them widely.
- Tim Bray developed "Minimal Generalized Markup Language" (MGML), defined in a paper for SGML '96 (www.textuality.com/mgml/index.html).

The archives of comp.text.sgml (available, among other places, at ftp.ifi.uio.no/pub/ SGML/comp.text.sgml) reveal many others advocating simplifications as well.

Nearly all these proposals take a basically similar approach, often including:

- Using no SGML features except **SHORTTAG**, sometimes **OMITTAG**, and occasionally **FORMAL**.
- Picking just some parts of **SHORTTAG** such as attribute defaulting and omission of quotes around attributes, while leaving out other parts such as **NET**-enabling start-tags, empty tags, and so on.
- Ruling out delimiter changes.
- Assuming larger limits (or no limits) on capacities and quantities.

- Requiring all constructs to be aligned with elements: no entities or marked sections containing an element's start but not its end, or vice versa (Questions 2.11 and 2.12).
- Ruling out constructs that have long-distance, unaligned effects, such as **`#CURRENT`** (see Question 5.16), **`USEMAP`** in the document instance (see Question 3.1), etc.

These changes have little to no effect on the range of structures SGML can represent, and they do not diminish SGML's key values and benefits. They do, however, greatly reduce the range of alternative ways to represent the same structures in raw form (for example, you can start a paragraph with "<P>" but not "<>"). User interfaces continue to advance while the amount of information to be managed increases, and so minimization features grow less crucial while structural power grows more crucial. Thus this kind of simplification is a sensible direction.

## SGML: It's 3, 3, 3 languages in one

One particular SGML simplification is often proposed, even though it is a bigger change than just ignoring options you don't need. This proposal arises from noticing that SGML is really three languages defined in one standard: one language for DTDs, one for SGML declarations, and one for structured document instances. Since DTDs and SGML declarations are obviously "structured documents" in the broad sense they ought to be expressible in the third language, and indeed they are. For example,

```
<!ELEMENT  p              - -  (#PCDATA)>
```

could certainly have other expressions such as shown below:

```
<ELEMENT gi="P" startMin="NO" endMin="NO">
   (#PCDATA)
</ELEMENT>
```

Obviously there are many variations possible. A straight conversion of DTD syntax to a slightly different representation is fairly simple; the difficulties arise if someone wants to tweak it a bit at the same time. Experts differ on the specific question of whether content models should be wholly converted to be composed of elements such as `GROUP`, `AND`, `REP`, and so on, or whether this particular part of DTDs should remain in an operator/parenthesis form (pretty much as-is). I favor the latter position, since I think SGML made just the right choice by using an expression language to represent content models, which are fundamentally expressions.

C. M. Sperberg-McQueen examined the SGML standard and counted the grammar rules for each of these three languages it defines. This led to some interesting findings (I quote here from his mail to the SGML-ERB on 8/29/96):

> ...Long ago, as an aid to study, I divided [the SGML grammar rules] into different files for the SGML declaration, the DTD, the instance, and common constructs. Here are the sizes of the files as I count them; the line counts include dependency trees and cross references. (The files are on the TEI file server, if anyone wants to check my logic or arithmetic.)

| [Item] | [Productions] | | [Lines] | |
|---|---|---|---|---|
| SGML declaration | 33 | | 401 | |
| DTD (w/Misc) | 92 | (139) | 970 | (1371) |
| Instance (w/Misc) | 448 | (849) | 39 | (86) |
| Basics (common constructs) | 47 | | 401 | |

Several early members of the SGML committee have told me that the idea of using instance syntax for DTDs simply never came up. With the benefit of time, the idea has been independently discovered several times since. Besides Sperberg-McQueen's work, Wayne Wohler raised it in July of 1994, and it is said that OmniMark Technologies once created a structured editor for DTDs by converting them back and forth from instance syntax and using an SGML editor (this seems a good tactic). Many SGML experts have advocated this syntax approach in various forums, so it may well occur someday.

## The SGML Review

All ISO standards are reviewed every five years, because changes in usage patterns, user requirements, and technological capabilities occur with time. The 1991 review of SGML showed that it remained effective and widely used (indeed it is one of the most successful ISO standards ever). An amendment earlier had already fixed several errors and added a few things like data entity attributes and the "DSM" recognition mode, so the 1991 review had impressively few problems to address.

The second review is going on now, with Charles Goldfarb remaining as editor, and at the SGML '96 conference SGML committee members Lynne Price and Dave Peterson summarized decisions made so far, including several simplification issues. As of this writing, it seems likely that ISO will quickly ballot a "Technical Corrigendum" (essentially a minor amendment) to implement the most pressing and uncontroversial changes rather than holding them until the end of the entire review (holding them would allow having only one vote instead of two, but it is felt that some minor adjustments are high enough priorities to justify the extra work).

Readers willing to participate in the SGML review process are urged to do so, either through their national standards organizations or through the International SGML User's Group. This group is an official liaison to the SGML committee, and can be reached at:

International SGML Users' Group
PO Box 361, Great Western Way
Swindon, Wiltshire SN5 7BF UK
Phone: +44 1793 512515
Fax: +44 1793 512516
Email: sug@dpsl.co.uk

My colleagues and I have attended ISO and ANSI meetings and keep in touch with those carrying out the review. We have sent numerous contributions and suggestions to the committee, and have presented the vast majority of this book's ideas to the committee and/or individual members of it.

## The W3C XML effort

A very important simplification effort dovetails with this ongoing process, and is sponsored by the World Wide Web Consortium (www.w3.org). The SGML Editorial Review Board (ERB) and SGML Working Group (WG) were chartered to develop a very easy to use, easy to implement subset of SGML for use on the Web and in similar applications. This subset is called XML, and is described in detail in this chapter.

Any valid XML document is also a valid SGML document, and XML and SGML parsers can produce the same structure out of such a document (that is, they'll find the same elements, attributes, etc. in the right places).

XML is a *subset* of SGML because it restricts syntactic options without prescribing a tag set, whereas HTML is an *application* because it mandates a particular set of tags (`P`, `H1`, `B`, etc.) but says little about what syntax features may be used. For example, XML says things like "thou shalt not omit end-tags", but HTML says things like "thou shalt have a `P` tag, but no `POEM` tag".

The XML committees have made swift progress in working out an elegant language that remains a subset of SGML but is easier to learn, implement, and use. The author is a co-editor of the XML specification, and has presented many of this book's ideas in the XML committees as well as learning many things there that have enhanced this book. The SGML-WG has about 100 members, most of whom are experts in SGML. The smaller SGML-ERB leads this effort, and each member has many years of SGML experience:

| | | |
|---|---|---|
| Jon Bosak (chair) | Sun Microsystems | jon.bosak@sun.com |
| Tim Bray | Textuality | tbray@textuality.com |
| James Clark | Individual | jjc@jclark.com |
| Steve DeRose | Inso Corp. Electronic Publishing Solutions (formerly EBT) | sderose@inso.com |
| Dave Hollander | Hewlett-Packard | dmh@hpsgml.fc.hp.com |
| W. Eliot Kimber | Highland Consulting | eliot@isogen.com |
| Tom Magliery | NCSA | mag@ncsa.uiuc.edu |
| Eve Maler | ArborText | elm@arbortext.com |
| Jean Paoli | Microsoft | jeanpa@microsoft.com |
| Peter Sharpe | SoftQuad | peter@sqwest.bc.ca |
| C. M. Sperberg-McQueen | University of Illinois, Chicago | tei@uic.edu |

## 8.2. Excerpts from the XML Working Draft

This section includes excerpts from the current *Working Draft* of the W3C XML specification, as of March 31, 1997. Its formal document number is "WD-xml-lang-970331". Such working drafts are meant for review by W3C members and "other interested parties", which by this time I hope you are. They are most definitely "works in progress" and are subject to being updated, replaced or obsoleted by other documents at any time. It is therefore very important that readers refer to the most recent version.

Web searches for XML show a large and growing number of press releases, analyses, FAQ lists, and other information about XML. There is information about all three parts of XML, not just the simplified SGML syntax part described here. The other two parts involve sophisticated hyperlinking and a very powerful stylesheet mechanism. The XML language specification from which these excerpts are drawn is available on the Web at:

**This version:** www.w3.org/pub/WWW/TR/WD-xml-lang-970331.html
**Previous:** www.w3.org/pub/WWW/TR/WD-xml-961114.html
**Latest:** www.textuality.com/sgml-erb/WD-xml-lang.html

The selections quoted here include parts of the rationale and general description and the formal grammar. Many parts have been omitted, such as descriptions of how the Unicode character set works with XML, and much of the supplemental descriptions of XML syntax (the XML standard itself, however, provides enough information to stand alone). This portion, while small, should give a feel for the general approach and rationale, in hopes you will be motivated to look further into XML.

For definitive information about the current state of any W3C specification, draft or otherwise, look to the official W3C Web site, not to any printed copy. A list of current W3C working drafts can be found at www.w3.org/pub/WWW/TR. The XML syntax specification was edited by Tim Bray and C. M. Sperberg-McQueen. Section numbers below correspond to the working draft (and therefore skip the sections that are not quoted).

## 1. Introduction

The Extensible Markup Language, abbreviated XML, describes a class of data objects called XML documents, and partially describes the behavior of computer programs which process them. XML is an application profile or restricted form of SGML, the Standard Generalized Markup Language [ISO 8879].

XML documents are made up of storage units called entities, which contain either text or binary data. Text is made up of characters, some of which form the character data in the document, and some of which form markup. Markup encodes a description of the document's storage layout and logical structure. XML provides a mechanism to impose constraints on the storage layout and logical structure.

### Design goals for XML

1. XML shall be straightforwardly usable over the Internet.
2. XML shall support a wide variety of applications.
3. XML shall be compatible with SGML.
4. It shall be easy to write programs which process XML documents.
5. The number of optional features in XML is to be kept to the absolute minimum, ideally zero.
6. XML documents should be human-legible and reasonably clear.
7. The XML design should be prepared quickly.
8. The design of XML shall be formal and concise.
9. XML documents shall be easy to create.
10. Terseness in XML markup is of minimal importance.

## 2.2 Well-Formed XML Documents

A textual object is said to be a well-formed XML document if, first, it matches the production labeled document, and if for each entity reference which appears in the document, either the entity has been declared in the document type declaration or the entity name is one of: amp, lt, gt, apos, quot.

Matching the document production implies that:

1. It contains one or more elements.
2. There is exactly one element, called the root, or document element, for which neither the start-tag nor the end-tag is in the content of any other element. For all other elements, if the start-tag is in the content of another element, the end-tag is in the content of the same element. More simply stated, the elements, delimited by start- and end-tags, nest within each other.

As a consequence of this, for each non-root element C in the document, there is one other element P in the document such that C is in the content of P, but is not in the content of any other element that is in the content of P. Then P is referred to as the parent of C, and C as a child of P.

## 2.8 White Space Handling

In editing XML documents, it is often convenient to use "white space" (spaces, tabs, and blank lines, denoted by the nonterminal `S` in this specification) to set apart the markup for greater readability. Such white space is typically not intended for inclusion in the delivered version of the document. On the other hand, "significant" white space that must be retained in the delivered version is common, for example, in poetry or source code.

An XML processor which does not read the DTD must always pass all characters in a document that are not markup through to the application. An XML processor which does read the DTD must always pass all characters in mixed content that are not markup through to the application. It may also choose to pass white space ocurring in element content to the application; if it does so, it must signal to the application that the white space in question is not significant.

A special attribute may be inserted in documents to signal an intention that the element to which this attribute applies requires all white space to be treated as significant by applications.

In valid documents, this attribute must be declared as follows, if used:

```
XML-SPACE (DEFAULT|PRESERVE) #IMPLIED
```

The value `DEFAULT` signals that applications' default white-space processing modes are acceptable for this element; the value `PRESERVE` indicates the intent that applications preserve all the white space.

The root element of any document, unless this attribute is provided or defaulted with a value of `PRESERVE`, is considered to have signaled no intentions as regards application space handling. Any space handling behavior specified for an element by the `XML-SPACE` attribute is inherited by that element's child elements as well.

## 2.9 Prolog and Document Type Declaration

XML documents may, and should, begin with an XML declaration which specifies, among other things, the version of XML being used.

The function of the markup in an XML document is to describe its storage and logical structures, and associate attribute-value pairs with the logical structure. XML provides a mechanism, the document type declaration, to define constraints on that logical structure and to support the use of predefined storage units. An XML document is said to be valid if there is an associated document type declaration and if the document complies with the constraints expressed in it.

## 4.1 Logical and Physical Structures

The logical and physical structures in an XML document must be synchronous. Tags and elements must each begin and end in the same entity, but may refer to other entities internally; comments, processing instructions, character references, and entity references must each be contained entirely within a single entity. Entities must each contain an integral number of elements, comments, processing instructions, and references, possibly together with character data not contained within any element in the entity, or else they must contain non-textual data, which by definition contains no elements.

## 4.3 Entity Declarations

The SystemLiteral that follows the keyword `SYSTEM` is called the entity's system identifier. It is a URL, which may be used to retrieve the entity. Unless otherwise provided by information outside the scope of this specification (e.g. a special XML element defined by a particular DTD, or a processing instruction defined by a particular application specification), relative URLs are relative to the location of the entity or file within which the entity declaration occurs. Relative URLs in entity declarations within the internal DTD subset are thus relative to the location of the document; those in entity declarations in the external subset are relative to the location of the files containing the external subset.

In addition to a system literal, an external identifier may include a public identifier. An XML processor may use the public identifier to try to generate an alternative URL. If the processor is unable to do so, it must use the URL specified in the system literal.

### XML and SGML

XML is designed to be a subset of SGML, in that every valid XML document should also be a conformant SGML document, using the same DTD, and that the parse trees produced by an SGML parser and an XML processor should be the same. To achieve this, XML was defined by removing features and options from the specification of SGML.

The following list describes syntactic characteristics which XML does not allow but which are legal in SGML. The list may not be complete.

- Comment declarations must have the delimiters `<!-- comment text -->` and can't have spaces within the markup of `<!--` or `-->`.
- No comments (`--` ... `--`) inside markup declarations.
- Comment declarations can't jump in and out of comments with `-- --`.
- No name groups for declaring multiple elements or making a single `ATTLIST` declaration apply to multiple elements.
- No `CDATA` or `RCDATA` declared content in element declarations.
- No exclusions or inclusions on content models.
- No minimization parameters on element declarations.
- Mixed content models must be optional-repeatable `OR`-groups, with `#PCDATA` first.
- No `AND` (&) content model groups.
- No `NAME[S]`, `NUMBER[S]`, or `NUTOKEN[S]` declared values for attributes.
- No `#CURRENT` or `#CONREF` declared values for attributes.
- Attribute default values must be quoted.
- Marked sections can't have spaces within the markup of `<![keyword[` or `]]>`.
- No `RCDATA`, `TEMP`, `IGNORE`, or `INCLUDE` marked sections in document instances.
- Marked sections in instances must use the `CDATA` keyword literally, not a parameter entity.
- No `SDATA`, `CDATA`, or bracketed internal entities.
- No `SUBDOC`, `CDATA`, or `SDATA` external entities.
- No public identifiers in `ENTITY`, `DOCTYPE`, and `NOTATION` declarations.
- No data attributes on `NOTATION`s or attribute value specifications on `ENTITY` declarations.
- No `SHORTREF` declarations.
- No `USEMAP` declarations.
- No `LINKTYPE` declarations.

- No `LINK` declarations.
- No `USELINK` declarations.
- No `IDLINK` declarations.
- No SGML declarations.

The specific SGML declaration needed to enable SGML systems to process XML documents will vary from document to document...

## 8.3. XML Grammar Productions

This section includes the formal grammar rules of XML as specified in the working draft of March 31, 1997. These are the rules which would guide an implementer building support for XML, although there is other material in the XML specification that would also be needed. The production rules are included to show how elegantly simple the language is, to give a flavor for what it does and does not include in the SGML subset it defines, and to provide a convenient introduction for the technically inclined reader. This grammar should not be taken as definitive, since the committees developing XML may make changes. Always consult the latest draft or version, available at the W3C web site, for accurate and up-to-date information.

<table>
<tr><th>#</th><th>Name</th><th>::=<br>/* comment */ or [well-formedness/validity constraints]</th></tr>
<tr><td>1</td><td>S</td><td>(#x0020 | #x0009 | #x000d | #x000a | #x3000)+</td></tr>
<tr><td>2</td><td>Char</td><td>#x09 | #x0A | #x0D | [#x20-#xFFFD]<br>| [#x00010000-#x7FFFFFFF]<br>/* any ISO 10646 31-bit code, FFFE and FFFF excluded */</td></tr>
<tr><td>3</td><td>MiscName</td><td>'.' | '-' | '_' | CombiningChar | Ignorable | Extender</td></tr>
<tr><td>4</td><td>NameChar</td><td>Letter | Digit | MiscName</td></tr>
<tr><td>5</td><td>Name</td><td>(Letter | '_') (NameChar)*</td></tr>
<tr><td>6</td><td>Names</td><td>Name (S Name)*</td></tr>
<tr><td>7</td><td>Nmtoken</td><td>(NameChar)+</td></tr>
<tr><td>8</td><td>Nmtokens</td><td>Nmtoken (S Nmtoken)*</td></tr>
<tr><td>9</td><td>EntityValue</td><td>'"' ([^%&"] | PEReference | Reference)* '"'<br>| "'" ([^%&'] | PEReference | Reference)* "'"</td></tr>
<tr><td>10</td><td>AttValue</td><td>'"' ([^<&"] | Reference)* '"'<br>| "'" ([^<&'] | Reference)* "'"</td></tr>
<tr><td>11</td><td>SystemLiteral</td><td>'"' URLchar* '"'<br>| "'" (URLchar - "'")* "'"</td></tr>
<tr><td>12</td><td>URLchar</td><td>/* See RFC 1738 */</td></tr>
<tr><td>13</td><td>PubidLiteral</td><td>'"' PubidChar* '"'<br>| "'" (PubidChar - "'")* "'"</td></tr>
<tr><td>14</td><td>PubidChar</td><td>#x0020 | #x0009 | #x000d | #x000a | #x3000<br>| [a-zA-Z0-9] | [-'()+,./:=?]</td></tr>
<tr><td>15</td><td>SkipLit</td><td>('"' [^"]* '"') | ("'" [^']* "'")</td></tr>
<tr><td>16</td><td>PCData</td><td>[^<&]*</td></tr>
<tr><td>17</td><td>Comment</td><td>'<!--' (Char* - (Char* '--' Char*)) '-->'</td></tr>
<tr><td>18</td><td>PI</td><td>'<?' Name S (Char* - (Char* '?>' Char*)) '?>'</td></tr>
<tr><td>19</td><td>CDSect</td><td>CDStart CData CDEnd</td></tr>
<tr><td>20</td><td>CDStart</td><td>'<![CDATA['</td></tr>
</table>

<table>
<tr><th>#</th><th>Name</th><th>::=<br>/* comment */ or [well-formedness/validity constraints]</th></tr>
<tr><td>21</td><td>CData</td><td>(Char* - (Char* ']]>' Char*))</td></tr>
<tr><td>22</td><td>CDEnd</td><td>']]>'</td></tr>
<tr><td>23</td><td>document</td><td>Prolog element Misc*</td></tr>
<tr><td>24</td><td>Prolog</td><td>XMLDecl? Misc* (doctypedecl Misc*)?</td></tr>
<tr><td>25</td><td>XMLDecl</td><td>'<?XML' VersionInfo EncodingDecl? RMDecl? S?<br>'?>'</td></tr>
<tr><td>26</td><td>VersionInfo</td><td>S 'version' Eq ('"1.0"' | "'1.0'")</td></tr>
<tr><td>27</td><td>Misc</td><td>Comment | PI | S</td></tr>
<tr><td>28</td><td>doctypedecl</td><td>'<!DOCTYPE' S Name (S ExternalID)? S?<br>('[' markupdecl* ']' S?)? '>'<br>[VC: Root Element Type]@@@[VC: Non-null DTD]</td></tr>
<tr><td>29</td><td>markupdecl</td><td>%( ( %elementdecl | %AttlistDecl | %EntityDecl<br>| %NotationDecl | %conditionalSect | %PI | %S<br>| %Comment )* )</td></tr>
<tr><td>30</td><td>RMDecl</td><td>S 'RMD' Eq "'" ('NONE' | 'INTERNAL' | 'ALL')<br>"'"<br>| S 'RMD' Eq '"' ('NONE' | 'INTERNAL' | 'ALL')<br>'"'</td></tr>
<tr><td>31</td><td>STag</td><td>'<' Name (S Attribute)* S? '>'<br>[WFC: Unique Att Spec]</td></tr>
<tr><td>32</td><td>Attribute</td><td>Name Eq AttValue<br>[VC: Attribute Value Type, No External Entity References]</td></tr>
<tr><td>33</td><td>Eq</td><td>S? '=' S?</td></tr>
<tr><td>34</td><td>ETag</td><td>'</' Name S? '>'</td></tr>
<tr><td>35</td><td>content</td><td>(element | PCData | Reference | CDSect | PI |<br>Comment)*<br>[VC: Content]</td></tr>
<tr><td>36</td><td>element</td><td>EmptyElement | STag content Etag<br>[WFC: GI Match]</td></tr>
<tr><td>37</td><td>EmptyElement</td><td>'<' Name (S Attribute)* S? '/>'</td></tr>
<tr><td>38</td><td>elementdecl</td><td>'<!ELEMENT' S %Name %S %contentspec S? '>'<br>[VC: Unique Element Declaration]</td></tr>
<tr><td>39</td><td>contentspec</td><td>'EMPTY' | 'ANY' | Mixed | elements</td></tr>
<tr><td>40</td><td>elements</td><td>(choice | seq) ('?' | '*' | '+')?</td></tr>
<tr><td>41</td><td>cp</td><td>(Name | choice | seq) ('?' | '*' | '+')?</td></tr>
<tr><td>42</td><td>cps</td><td>S? %cp S?</td></tr>
<tr><td>43</td><td>choice</td><td>'(' S? %(cps ('|' cps)+) S? ')'</td></tr>
<tr><td>44</td><td>seq</td><td>'(' S? %(cps (',' cps)*) S? ')'</td></tr>
<tr><td>45</td><td>Mixed</td><td>'(' S? %( %'#PCDATA' ( S? '|' S? %(%Name (S?<br>'|' S? %Name)*) )* ) S? ')*'<br>| '(' S? %('#PCDATA') S? ')' '*'?</td></tr>
<tr><td>46</td><td>AttlistDecl</td><td>'<!ATTLIST' S %Name S? (%AttDef+)+ S? '>'</td></tr>
<tr><td>47</td><td>AttDef</td><td>S %Name S %AttType S %Default</td></tr>
<tr><td>48</td><td>AttType</td><td>StringType | TokenizedType | EnumeratedType</td></tr>
<tr><td>49</td><td>StringType</td><td>'CDATA'</td></tr>
<tr><td>50</td><td>TokenizedType</td><td>'ID' | 'IDREF' | 'IDREFS' | 'ENTITY' |<br>'ENTITIES' | 'NMTOKEN' | 'NMTOKENS'<br>[VC: [value must fit type]]</td></tr>
<tr><td>51</td><td>EnumeratedType</td><td>NotationType | Enumeration</td></tr>
</table>

<table>
<tr><th>#</th><th>Name</th><th>::=<br>/* comment */ or [well-formedness/validity constraints]</th></tr>
<tr><td>52</td><td>NotationType</td><td>%('NOTATION') S %( '(' S? %( %Name (S? '|' S? %Name)* ) S? ')' )<br>[VC: Notation Attributes]</td></tr>
<tr><td>53</td><td>Enumeration</td><td>'(' S? %( %( %Nmtoken (S? '|' S? %Nmtoken)* S? ) ( '|' %( %Nmtoken (S? '|' S? %Nmtoken)* S? ) )* ) ')'<br>[VC: Enumeration]</td></tr>
<tr><td>54</td><td>Default</td><td>'#REQUIRED' | '#IMPLIED'<br>| ((%'#FIXED' S)? %AttValue)<br>[VC: Attribute Default Legal]</td></tr>
<tr><td>55</td><td>conditionalSect</td><td>includeSect | ignoreSect</td></tr>
<tr><td>56</td><td>includeSect</td><td>'<![' %'INCLUDE' '[' (%markupdecl*)* ']]>'</td></tr>
<tr><td>57</td><td>ignoreSect</td><td>'<![' %'IGNORE' '[' ( ((SkipLit | Comment | PI) - (Char* ']]>' Char*)) | ignoreSect | (Char - ([<'"] | ']'))* | ('<!' (Char - ('-' | '['))*) ) ']]>'</td></tr>
<tr><td>58</td><td>Hex</td><td>[0-9a-fA-F]</td></tr>
<tr><td>59</td><td>CharRef</td><td>'&#' [0-9]+ ';' | '&#x' Hex+ ';'</td></tr>
<tr><td>60</td><td>Reference</td><td>EntityRef | CharRef</td></tr>
<tr><td>61</td><td>EntityRef</td><td>'&' Name ';'<br>[WFC: Entity Declared, Text Entity, No Recursion]</td></tr>
<tr><td>62</td><td>PEReference</td><td>'%' Name ';'<br>[WFC: Entity Declared, Text Entity, No Recursion, In DTD]</td></tr>
<tr><td>63</td><td>EntityDecl</td><td>'<!ENTITY' S %Name S %EntityDef S? '>'<br>/* General entities */<br>| '<!ENTITY' S '%' S %Name S %EntityDef S? '>'<br>/* Parameter entities */</td></tr>
<tr><td>64</td><td>EntityDef</td><td>EntityValue | ExternalDef</td></tr>
<tr><td>65</td><td>ExternalDef</td><td>ExternalID NDataDecl?</td></tr>
<tr><td>66</td><td>ExternalID</td><td>'SYSTEM' S SystemLiteral<br>| 'PUBLIC' S PubidLiteral S SystemLiteral</td></tr>
<tr><td>67</td><td>NDataDecl</td><td>S %'NDATA' S %Name<br>[VC: Notation Declared]</td></tr>
<tr><td>68</td><td>EncodingDecl</td><td>S 'encoding' Eq QEncoding</td></tr>
<tr><td>69</td><td>EncodingPI</td><td>'<?XML' S 'encoding' Eq QEncoding S? ?></td></tr>
<tr><td>70</td><td>QEncoding</td><td>'"' Encoding '"' | "'" Encoding "'"</td></tr>
<tr><td>71</td><td>Encoding</td><td>LatinName</td></tr>
<tr><td>72</td><td>LatinName</td><td>[A-Za-z] ([A-Za-z0-9._] | '-')*<br>/* Name containing only Latin characters */</td></tr>
<tr><td>73</td><td>NotationDecl</td><td>'<!NOTATION' S %Name S %ExternalID S? '>'</td></tr>
</table>

# 8.4. Trivial text grammar for XML

The grammar given in the body of this specification is relatively simple, but for some purposes it is convenient to have an even simpler one. A very simple XML processor could parse a well-formed XML document, recognizing all element boundaries correctly (though not expanding entity references) using the following grammar.

<table>
<tr><th>#</th><th>Name</th><th>::=<br>/* comment */ or [well-formedness/validity constraints]</th></tr>
<tr><td>81</td><td>Trivial</td><td>(PCData | Markup) *</td></tr>
<tr><td>82</td><td>Eq</td><td>S? '=' S?</td></tr>
<tr><td>83</td><td>Markup</td><td>'<' Name (S Name Eq AttValue)* S? '>'<br>/* start-tags */<br>| '</' Name S? '>'<br>/* end-tags */<br>| '<' Name (S Name Eq AttValue)* S? '/>'<br>/* empty elements */<br>| '&' Name ';'<br>/* entity references */<br>| '&#' [0-9]+ ';'<br>/* character references */<br>| '&#x' Hex+ ';'<br>/* character references */<br>| '<!--' (Char* - (Char* '--' Char*) '-->'<br>/* comments */<br>| '<![CDATA[' CData ']]>'<br>/* CDATA sections */<br>| '<!DOCTYPE' [^]]+ ('[' (Comment | TrivialLit<br>| conditionalSect | [^]]* )* ']')? '>'<br>/* doc type declaration */<br>| '<?' [^?]* ('?' [^>]+)* '?>'<br>/* processing instructions */</td></tr>
<tr><td>84</td><td>TrivialLit</td><td>('"' [^"]* '"') | ("'" [^']* "'")</td></tr>
</table>

Most processors will require the more complex grammar given in the body of this specification.

# Appendix A: Introduction to SGML

This appendix gives a very brief introduction to SGML. This should be enough to carry a reader through the first part of this book. If you are not already familiar with SGML, you will benefit from some additional reading. The bibliography lists several books on SGML; van Herwijnen 1994 is a popular and accessible introduction.

## What is SGML, really?

SGML is short for Standard Generalized Markup Language, and it is defined by ISO Standard 8879 (1986). It provides a flexible and portable way of representing documents on computers, where you can choose what kinds of components occur in each particular type of document, and then clearly label those parts as they occur.

The foundation of SGML, and to my thinking the primary reason it has gained such wide acceptance, is very simple: It lets you describe document structures directly, rather than describing something temporary like formatting, that *depends on* the structure. Simply put, SGML lets you tell the truth about your documents. This is reflected in five key characteristics that form the basis of its wide acceptance:

- **Descriptive markup**: An SGML document consists of objects of various classes (chapters, titles, references, repair procedures, graphic objects, poems, etc.), not sequences of formatting instructions. These objects are called **elements**, and each one has a generic **element type**. SGML marks the boundaries of elements using start- and end- **tags** . For example, a quotation could be stored as:

```
<QUOTATION>Full speed ahead</QUOTATION>
```

By labeling elements *themselves* rather than saying what to do with them, SGML avoids locking information into one program or even one purpose. Processing for various purposes is specified separately, often by style sheets or similar mechanisms.

- **Hierarchical structure**: Elements can contain one another in a hierarchy (a chapter can contain a title and several sections which in turn contain other elements). Therefore one can create, manipulate and manage not only "chapter titles," as in word processors, but also chapters as complete units. Hierarchies are also called "trees" because they branch repeatedly, and every sub-branch comes from only one "parent" branch. For example, a chapter might be stored as:

```
<CHAPTER><TITLE>Getting Started</TITLE>
<SECTION><TITLE>Overview of SGML</TITLE>
<P>SGML is…</P>
…
</SECTION></CHAPTER>
```

  A tree is a significantly different and more powerful model than the flat list or slightly hierarchical structures used in many word processor and database products.

- **Flexibility**: SGML does not dictate what types of components may appear in a document or how they relate. Individuals or groups can define types appropriate for their kinds of documents. For example, manuals need parts lists and procedures, catalogs needs prices and descriptions, while literary texts need a quite different variety of structures. Nevertheless, a single SGML implementation can work with all of these. There is no need for new software for each new set of element types.

- **Formal specification**: The specific elements contained in an SGML document are declared before the document begins in the **DTD**, or Document Type Declaration. After reading a DTD, programs called **validating parsers** can check SGML documents and detect many kinds of errors. Of course they cannot detect all errors: If you create a poem and tell the computer it is just a plain paragraph (or a repair procedure), validity checking won't help much.

- **Human-readable representation**: Finally, SGML provides a plain-text format for all this information. This means that one can read and write SGML documents not only with sophisticated SGML-aware tools, but even with *no* tools beyond any computer's everyday text handling commands (such as "type" or "edit"). Even without knowing SGML it isn't hard to figure out that this represents an emphasized word:

```
<EMPH>very</EMPH>
```

Simple yet formal representations based on readable embedded **markup** within the data have another important advantage: they are machine-independent. The internal file formats most programs use seldom survive transfer across networks, from one make of computer to another, or across national borders. SGML does. This is a vast improvement, especially over the proprietary binary representations programs typically use for optimizing internal operations.

SGML's key characteristics have little to do with specific kinds of processing (such as formatting or retrieval) or specific interfaces. By leaving these issues undefined (while ensuring that the structural information needed to determine them *is* defined), SGML encourages building systems that use the best processing and interface technologies available in any situation. Because of this SGML data lasts far longer than other representations, and a single SGML source document can be "re-purposed" for a wide variety of uses, often with no changes at all.

The key characteristics also have very little to do with syntax, or the formal grammar rules that govern just *how* SGML represents structured information. Syntax is important because only after agreeing on some syntax can programs exchange data. However, the greatest value of SGML stems from its use of descriptive markup methodology, not from the details of its rules. The syntax could have been standardized in a number of other ways without diminishing that value or the others described above.

SGML documents can be created, edited and otherwise processed with generic editors or with WYSIWYG editors that look like typical word processors. Cooperating authors often use different methods and programs on the same documents. In the same way, the result of authoring can be processed unchanged for many different purposes, such as local printing, high-quality typesetting, display in Braille, information retrieval, linguistic analysis, or hypertext browsing. No representation that is based mainly on formatting can do that.

### Formatting and structure

Strong separation of formatting from structure is a hallmark of good SGML use. However, just using the standard cannot ensure such good practice. It is possible, even easy, to use "legal" SGML syntax with tags that represent only formatting information, but doing this loses many benefits SGML is meant to provide. For example, it is easy to make a set of SGML element types that looks like a raw formatting language. A block quote might then be tagged as follows:

```
<SK><DS><IN L="+10" R="-10">The quotation…
<SK><IL L="+10">The following paragraph…
```

Even worse, someone could just put "<DOC>…</DOC>" around a document in any other representation and call it SGML:

```
<DOC>
.sk;.ds;.in +10 -10;
The quotation…
.sk;.il +10;
The following paragraph…
<DOC>
```

Given corresponding DTDs, both these approaches yield perfectly legal, syntactically correct SGML for which a validating SGML parser would report no errors. However, the information is no more portable or communicative than if it were not using SGML: SGML syntax is merely being a veneer over non-descriptive, non-hierarchical markup, whose meaning is not accessible to the SGML processor for validation or use.

In contrast, the following SGML coding is clearer, more concise, easier to maintain, more efficient and more useful for a wide range of purposes:

```
<QUO>The quotation…</QUO>
<P>The following paragraph…</P>
```

# Parts of an SGML document

An SGML document is divided into three major parts:

- An **SGML declaration** gives general information about SGML syntax options. It says what character set is used, how long element type names can be, what **delimiter strings** (such as "<" and "</") separate tags from content, what optional SGML features are used, and so on. Many SGML parsers allow the declaration to be omitted. Then standard default settings are used, called the **reference concrete syntax**. This book assumes these settings except that element and other names may exceed the default eight-character limit.
- A **Document Type Declaration** or **DTD** says what element types and other components are permitted in the document, using detailed **markup declarations**. The declarations also say which element types can contain which others. For example, footnotes might not be allowed to contain chapters.
- A **document instance** includes the content of a document as well as the tags and other markup that indicate where elements of each type start and end. A document instance can be stored in more than one file by dividing it up into parts called **entities**, and may include data in other media and formats by reference as described below.

## Parts of an SGML document instance

This section gives a brief review of how documents are tagged using SGML and how tagging schemes are declared in DTDs, then shows the complete SGML markup for a short example document. Conceptually, an SGML document instance includes content and structure, such as graphics, video, text, indications of structural components, and links. In terms of syntax or representation, it has four major kinds of objects each of which has a corresponding type of declaration that can appear in the DTD. Once declared, actual instances of these objects may be used in the document instance.

**Elements** divide the document into meaningful conceptual components, each of which has some name, such as `chapter`, `part-number`, or `task`. The name is called an **element type** or **generic identifier** ("GI"). Elements are marked by **tags** at their start and end, that in turn are marked off by special strings called **delimiters**.

**Attributes** may be specified for elements and give information about a particular instance of the element type such as a security level or a unique identifier. Each attribute has a name, a type, and a rule about default values. Attributes appear within start-tags.

**Entity references** are a way to include data by reference, and are **resolved** by the SGML parser and replaced by their values: either externally stored information or strings defined in the DTD. Entities can even be data in non-SGML representations.

**Data content** is called **#PCDATA**, and occurs within elements where permitted by the DTD. This is typically the bulk of the information to be read or viewed, though there is not a perfect separation between attributes and data content in this respect.

These objects form the basic structure of an SGML document. They are all distinguished from actual text content, because they are marked off by "markup" characters and sequences, known as "delimiters". Each delimiter in SGML has a name, and a string that usually serves as the delimiter (the string, however, can be changed).

There are other SGML constructs. One is the **marked section**, a way of including parts of a document conditionally and of suppressing recognition of markup delimiter. Some others are **processing instructions** and **comments**, whose content is generally not considered part of the document content. These constructs mainly come up in this book because they may show up unintentionally, such as if you insert their delimiters, intending them as text content.

## Elements

Elements represent chapters, links, footnotes, graphic references, and so on. The beginning and end of each element are marked by **tags**, that state what element type is starting or ending:

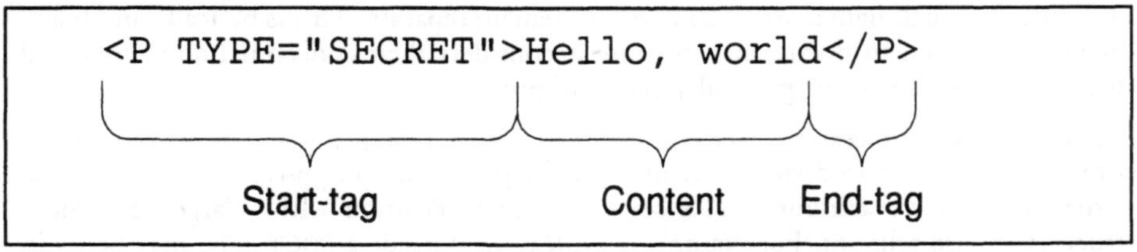


By default the tags are enclosed between special delimiter strings, normally less-than and greater-than signs or "angle brackets" (plus slash to distinguish end-tags from start-tags). Tags contain names to identify the element type, that are known as **generic identifiers** (commonly abbreviated "GIs"), or as element type names or tag names. These names normally disregard upper/lower case distinctions and can contain letters, digits, periods and hyphens, beginning with a letter. The parts of a tag are illustrated here:

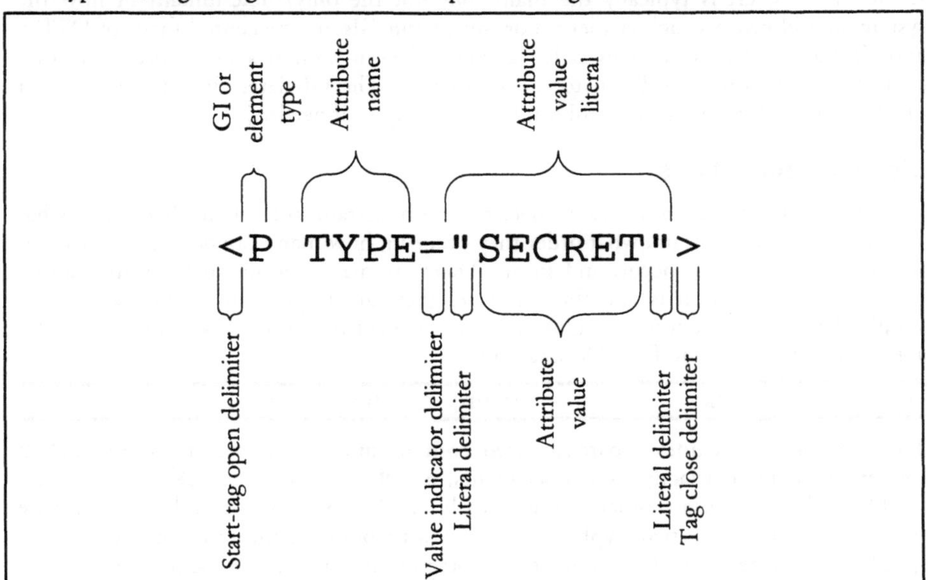


The element type names can be anything the DTD designer chooses (along with their permitted relationships). Of course, mnemonic names are better: `QUOTE` is superior to `Q`, which is in turn superior to `TAG37`. With modern editing software any of these can be entered with equal ease via a single menu selection or command key, so keeping names short to save typing is false economy.

Although examples show the actual file representation of SGML, remember that this need not be what authors or other users see. SGML editing software can hide all this, just as word processors hide their arcane proprietary formats. It is an advantage, however, that one *can* edit SGML with any text editor; this is not possible with proprietary word-processor formats.

### The GI as major class identifier

For most SGML applications the generic identifier tells what an element is and thus what kind of processing is appropriate. This reflects the fundamental descriptive markup approach: name things by what they are and expect the computer to use that name. Deciding *how* such names are to be used can remain separate. This is basically an object-oriented approach to documents, because it considers their conceptual and functional structure primary, and the particular details of processing methods secondary.

However, much processing needs more information that just the GI. Attributes are commonly used to sub-divide element types for processing purposes, such as hiding all elements that have attribute `TYPE` set to `SECRET`. Position within larger document structures is also relevant. For example, a `PARAGRAPH` inside a `FOOTNOTE` may be set in smaller type than other paragraphs, or the first paragraph of each section may be unindented (except, perhaps, in the front matter). These are very simple cases; countless other examples exist, and so stylesheet mechanisms need to provide ways of referring to locations in documents and examining their contexts in order to control formatting adequately.

In SGML, the GI is typically the main (but not the only) determinant of how the system should process each element. For this reason GIs are the central focus of DTDs, and why a DTD is sometimes called a "tag set" even though a DTD provides other critical information in addition to the set of tags. The GI determines processing not directly, but indirectly; the control can be very complex if needed.

### Element declarations

Each element type in a DTD is declared with certain rules that determine what subelements it can contain, what order they occur in, how many can occur, whether and where text content can occur, and so on. There are many reasons such control can be useful; in cases where it is not, the DTD designer can simply state very loose rules. A simple element declaration for a glossary entry element might look like this, and would appear in the Document Type Declaration:

```
<!ELEMENT  ENTRY        - -  (WORD, DEFN)>
```

This declaration includes a parenthesized **content model** that requires every `ENTRY` element to contain exactly two subelements, a `WORD` and then a `DEFN`. A complete DTD would also declare other elements to hold `ENTRY` elements and would declare `WORD` and `DEFN`. The two hyphens are used with optional minimization features to specify that neither an `ENTRY` element's start-tag nor its end-tag may be omitted.

The definitions for `GLOSSARY` (consisting of a list of one or more `ENTRY` elements) and for `WORD` and `DEFN`(consisting of strings of characters) could be:

```
<!ELEMENT  GLOSSARY     - -  (ENTRY)+>
<!ELEMENT  WORD         O O  (#PCDATA)>
<!ELEMENT  DEFN         - O  (#PCDATA)>
```

This defines both WORD and DEFN to contain "parsed character data". This basically means plain text. Since the characters that start a tag (like "<") might be needed literally in text, SGML provides mechanisms to include them without confusing them with their use as markup (see Question 1.1).

The WORD element has an "O" (capital letter O, not zero) in both of its minimization specifications, indicating that it is permissible to omit either the start-tag, end-tag, or both in certain circumstances. A DEFN element may only have its end-tag omitted. Questions 2.1 through 2.3 discuss minimization in particular detail.

The GLOSSARY element itself is declared to contain one or more ENTRY elements. The "+" means that the preceding item can be repeated one or more times. Other operators allow optional elements, choices between elements, and elements that can be arbitrarily re-ordered.

Content models may contain sub-models separated by **connectors** which specify what elements are required by a content model:

| | |
|---|---|
| , | The sequence connector (**SEQ**) separates sub-models that must appear in the particular order specified. |
| \| | The **OR** connector separates sub-models either of which can appear (but not both, unless the sub-model itself is repeatable). |
| & | The **AND** connector separates sub-models that must both appear, but can occur in any order. |

Content models may contain **occurrence indicators** that indicate how many times a sub-model must occur when it appears. These indicators follow the sub-model to which they apply:

| | |
|---|---|
| ? | The "optional" (**OPT**) occurrence indicator specifies that the sub-model is optional. |
| + | The "required and repeatable" (**PLUS**) occurrence indicator specifies that one or more instances of the sub-model may occur. |
| * | The "optional and repeatable" (**REP**) occurrence indicator specifies that zero or more instances of the sub-model may occur. |
| none | If no occurrence indicator is given, the sub-model must occur exactly once in each element instance. |

Examples of all the connectors and occurrence indicators appear below. Parentheses can be used to build more complex content models and sub-models (called **groups**); only one type of connector can be used in any given group, and the group may have a single occurrence indicator after the close parenthesis.

```
<!ELEMENT  CHP          - -  (CT, SEC*)>
<!ELEMENT  SEC          - -  (ST?, (SUBSEC | P)*)>
<!ELEMENT  BIBENTRY     - -  (AUTHOR & TITLE & DATE)>
<!ELEMENT  LIST         - -  (ITEM)+>
```

Instead of a parenthesized content model, a declaration may also use one of these special keywords (*not* in parentheses):

**CDATA** means that delimiters inside the element will be treated as literal data instead of as delimiters. No subelements can occur inside one of these. An end-tag will still be recognized, however, since it is needed to end the **CDATA** element.

**RCDATA** is like **CDATA**, but permits entity references to be resolved within the element.

**EMPTY** means that the element is a point event and cannot contain any text or other elements.

**ANY** means the element can contain any mixture of text and other elements declared in the DTD.

## Attributes

An instance of an element may have associated information in the form of attributes which usually express properties or characteristics of an entire element (this is discussed in Question 5.10). Thus, a footnote may have a reference code, a paragraph may have a security level, or a list may specify whether its items should be shown with automatic numbering, with bullet characters in front, or plain. Attributes appear only within start-tags, at the start of the elements to which they apply:

```
<LIST TYPE="BULLETED">
   <ITEM>...</ITEM>
   ...
</LIST>
```

### Attribute declarations

The attributes permitted for an element type are declared all at once in the DTD using an **attribute list declaration**. Each attribute has a name by which it is referenced, a type that determines the sort of value it can have (SGML identifier, number, etc.), and a default value to be used if the attribute is not specified. A declaration for two attributes that can apply to elements of type LIST might look like this:

```
<!-- Declare two attributes for 'LIST' element -->
<!ATTLIST  LIST
   AUTHOR   CDATA         #IMPLIED
   TYPE     (BULLETED  |  NUMBERED)
                          "BULLETED">
```

After a comment, this declares that each LIST element has two attributes. One, called AUTHOR, takes a string as value. The keyword **#IMPLIED** specifies that AUTHOR is optional for LIST element instances. The other attribute, called type, can have either the value BULLETED or the value NUMBERED; it defaults to BULLETED if a value is not specified.

## Attribute types

An attribute's type is known as its **declared value**. The various declared value types constrain the form of permitted values, such as to being a number, a single word, an SGML name, or unrestricted. Alternatively, an attribute can be constrained to one of an enumerated list of specific values, each of which must be a single SGML name. The declared value types known to SGML are **ENTITY**, **IDREF**, **NAME**, **NMTOKEN**, **NUMBER**, **NUTOKEN** (all with corresponding plurals that allow multiple tokens separated by whitespace), as well as **CDATA**, **ID** and **NOTATION**.

A few of these declared value types do not just constrain the form of their values, but also impose a semantic restriction. Those declared values are **ID**, **IDREF**, **IDREFS**, **ENTITY**, **ENTITIES**, and **NOTATION**, and they are discussed in Question 5.14.

## Attribute defaults

Each attribute must specify what happens if no value is given on the start-tag for its element type. The declaration can specify a default value (as for the TYPE attribute above), or some special keywords can be used:

**#IMPLIED** means it is optional but has no default value unless one is supplied by the application later,

**#REQUIRED** means omitting it is an error,

**#CURRENT** means the value is the same as last time,

**#CONREF** is a special case. If a **#CONREF** attribute has a value, then the element must be empty,

**#FIXED** means only one value given in the DTD is permitted; specifying any other value causes a validating SGML parser to report a syntax error.

### ID and IDREF

Two types of SGML attributes are especially important because of their use in creating hypertext links: **ID** and **IDREF**. These permit attaching unique identifiers to elements and referencing them from other elements. There may be at most one attribute with declared value **ID** for a given element type, and its instances must have these properties:

- Any value specified for the attribute must be a valid SGML name: that is, a name start character (normally a letter) followed by any number of name characters (letters, digits, hyphen and period), up to some maximum length.
- The values of all **ID** attributes in a single document must be distinct (**ID**s that differ only in case count as equal, such as chap1 and CHAP1).

Attributes with declared value **IDREF** (short for "**ID** reference") need not each have distinct value, but each such value must match the value of *some* **ID** attribute elsewhere in the same document.

Because all **ID**s must be distinct they provide a natural way to refer to a particular element — a way that a validating SGML parser can check. **ID**s and **IDREF** attributes are used very heavily for linking in SGML documents. Here are some examples of declaring **ID** and **IDREF** attributes for particular elements:

```
<!-- Declare chapter element with mandatory ID -->
<!ELEMENT  CHAPTER     - - (CT, P+)>
<!ATTLIST  CHAPTER
   ID       ID          #REQUIRED>

<!-- Paragraph element has optional ID attribute -->
<!ELEMENT  P           - - (#PCDATA)>
<!ATTLIST  P
   ID       ID          #IMPLIED>

<!-- Cross-reference element has mandatory 'target'
     attribute to point to any element with an ID -->
<!ELEMENT  XREF        - - (#PCDATA)>
<!ATTLIST  XREF
   TARGET   IDREF       #REQUIRED>
```

Given these declarations, CHAPTER elements *must* have unique identifier attributes and P elements *may* have them. Each XREF element *must* have a TARGET attribute that points to an element by identifier. An example of this tagging scheme is:

```
<CHAPTER ID="chap1">
   ...
   <P ID="main.point">...</P>
</CHAP>
...
<XREF TARGET="chap1">See also Chapter 1</XREF>
```

## Entities and notations

An entity is some piece of data that can be referenced using a normally case-sensitive name declared for it. The entity itself may be something as simple as an abbreviation for a literal string, or may represent an external data object such as a file of SGML or non-SGML data. The former are called **internal entities**, the latter **external entities**.

Entities can be used to avoid redundant copies of data and to help organize the parts of documents into files or other storage units. They are important for referring to locations outside a single document by naming the entity that contains the location (such as a video sequence). Some links then add a more specific place within the entity (such as a range of frames). A declaration for a non-SGML entity also states what representation the entity is in, to enable proper processing of the data.

Internal entity declarations, placed in the DTD, merely give the entity name and a quoted string that represents the value or **replacement text** that is substituted for each reference to the entity in the document:

```
<!ENTITY   safety
   "Ensure that red 'armed' light is not flashing.">
```

An entity reference in the document normally consists of an ampersand, the entity name and a semicolon, as in the example below:

```
<procedure>
   <step>After opening the box, do the following
      safety checks: &safety;</step>
   <step>Replace the entire unit.</step>
</procedure>
```

The effect of this is to include the text "`Ensure that red 'armed' light is not flashing.`" in the document in place of the entity reference "`&safety;`".

### Parameter entities

Some entities are intended to contain information that should be substituted within the DTD rather than the document. These are called **parameter entities** and they are syntactically separate from other entities. Names of parameter entities and ordinary entities cannot conflict because they are separately defined. A parameter entity is declared like any other internal entity with the addition of a special signal, the character "%" following the keyword **ENTITY**, for example:

```
<!ENTITY   % para-stuff "P | FN | BQ">
```

This entity is called `para-stuff` and can be referenced later in the DTD with the string "`%para-stuff;`". The following two declarations, for example, have the same effect:

```
<!ELEMENT  TEXT          - - (%para-stuff;)>

<!ELEMENT  TEXT          - - (P | FN | BQ)>
```

Parameter entities can occur in exactly one place within document content: as a way of turning parts of the content on and off using an SGML construct called a marked section. Marked sections are discussed further in Questions 2.9 through 2.11. In short, they take a keyword that indicates how their context is to be processed. For conditional text the keyword is **INCLUDE** or **IGNORE**. Keywords can be specified literally or via parameter entities:

```
<P>The <![ IGNORE [ quick ]]> brown fox.</P>
<P>The <![ %fox.entity; [ quick ]]> brown fox.</P>
```

### External entities

External entities typically correspond to individual computer files (though this need not be true). For them the keyword **PUBLIC** or **SYSTEM** appears, followed by quoted identifiers that enable an SGML parser to locate the data that the entity represents (for further details see Question 5.22):

```
<!ENTITY   chap1       SYSTEM "/u/sjd/docs/faq/chap1.sgm">
```

### Entities with special parsing constraints

Several other keywords can appear with an entity's value specification to specify how it is to be parsed, as discussed in Question 5.22. Several are used for "data entities" whose replacement text is not to be parsed by the SGML parser. They include:

**CDATA** The replacement text is content, but may contain SGML delimiter strings (such as "<") as literal data without their being recognized as markup by the SGML processor.

**SDATA** The replacement text is "specific character data" that is by definition system-dependent; this is commonly used for special characters that are not shared among the character sets of various computer systems.

**NDATA** The replacement text is in some format or data content notation (usually other than SGML), named following the word **NDATA**. It should be passed for processing to some other program that knows that notation.

When a data content notation is used, there must be a **NOTATION** declaration that relates the notation name to a reference describing that data format.

Here are some examples of these entity types:

```
<!-- Specify CDATA so journal title is not taken
     as a tag instead of literal characters -->
<!ENTITY   tag.letter  CDATA
   "<TAG>: The SGML newsletter">

<!-- Declare needed Hebrew letter -->
<!ENTITY   aleph       SDATA
   "font(Hebrew) charset(ISO8859-8) codepoint(224)">

<!-- Declare graphic notation and entity using it -->
<!NOTATION TIFF        PUBLIC
   "+//ISBN 0-7923-9432-1::Graphic Notation//NOTATION
   Aldus/Microsoft
   Tagged Interchange File Format//EN">

<!ENTITY   wheel       SYSTEM
   "fig29.tif" NDATA TIFF>
```

The value for `aleph` would vary from system to system. The `wheel` entity is declared to be in the `TIFF` notation, which allows the external graphics data to be directed to an appropriate processing program.

### The SGML declaration

The optional features, character set used and any syntactic changes to SGML are described in an **SGML declaration**. Documents that use no optional features and the default settings are called **minimal SGML documents** because only the minimal subset of SGML is used. Sometimes the terms "normalized documents" or "canonical documents" are used to mean much the same thing. **Basic SGML documents** are those that use only a certain few optional features. They are quite common. There is seldom a reason to change SGML delimiters, but the default limits on lengths of tag names and other strings, controlled by the **quantity set**, are often increased.

## A sample SGML document

This section presents a small sample document, along with a complete SGML DTD and document instance, showing each of the items described above (the headings separating the three major parts would not be part of the document). The SGML Declaration is not included here.

First, a formatted version of the sample document:

January 27, 1993

Dear Jean Luc,

How are you doing?
Isn't it *about time* you visited?

See you soon,

Genise

### The document type declaration

The DTD contains declarations for all the kinds of units that will occur in the document. The DTD, for example, declares various elements, attributes and entities that can be used to encode documents such as the one above. The declarations are enclosed in a **DOCTYPE declaration**, within a **declaration subset** enclosed within square brackets.

```
<!DOCTYPE  letter [

<!-- declare root element type for document -->
<!ELEMENT  letter       - - (date, greeting,
                              body, closing, sig)>
<!ATTLIST  letter
   filecode NUMBER      #REQUIRED
   secret   (yes|no)    "no">

<!ELEMENT  body         - - (p)*>
<!ELEMENT  (date, greeting, closing, sig)
                        - - (#PCDATA)>
<!ELEMENT  p            - - (#PCDATA | emph)*>
<!ELEMENT  emph         - - (#PCDATA)>

<!-- Provide a handy, replaceable greeting -->
<!ENTITY   salute       "Dear">
]>
```

The DTD as shown above can be placed right at the top of the document in the same file. It is also common to place the **`DOCTYPE`** line there along with any document-specific declarations (called the "internal declaration subset"), but refer to most of the declarations externally using a **PUBLIC** or **SYSTEM** identifier as shown here:

```
<!DOCTYPE  letter SYSTEM "Slack:sgml:dtds:letter.dtd" [
<!-- any additional declarations for document -->
<!ENTITY   fig1       SYSTEM "Slack:pix:runes.tiff">
]>
```

### The document instance

With this DTD, the document instance below is valid in SGML. The indentation is added for clarity to show the hierarchical structure; it would probably not appear in the document (although with this DTD it could). Question 1.8 discusses SGML's rules about exactly where whitespace can go.

```
<letter filecode="97022701">
   <date>January 27, 1997</date>
   <greeting>&salute; Jean Luc,</greeting>
   <body>
      <p>How are you doing?</p>
      <p>Isn't it <emph>about time</emph> you visited?</p>
   </body>
   <closing>See you soon,</closing>
   <sig>Genise</sig>
</letter>
```

### A non-SGML equivalent

Lest anyone think this representation seem unduly complicated, the way one popular WYSIWYG word processing system encodes the same document is shown below. This puts the comparison on the same terms as above: showing what's underneath the interface (which you should not need to see in practice, but which largely determines what you can ultimately do with your data). In this case, it directly represents instructions for formatting the document in a certain way. It is obviously much less readable than the SGML representation above, as well as being less maintainable and less useful for other processing such as retrieval:

```
\widowctrl\fracwidth \sectd \sbknone\linemod0
\linex0\cols1\endnhere \pard\plain \s1\li360
\sl280\tx720\tx1080\tx1440\tx1800\tx2160 \f22
{\v 93020401}\par \pard
\s1\qr\li360\sl280\tx720\tx1080\tx1440\tx1800\tx2160
January 27, 1993\par\pard
\s1\li360\sb1440\sa240\sl280\tx720\tx1080
\tx1440\tx1800\tx2160
Dear Jean Luc,\par\pard\s1
\li360\sl280\tx720\tx1080\tx1440\tx1800\tx2160
How are you doing?\par Isn\rquote t it
{\i about time} you visited?\par\pard\s1
\li360\sb240\sl280\tx720\tx1080\tx1440\tx1800\tx2160
See you soon,\par\pard \s1\li360\sb1440\sl280
\tx720\tx1080\tx1440\tx1800\tx2160
Genise\par \pard\plain \f20\fs28 \par
```

Most writers using a word processor do not see all these backslashes there, just as most writers using an SGML editor do not see angle brackets there. Even so, the SGML representation is both cleaner and shorter; most importantly, the information it contains is more generally useful. Both user interfaces and data representations are very important. There is no need to accept good interfaces on bad data representations or bad interfaces on good ones. Only a system that does both things well is adequate. SGML documents can be edited with a pleasant, WYSIWYG interface. Several such environments are available.

SGML provides several intrinsic features that are useful to represent hypertext as well, and so SGML-based hypertext systems have become important. Document structure is a crucial means of navigation and orientation, and hypertext systems lacking support for component structure such as SGML provides usually have problems with users becoming "lost in hyperspace". SGML also provides reference mechanisms that can express fine-grained connections between components of documents, providing excellent precision and robustness for hypertext links.

# Optional SGML features

This section discusses SGML's **optional features** briefly. Many of them provide more compact ways of manually keying markup should that be necessary. They may also reduce visual distraction if you have to read or edit SGML with non-SGML-aware text editors. Other features involve the interactions between documents and various DTDs, and the way in which entities are formally named.

For example, the markup in the first line below may be a bit imposing to type or read as-is, and so one might use minimization instead such as shown in the second line. However, this can only be done when the context and the DTD permit it, and should only be done if it does not end up detracting from portability, readability, and ease of maintenance for authors down the line:

```
<QUOTE TYPE="long">…</QUOTE>
<>…</>
```

Current software typically shields the user from such details by providing graphical interfaces for data entry, editing, and display. Authors might pick an "Insert quotation" menu item (or press alt-control-q) and be done; for display they might choose to see no tags, but only quotation marks, a formatting distinction, or some other graphical indication of the element's presence. Regardless of such syntactic and interface variations, the fundamental notion of descriptive markup remains essential; minimization does not introduce new markup structures, just alternative ways of expressing the same structures.

## Minimization features

The first of SGML's **markup minimization features** is quite simple. **SHORTTAG** provides ways to make start and end-tags shorter although it never permits omitting them completely. It has several aspects:

- Leaving out quotes around attribute values when they contain only name characters (normally letters, digits, hyphen and period):

```
<LIST TYPE=NUMBERED>
```

- Leaving out attributes that have default values. For example, given this declaration:

```
<!ATTLIST  LIST
   TYPE     (NUMBERED | BULLETED | PLAIN)
                        "PLAIN"
   STARTAT  NUMBER       1>
```

the following LIST start-tags are both valid and equivalent, because the SGML parser will fill in default values:

```
<LIST STARTAT="1" TYPE="PLAIN">…</LIST>
<LIST>…</LIST>
```

- Leaving out the tag name from start and end-tags when it can be inferred from context (see Question 2.1):

```
<LIST>
   <ITEM>Item 1</>
   <ITEM>Item 2</>
</>
```

- Substituting "/" for ">" on a start-tag to declare that the next freestanding "/" in the document will be treated as the corresponding end-tag. This feature is rarely used and should be treated with care (see Questions 1.4 and 1.5):

```
<LIST/
   <ITEM/Item 1/
   <ITEM/Item 2/
/
```

**OMITTAG** saves keying tags entirely when the DTD permits them to be inferred. For example, if LIST elements are declared to *require* at least one ITEM, then the start-tag for the first ITEM element can be omitted. In the same way, if ITEM elements are *required* never to directly contain other ITEM elements, the end-tags for most or all of them can be omitted:

```
<list>
   Item 1
   <item>Item 2
</list>
```

A third feature is called **SHORTREF**. It lets you define **maps**, which are lists of synonyms for markup. For example, you could declare "|" to be an synonym for "<CELL>" and then enter a table as shown below (this example also assumes **OMITTAG** is used to infer the end-tag for each CELL element):

```
<TABLE>
   <ROW>| China   | 1400 million
   <ROW>| India   | 800 million
   <ROW>| USA     | 250 million
   <ROW>| France  | 50 million
   <ROW>| Canada  | 25 million
</TABLE>
```

### Other SGML features

While the remaining SGML features add capability, they are less commonly used. Three features are together known as **LINK**. They provide a possible way of associating processing information with elements in an SGML document (through associating a new GI or attributes with elements, though not with anything that isn't already an element). The LINK features are unrelated to hypertext linking.

The SGML **SUBDOC** feature lets an entire document embed within another as a single element, even if the two use completely different DTDs, though not different SGML declarations (see Question 2.13). **CONCUR** permits two or more completely separate markup structures (defined by separate DTDs) for the same document (it is discussed a bit further in Question 5.9).

The final SGML feature is **FORMAL**, which can be used to require that public names for documents and entities be in a special form known to SGML. This is called a **Formal Public Identifier**, and a registered one constructed it the specified way should be globally unique. An FPI does not depend on any particular computer implementation as a filename or network address does (Questions 4.9 through 4.16 discuss these).

An entity declaration for an external entity can supply two kinds of identifiers: **PUBLIC** and **SYSTEM** (see Clause 10 of the SGML standard); the **FORMAL** feature only imposes requirements on the **PUBLIC** kind. Except for FPIs, which must include certain sub-parts as described below, these identifiers can be in any form at all so long as

- they are quoted using either single or double quotes (the "**LIT**" and "**LITA**" delimiters); and
- they contain only "minimum data characters:" letters, digits, white-space and "special" characters, namely `()+,-./:=?` (see Question 4.11).

Any leading or trailing white-space characters in these identifiers are ignored and any multiple internal white-space characters are treated as a single space. This is done in the same way as for SGML attribute values (except those of type **ENTITY**, **ENTITIES** and **CDATA**, which are not normalized in this way).

## Formal public identifiers

Formal public identifiers, or FPIs, have a useful internal structure. When this feature is used, an SGML parser will check that all public identifiers conform to the proper syntax. ISO Standard 9070 describes this syntax and the registration procedures to be used to make an identifier publicly accessible.

One simple way to create a registered FPI is to use an International Standard Book Number, or ISBN, using the registration authority established by the publishing industry. For example:

```
+//ISBN 0-7923-9943-9//TEXT The SGML FAQ Book//EN
```

An entity representing the book could thus be declared and used to link to the book:

```
<!ENTITY   book1       PUBLIC
   "+//ISBN 0-7923-9943-9//TEXT
   The SGML FAQ Book//EN">
```

A formal public identifier has several parts, separated by pairs of slash characters. The double slash sequence may not occur except where specified by the FPI syntax. The FPI above is broken down in the table below:

| Part | Function |
|---|---|
| `+//` | The **owner prefix**, one of:<br>`+//` An owner formally registered under the rules of ISO 9070<br>`-//` Any unregistered owner prefix<br>(other) Must be an ISO publication number, such as "`ISO 8879:1986`" |
| `ISBN 0-7923-9943-9` | The **owner name**, that identifies who owns the FPI (not necessarily who owns the data it points to — see Question 4.13) |
| `//` | Separator |
| **`TEXT`** | The **public text class**, usually one of these values (see also Question 4.11):<br>**`TEXT`** An SGML document or portion<br>**`DOCUMENT`** A complete SGML document<br>**`NONSGML`** Data not in SGML (the declaration should include an **`NDATA`** specification to describe the data format)<br>**`NOTATION`** A definition for a notation (as opposed to data expressed in the notation) |
| | An optional "`-//`" to indicate that the replacement text is unavailable for some reason (not used in this example) |
| `Making...` | The **public text description** or name identifying the particular entity among all those whose FPIs have the same owner id. |
| `//` | Separator |
| `EN` | The **public text language** in which the data is encoded ("`EN`" means English). This should be a language code according to ISO 639, but need not be (see Question 4.14 for more on this) |
| | An optional description of the display device for which the entity is set up, in case there are versions for different devices (not used in this example, but see Question 4.15) |

When creating a formal public identifier, an organization takes on the responsibility to ensure that any changes in the content of the entity are properly reflected in the name, etc. To create a registered public identifier, the owner name must be registered according to ISO 9070. To make this process of name assignment easier, owner names can be divided into parts by occurrences of the marker "`::`". The first field of the name must specify the issuing authority for the name, and the remaining parts can give any additional information needed to identify the object. To create a public owner name from an ISBN, put the string "`ISBN`" followed by the ISBN publisher or book number designating the issuer or a published reference.

# Appendix B: SGML Delimiters

The strings that indicate markup in SGML are called delimiters, and each one has a name as well as a default ("reference concrete syntax") setting. This table is based on Figure 3 and Clause 9.6 in the standard, and provides those names and values along with the "recognition modes" and "contextual constraints" under which each delimiter is recognized. An unrecognized delimiter is just data to SGML. Following the delimiter table is a table showing which delimiters are recognized in each mode.

## Delimiter names, strings, and contexts

| Name | String | Mode | Constraint | Description |
|---|---|---|---|---|
| AND | & | GRP | | And connector |
| COM | -- | CXT MD | | Comment start or end |
| CRO | &# | CON LIT | CREF | Character reference open |
| DSC | ] | DS MD | ENT | Declaration subset close |
| DSO | [ | CXT MD | | Declaration subset open |
| DTGC | ] | GRP | | Data tag group close |
| DTGO | [ | GRP | | Data tag group open |
| ERO | & | CON LIT | NMS | Entity reference open |
| ETAGO | </ | CON TAG | GI | End-tag open |
| GRPC | ) | GRP | | Group close |
| GRPO | ( | CXT GRP MD | | Group open |
| LIT | " | GRP LIT MD TAG | | Literal start or end |
| LITA | ' | GRP LIT MD TAG | | Literal start or end (alternative) |
| MDC | > | CXT MD | | Markup declaration close |
| MDO | <! | CON DSM | DCL | Markup declaration open |
| MINUS | - | MD | EX | Exclusion |

| Name | String | Mode | Constraint | Description |
|---|---|---|---|---|
| **MSC** | ]] | **CON DSM** | **MSE** | Marked section close |
| **NET** | / | **CON TAG** | **ELEM** | Null end-tag |
| **OPT** | ? | **GRP** | | Optional occurrence indicator |
| **OR** | \| | **GRP** | | Or connector |
| **PERO** | % | **DSM GRP MD LIT** | **NMS** | Parameter entity reference open |
| **PIC** | > | **PI** | | Processing instruction close |
| **PIO** | <? | **CON DSM** | | Processing instruction open |
| **PLUS** | + | **GRP MD** | **EX** | Required and repeatable; inclusion |
| **REFC** | ; | **REF** | | Reference close |
| **REP** | * | **GRP** | | Optional and repeatable |
| **RNI** | # | **GRP MD** | | Reserved name indicator |
| **SEQ** | , | **GRP** | | Sequence connector |
| **STAGO** | < | **CON TAG** | **GI** | Start-tag open |
| **TAGC** | > | **CXT TAG** | | Tag close |
| **VI** | = | **TAG** | | Value indicator |

Of the 31 named delimiters, 11 cannot occur in document instances; 2 more only occur there with the **CONCUR** feature, and 3 more only for marked sections; a few more have very restricted uses, such as **NET**.

**Note**: Recognition modes resemble the states of a Finite State Automaton in standard parsing technology (see for example Aho and Ullman 1977), but they are not the same. Amendment 1 added a recognition mode to SGML that co-occurs with one of the others, unlike states. Also, FSA states follow from the grammar rules automatically: each symbol of the grammar is in effect a recognition mode, in which the allowed things are recognized.

### Delimiters recognized in each recognition mode

| Mode | Applies inside... | Delimiters recognized |
|---|---|---|
| **CON** | **#PCDATA** or other content | **MDO MSC PIO CRO ERO ETAGO NET STAGO** |
| **CXT** | | **GRPO COM DSO MDC TAGC** |
| **DS** | the declaration subset | **DSC** |
| **DSM** | DS + marked sections in it (co-occurs w/ DS) | **MDO MSC PIO PERO** |
| **GRP** | a parenthesized group such as a content model | **AND DTGC DTGO GRPC OPT OR REP SEQ LIT LITA GRPO PLUS RNI PERO** |
| **LIT** | a quoted literal | **CRO ERO LIT LITA PERO** |
| **MD** | a markup declaration | **GRPO PLUS RNI DSC COM DSO MDC MINUS PERO LIT LITA** |
| **PI** | a processing instruction | **PIC** |
| **REF** | an entity reference | **REFC** |
| **TAG** | a start- or end-tag | **LIT LITA TAGC ETAGO NET STAGO VI** |

# Appendix C: SGML Productions (Grammar Rules)

This index lists the actual grammar rules of SGML in alphabetical order, but only through Clause 11. It omits link processes, SGML declarations, and system declarations. For each other rule, the table lists its sequence number, its name, and where it occurs in the SGML standard (as a production, and when applicable, as a defined term) and in *The SGML Handbook.*

Many of the lower-level productions in the SGML grammar mention character classes, such as "LC Letter". These classes are defined in Clause 9.2 of the SGML standard, the table also appears on p. 345 of *The SGML Handbook.* Smith and Stutely (1988) is also an excellent reference for information on the SGML grammar.

| Number | Symbol | Production | Definition | *Handbook* |
|---|---|---|---|---|
| 72 | associated element type | 10.1.5 | 4.8 | 377 |
| 149.1 | associated notation name | 11.4.1.1 | 4.8.1 | 428 |
| 143 | attribute definition | 11.3 | 4.10 | 421 |
| 142 | attribute definition list | 11.3 | 4.11 | 420 |
| 141 | attribute definition list declaration | 11.3 | 4.12 | 420 |
| 144 | attribute name | 11.3.2 | | 421 |
| 32 | attribute specification | 7.9 | 4.15 | 327 |
| 31 | attribute specification list | 7.9 | 4.16 | 327 |
| 35 | attribute value | 7.9.4 | | 333 |
| 34 | attribute value literal | 7.9.3 | 4.17 | 331 |
| 33 | attribute value specification | 7.9.3 | | 331 |
| 11 | base document element | 7.2 | 4.20 | 306 |
| 9 | base document type declaration | 7.1 | (4.21) | 303 |

| Number | Symbol | Production | Definition | *Handbook* |
|---|---|---|---|---|
| 107 | bracketed text | 10.5.4 | | 399 |
| 49 | character | 9.2 | 4.31 | 344 |
| 47 | character data | 9.2 | 4.33 | 344 |
| 5.1 | character data entity | 6.3 | 4.34 | 300 |
| 64 | character number | 9.5 | 4.36 | 357 |
| 62 | character reference | 9.5 (9.2) | 4.37 | 356 |
| 92 | comment | 10.3 | 4.46 | 391 |
| 91 | comment declaration | 10.3 | 4.47 | 391 |
| 131 | connector | 11.2.4.1 | 4.1 | 413 |
| 24 | content | 7.6 | 4.53 | 320 |
| 126 | content model | 11.2.4 | 4.55 | 410 |
| 128 | content token | 11.2.4 | | 410 |
| 149.2 | data attribute specification | 11.4.1.2 | | 428 |
| 48 | data character | 9.2 | 4.73 | 344 |
| 133 | data tag group | 11.2.4.4 | 4.77 | 415 |
| 137 | data tag padding template | 11.2.4.4 | | 416 |
| 134 | data tag pattern | 11.2.4.4 | 4.78 | 416 |
| 136 | data tag template | 11.2.4.4 | | 416 |
| 135 | data tag template group | 11.2.4.4 | | 416 |
| 106 | data text | 10.5.3 | | 396 |
| 125 | declared content | 11.2.3 | | 409 |
| 145 | declared value | 11.3.3 | | 422 |
| 147 | default value | 11.3.4 | 4.84 | 425 |
| 12 | document element | 7.2 | 4.99 | 306 |
| 10 | document instance set | 7.2 | 4.101 | 306 |
| 110 | document type declaration | 11.1 | 4.103 | 403 |
| 112 | document type declaration subset | 11.1 | 4.104 | 404 |
| 111 | document type name | 11.1 | | 404 |
| 28 | document type specification | 7.7 | 4.106 | 325 |
| 71 | ds | 10.1.4 | 4.107 | 376 |
| 13 | element | 7.3 | 4.110 | 308 |
| 26 | element content | 7.6 | | 320 |
| 116 | element declaration | 11.2 | 4.111 | 405 |
| 114 | element set | 11.1 | 4.112 | 404 |
| 130 | element token | 11.2.4 | | 410 |
| 117 | element type | 11.2.1 | 4.114 | 406 |
| 21 | empty end-tag | 7.5.1.1 | | 318 |
| 16 | empty start-tag | 7.4.1.1 | | 315 |
| 19 | end-tag | 7.5 | 4.119 | 317 |
| 124 | end-tag minimization | 11.2.2 | | 408 |
| 101 | entity declaration | 10.5 | 4.121 | 394 |
| 102 | entity name | 10.5.1 | | 395 |
| 113 | entity set | 11.1 | 4.125 | 404 |
| 105 | entity text | 10.5.2 | 4.127 | 396 |
| 109 | entity type | 10.5.5 | | 400 |
| 138 | exceptions | 11.2.5 | 4.130 | 418 |

| Number | Symbol | Production | Definition | *Handbook* |
|---|---|---|---|---|
| 140 | exclusions | 11.2.5.2 | 4.131 | 419 |
| 108 | external entity specification | 10.5.5 | | 400 |
| 73 | external identifier | 10.1.6 | | 379 |
| 79 | formal public identifier | 10.2 | 4.137 | 382, 183 |
| 54 | function character | 9.2.2 | 4.139 | 346 |
| 63 | function name | 9.5 | | 356 |
| 103 | general entity name | 10.5.1 | | 395 |
| 35.1 | general entity name list | 7.9.4 | | 333 |
| 59 | general entity reference | 9.4.4 | 4.144 | 350 |
| 30 | generic identifier | 7.8 | 4.145 | 325 |
| 29 | generic identifier specification | 7.8 | | 325 |
| 37 | id reference list | 7.9.4 | 4.151 | 333 |
| 38 | id reference value | 7.9.4 | 4.152 | 333 |
| 36 | id value | 7.9.4 | 4.153 | 333 |
| 139 | inclusions | 11.2.5.1 | | 418 |
| 81 | ISO owner identifier | 10.2.1.1 | 4.162 | 383 |
| 87.1 | ISO text description | 10.2.2.2 | 4.163 | 387 |
| 151 | map name | 11.5 | | 429 |
| 153 | map specification | 11.6 | | 430 |
| 96 | marked section | 10.4 | 4.179 | 392 |
| 93 | marked section declaration | 10.4 | 4.180 | 391 |
| 95 | marked section end | 10.4 | 4.181 | 392 |
| 94 | marked section start | 10.4 | 4.182 | 392 |
| 51 | markup character | 9.2.1 | 4.184 | 345 |
| 20 | minimized end-tag | 7.5.1 | | 318 |
| 15 | minimized start-tag | 7.4.1 | | 314 |
| 77 | minimum data | 10.1.7 | | 381 |
| 78 | minimum data character | 10.1.7 | | 381 |
| 76 | minimum literal | 10.1.7 | | 381 |
| 25 | mixed content | 7.6 | | 320 |
| 127 | model group | 11.2.4 | 4.194 | 410 |
| 55 | name | 9.3 | 4.198 | 346 |
| 52 | name character | 9.2.1 | 4.199 | 345 |
| 69 | name group | 10.1.3 | 4.200 | 374 |
| 99 | name group<br>(deleted by Amendment 1) | 10.4.2 | | 393 |
| 39 | name list | 7.9.4 | | 333 |
| 53 | name start character | 9.2.1 | 4.201 | 346 |
| 57 | name token | 9.3 | 4.202 | 347 |
| 68 | name token group | 10.1.3 | 4.203 | 374 |
| 40 | name token list | 7.9.4 | | 333 |
| 18 | net-enabling start-tag | 7.4.1.3 | | 316 |
| 6 | non-SGML data entity | 6.3 | 4.208 | 300 |
| 146 | notation | 11.3.3 | | 423 |
| 148 | notation declaration | 11.4 | 4.212 | 426 |
| 149 | notation identifier | 11.4 | 4.213 | 427 |

| Number | Symbol | Production | Definition | *Handbook* |
|---|---|---|---|---|
| 41 | notation name | 7.9.4 | 4.214 | 333 |
| 23 | null end-tag | 7.5.1.3 | | 319 |
| 56 | number | 9.3 | 4.215 | 347 |
| 42 | number list | 7.9.4 | | 333 |
| 58 | number token | 9.3 | 4.216 | 347 |
| 43 | number token list | 7.9.4 | | 333 |
| 132 | occurrence indicator | 11.2.4.2 | | 413 |
| 122 | omitted tag minimization | 11.2.2 | (4.219) | 408 |
| 27 | other content | 7.6 | | 320 |
| 8 | other prolog | 7.1 | | 303 |
| 80 | owner identifier | 10.2.1 | 4.223 | 383, 183 |
| 104 | parameter entity name | 10.5.1 | | 395 |
| 60 | parameter entity reference | 9.4.4 | 4.226 | 350 |
| 66 | parameter literal | 10.1.2 | 4.227 | 373 |
| 129 | primitive content token | 11.2.4 | | 410 |
| 44 | processing instruction | 8 | | 339 |
| 7 | prolog | 7.1 | 4.236 | 303 |
| 65 | ps | 10.1.1 | 4.238 | 372 |
| 74 | public identifier | 10.1.6 | 4.239 | 379 |
| 86 | public text class | 10.2.2.1 | 4.241 | 386 |
| 87 | public text description | 10.2.2.2 | 4.242 | 387 |
| 89 | public text designating sequence | 10.2.2.4 | 4.243 | 388 |
| 90 | public text display version | 10.2.2.5 | 4.244 | 390 |
| 88 | public text language | 10.2.2.3 | 4.245 | 388 |
| 98 | qualified status keyword (deleted by Amendment 1) | 10.4.2 | | 393 |
| 120 | rank stem | 11.2.1.1 | | 407 |
| 121 | rank suffix | 11.2.1.1 | | 407 |
| 118 | ranked element | 11.2.1.1 | 4.248 | 407 |
| 119 | ranked group | 11.2.1.1 | 4.249 | 407 |
| 61 | reference end | 9.4.5 | | 352 |
| 82 | registered owner identifier | 10.2.1.2 | 4.262 | 384, 183 |
| 46 | replaceable character data | 9.1 | 4.263 | 343 |
| 67 | replaceable parameter data | 10.1.2 | 4.264 | 373 |
| 5 | s | 6.2.1 | 4.273 | 297 |
| 50 | SGML character | 9.2.1 | 4.280 | 345 |
| 1 | SGML document | 6.1 | 4.282 | 294 |
| 2 | SGML document entity | 6.2 | 4.283 | 295 |
| 3 | SGML subdocument entity | 6.2 | 4.286 | 296 |
| 4 | SGML text entity | 6.2 | 4.288 | 296 |
| 150 | short reference mapping declaration | 11.5 | 4.293 | 429 |
| 115 | short reference set | 11.1 | 4.294 | 404 |
| 152 | short reference use declaration | 11.6 | 4.296 | 430 |
| 5.2 | specific character data entity | 6.3 | 4.304 | 300 |
| 14 | start-tag | 7.4 | 4.306 | 314 |
| 123 | start-tag minimization | 11.2.2 | | 408 |

| Number | Symbol | Production | Definition | *Handbook* |
|---|---|---|---|---|
| 100 | status keyword | 10.4.2 | 4.307 | 393 |
| 97 | status keyword specification | 10.4.2 | | 393 |
| 45 | system data | 8 | | 339 |
| 75 | system identifier | 10.1.6 | 4.313 | 379 |
| 84 | text identifier | 10.2.2 | | 385 |
| 70 | ts | 10.1.3 | | 375 |
| 85 | unavailable text indicator | 10.2.2 | (4.18, 4.323) | 385, 182 |
| 22 | unclosed end-tag | 7.5.1.2 | | 318 |
| 17 | unclosed start-tag | 7.4.1.2 | | 316 |
| 83 | unregistered owner identifier | 10.2.1.3 | 4.325 | 385, 183 |

## Technophile's note on grammar rules

SGML's approach to entities differs from most computer languages, which separate inclusion from grammar, such that the grammar applies to data regardless of whether it was included physically or by logical inclusion. SGML instead mentions entity references as part of the grammar rules, for example under "other content" in Clause 7.6:

[24] content = *mixed content* | *element content* | *replaceable character data* | *character data*

[25] mixed content = (*data character* | *element* | *other content*)*

[26] element content = (*element* | *other content* | *s*)*

[27] other content = *comment declaration* | *short reference use declaration* | *link set use declaration* | *processing instruction* | **shortref** | *character reference* | *general entity reference* | *marked section declaration* | **Ee**

But the entity reference (typically an ampersand, some name characters, and a semicolon) is not what satisfies an SGML grammar rule: the result of resolving it must. For example, although "element content" allows "other content" this refers only to what happens *before* replacement; other required tokens may be buried within the entity's replacement text, and must be counted *after* replacement. This is especially important for separators, as discussed in Question 7.8: the replacement text of the entity usually (with ts, always) contains tokens that are not part of the separator, but fulfill a different rule or rules in the grammar.

# Bibliography


Agosti, Maristelle and Alan Smeaton. 1996. *Information Retrieval and Hypertext.* Boston: Kluwer Academic Publishers. ISBN 0-7923-9710-X.

Aho, Alfred V. and Jeffrey D. Ullman. 1977. *Principles of compiler design.* Reading, MA: Addison-Wesley. ISBN 0201000229.

Alschuler, Liora. 1995. *ABCD...SGML: A User's Guide to Structured Information.* Boston: International Thomson Computer Press. ISBN 1850321973.

American National Standards Institute. 1992. *Text and Office Systems — Conformance Testing for Standard Generalized Markup Language (SGML) Systems.* New York: ANSI, standard X3.190-1992.

André, Jacques, Richard Furuta, and Vincent Quint (eds). 1989. *Structured Documents.* Cambridge: Cambridge University Press. ISBN 0521365546.

Barnard, David T., Lou Burnard, Steven J. DeRose, David G. Durand, and C. Michael. Sperberg-McQueen. 1995. "Lessons for the World Wide Web from the Text Encoding Initiative". *World Wide Web Journal.* Issue One: Conference Proceedings, Fourth International World Wide Web Conference, Boston (December), 349-357. ISBN 1565921690.

Barnard, D.T., L. Burnard, J.-P. Gaspart, L. Price, C.M. Sperberg-McQueen, and G.B. Varile 1995. "Hierarchical Encoding of Text: Technical Problems and SGML Solutions". *Computers and the Humanities* 29,3: 211-231. Reprinted in Ide and Véronis, eds. (1995).

Barnard, D.T., L. Burnard and C.M. Sperberg-McQueen. 1996. "Lessons Learned from Using SGML in the Text Encoding Initiative". *Computer Standards and Interfaces* 18: 3-10. Also appeared as Technical Report 95-375, Department of Computing and Information Science, Queen's University (1995).

Berners-Lee, Tim, Robert Cailliau, Jean-François Groff, Bernd Pollermann. 1992. "World-Wide Web: The Information Universe". *Electronic Networking: Research, Applications and Policy* 1(2): 74-82.

Berners-Lee, Tim, Robert Cailliau, Ari Luotonen, Henrik Frystyk Nielsen, Arthur Secret. 1994. "The World-Wide Web". *Communications of the Association for Computing Machinery* 37(8): 76-82.

Bryan, Martin. 1988. *SGML: An Author's Guide to the Standard Generalized Markup Language.* Wokingham, England: Addison-Wesley. ISBN 0-201-17535-5.

--------. 1997. *SGML and HTML Explained.* Reading, Massachusetts: Addison-Wesley. ISBN 0201403943.

Cline, Marshall P. and Greg A. Lomow. 1995. *C++ FAQs: Frequently Asked Questions.* Reading, Massachusetts: Addison-Wesley. ISBN 0-201-58958-3.

Cohen, Ben. 1996. *VHDL: Answers to Frequently Asked Questions.* Boston: Kluwer Academic Publishers. ISBN 0-7923-9791-6.

Coombs, James H., Allen H. Renear, and Steven J. DeRose. 1987. "Markup Systems and the Future of Scholarly Text Processing". *Communications of the Association for Computing Machinery* 30 (11): 933-947.

Cover, Robin C., Nicholas Duncan, and David T. Barnard. 1991. *Bibliography on SGML (Standard Generalized Markup Language) and Related Issues.* Technical Report 91-299. Kingston, Ontario: Queen's University, February, 1991. Extract reprinted in *Literary and Linguistic Computing* 6 (3): 197-209.

DeRose, Steven J. 1993. "Markup Systems in the Present". In *The Digital Word: Text-Based Computing in the Humanities,* ed. by George Landow and Paul Delany. Cambridge: MIT Press: 119-135. ISBN 0-262-12176-x.

DeRose Steven J. and David G. Durand. 1994. *Making Hypermedia Work: A User's Guide to HyTime.* Boston: Kluwer Academic Publishers. ISBN 0-7923-9432-1.

DeRose Steven J., David G. Durand, Elli Mylonas, and Allen H. Renear. 1990. "What is Text, Really?" *Journal of Computing in Higher Education* 1 (2): 3-26.

DeRose, Steven J. and Paul Grosso. 1996. "Fragment Interchange". SGML Open Technical Resolution 9601:1996. www.sgmlopen.org/sgml/docs/techpubs.htm.

Durand, David G., Elli Mylonas, and Steven J. DeRose. 1996. "What Should Markup Really Be? Applying theories of text to the design of markup systems". Paper at *The 1996 Joint International Conference of the Association for Literary and Linguistic Computing and the Association for Computers and the Humanities,* June 25-29, 1996, Bergen, Norway. Abstract published as No. 70 in the Report Series of the Norwegian Computing Center for the Humanities: 67-70. ISBN 82-7283-083-3.

Engelbart, Douglas C. 1963. "A Conceptual Framework for the Augmentation of Man's Intellect". In *Vistas in Information Handling,* Vol. 1 (P. Howerton, ed.). Washington, DC: Spartan Books: 1-29. Reprinted in Greif (1988): 35-65.

Exoterica Corporation. 1992. "Record Boundary Processing in SGML". Technical report ETR13-1092, October, 1992. Ottawa: Exoterica Corporation (now OmniMark Technologies).

Furuta, Richard. 1991. *Important Papers in the History of Document Preparation Systems: Basic Sources.* Technical Report UMIACS-TR-91-7, January, 1991. College Park: University of Maryland Department of Computer Science.

Goldfarb, Charles F. 1990. *The SGML Handbook.* Edited and with a foreword by Yuri Rubinsky. Oxford University Press. ISBN 0198537379.

Greif, Irene (ed.). 1988. *Computer-Supported Cooperative Work: A Book of Readings.* San Mateo, California: Morgan Kaufmann Publishers. ISBN 0934613575.

Ide, Nancy and Jean Veronis (eds.). 1995. *Text Encoding Initiative: Background and Context.* Boston: Kluwer Academic Publishers. ISBN 0792336895

International Organization for Standardization. 1986. ISO 8879. *Information Processing — Text and Office Information Systems — Standard Generalized Markup Language.*

--------. 1988. ISO 639. *Codes for the representation of names of languages.*

--------. 1988. ISO 9069. *Information Processing — SGML Support Facilities — SGML Document Interchange Format.*

--------. 1991. ISO/IEC 9070. *Information Processing — SGML Support Facilities — Registration procedures for public text owner identifiers.*

--------. 1991. ISO/IEC TR 10037. *Information Technology — SGML and Text Entry Systems — Guidelines for Syntax-Directed Editing Systems.*

--------. 1992. ISO/IEC 10744. *Information technology — Hypermedia/Time-based Structuring Language (HyTime).*

--------. 1993. ISO/IEC 9573. *Information technology — SGML Support Facilities — Techniques for Using SGML.* Available in several separate parts.

--------. 1994. ISO/IEC 10179. *Information technology — Processing languages — Document Style Semantics and Specification Language (DSSSL).*

Huitfeldt, Claus. 1995. "Multi-dimensional texts in a one-dimensional medium". *Computers and the Humanities* 28(4-5), '94/'95: 235-41.

Kernighan, Brian. 1990. "Issues and Tradeoffs in Document Preparation Systems". In *EP90: Proceedings of the International Conference on Electronic Publishing, Document Manipulation & Typography, Gaithersburg, Maryland, September.* Richard Furuta (ed.). Cambridge: Cambridge University Press: 1-16. ISBN 0521402468.

Koenig, Andrew W. 1989. *C Traps and Pitfalls.* Reading, Massachusetts: Addison-Wesley. ISBN 0-201-17928-8.

Maler, Eve and Jeanne El Andaloussi. 1996. *Developing SGML DTDs: From Text to Model to Markup.* Upper Saddle River, NJ: Prentice Hall. ISBN 0-13-309881-8.

Maloney, Murray and Yuri Rubinsky. 1997. *Beyond Html: Sgml Publishing on the World Wide Web.* Prentice Hall. ISBN 0135199840.

Prusky, John. 1978. *FRESS Resource Manual.* Providence: Brown University Division of Applied Mathematics.

Raggett, Dave, Jenny Lam, and Ian Alexander. 1996. *HTML 3: Electronic Publishing on the World Wide Web.* Reading, MA: Addison-Wesley. ISBN 0-201-87693-0.

Reid, Brian. 1980. "A high-level approach to computer document formatting". *Conference Record of the Seventh Annual ACM Symposium on Principles of Programming Languages,* January.

Reid, Brian. 1981. *Scribe: A Document Specification Language and its Compiler.* Ph.D. thesis, Carnegie-Mellon University, Pittsburgh, PA. Also available as Technical Report CMU-CS-81-100.

Rice, Stanley. 1970. "Editorial Text Structures (with some relations to information structures and format controls in computerized composition)". Memo to ANSI Standards Planning and Requirements Committee. March 17.

SGML Open. 1996. *Fragment Interchange.* Technical Resolution 9601:1996. Steven J. DeRose and Paul Grosso, eds. (www.sgmlopen.org/sgml/docs/techpubs.htm).

Simons, Gary F. 1990. "A Conceptual Modeling Language for the Analysis and Interpretation of Text". Chicago: Text Encoding Initiative. Committee on Text Analysis and Interpretation, document AIW12, January 16.

Smith, Joan M. and Robert Stutely. 1988. *SGML: The User's Guide to ISO 8879.* Chichester: Ellis Horwood Limited. ISBN 0-7458-0221-4, 0-470-21126-1.

Sperberg-McQueen, C. Michael and Lou Burnard (eds). 1994. *Guidelines for Electronic Text Encoding and Interchange.* Chicago, Oxford: Text Encoding Initiative. Also available online from ftp://ftp-tei.uic.edu/pub/tei and many other places, most of which are pointed to from www.sil.org/sgml/acadapps.html#tei (part of Robin Cover's extensive SGML information guide at that site).

Stanek, William Robert. With Steven J. DeRose, Mary Jo Fahey, John J. Kottler, Adrian Scott, Gregory Stenstrom, Richmond Tuttle, and Sandra Tuttle. 1996. *Web Publishing Unleashed.* Indianapolis: Sams.net Publishing. ISBN 1575210517.

Summit, Steve. 1996. *C Programming FAQs: Frequently Asked Questions.* Reading, Massachusetts: Addison-Wesley. ISBN 0-201-84519-9.

Text Encoding Initiative. *Guidelines for Electronic Text Encoding and Interchange.* See Sperberg-McQueen and Burnard, eds (1994).

Tompa, Frank W. 1989. "What is (tagged) text?" In *Dictionaries in the Electronic Age: Proceedings of the Fifth Annual Conference of the UW Centre for the New OED:* 81-93.

Travis, B. and D. Waldt. 1995. *The SGML Implementation Guide: A Blueprint for SGML Migration.* Berlin: Springer-Verlag. ISBN 3-540-57730-0.

van Herwijnen, Eric. 1993. *SGML Tutorial.* Providence: Electronic Book Technologies.

--------. 1994. *Practical SGML: Second Edition.* Boston: Kluwer Academic Publishing. ISBN 0-7923-9434-8.

Yankelovich, Nicole, Norman Meyrowitz, and Andries van Dam. 1985. "Reading and Writing the Electronic Book". *IEEE Computer* 18 (October): 16-30.

# Glossary

**Ambiguous content model**
An SGML content model that permits documents to be constructed whose structure could not be unambiguously interpreted. Such content models are prohibited. For example, a long series of elements of type ITEM could satisfy the model below in several ways (it would be unclear how many were part of the first ITEM+ requirement, and how many were part of the second):

```
<!-- WRONG -->
<!ELEMENT  AMBIGUOUS-LIST           - -  (ITEM+, ITEM+)>
```

**Ancestor**
Any element instance that contains a given element instance. For example, BOOK and CHAPTER may be ancestors of a given P.

**Anchor**
The actual data at one end of a hypertext link. It is pointed to (directly or indirectly) by a "linkend" of a link. A single anchor can be pointed to by link ends in many different links.

**Anchor role**
The conceptual function that a particular anchor of a hypertext link has, such as "subject of criticism", "source", "origin", and so on, commonly indicated on an attribute.

**Architectural form**
A template for a class of SGML elements or a set of attributes to be used by multiple DTDs. Specific DTDs may declare element types to be subclasses of such a class by giving them a **#FIXED** attribute with a special name, whose value is the architectural form name. In HyTime, the special attribute is called HyTime.

**Attribute**
Data on some or all instances of an SGML element type, typically giving specific information about the properties or significance of the instance. Unique identifiers are also specified on elements via attributes.

**Basic SGML document**
A Basic SGML document uses those SGML features most commonly considered useful and thus is quite portable. It uses only the **SHORTTAG** and **OMITTAG** features, and only a few predetermined short references.

**CALS**
An initiative by the U.S. military to apply SGML to documentation, repair manuals, etc. CALS adopted SGML early and made several contributions that are now more widely used, such as its tag set for marking up tables.

**Case-folding**
The operation of making all letters in a string be capitals, or all be lower-case. In SGML, most kinds of attribute values are forced to upper-case before other processing. Internationally, not all characters have meaningful case-distinctions: ideographic writing systems use case sparingly (though Japanese has wide and narrow versions of its phonetic characters, which are somewhat similar to case distinctions); writing systems with many accents or other diacritic marks often delete them from the upper-case form, which means there is no exact upper-case equivalent to some accented lower-case forms.

**CDATA (Character data)**
A keyword applicable to various SGML constructs. An element, entity, or marked section of type **CDATA** can contains no markup (delimiters other than those specifically needed to end the constructed are treated as literal data).; **CDATA** attributes still recognize entity references, but are unrestricted in their string form unlike other declared values. Related to, but not the same as, **#PCDATA** and **RCDATA**. See Question 2.4 for more details.

**Connector**
Any of the delimiters used between two element type names in an SGML content model, to indicate their co-occurrence restrictions. Connectors include "|" (**OR**) meaning that either may occur but not both, "," (**SEQ**) meaning that both may occur, and "&" (**AND**), meaning that both may occur in either order. See also "occurrence indicator."

CONREF **attribute**
An SGML attribute that has been assigned the default value **#CONREF**. This means that if the attribute is specified on an instance of the element, that instance can have no content or subelements. A **CONREF** attribute may be of type **CDATA**, **ID**, **IDREF**, or any other type supported by SGML.

**Content model**
An expression in an element declaration in an SGML DTD that specifies what kinds of subelements can be directly contained in the element being declared. A content model appears as a parenthesized expression containing element names, occurrence indicators, and connectors. See also "declared content."

**Contextual constraint**
One of the rules in Clause 9.6.2 about what characters must immediately follow an SGML delimiter for it to count as markup rather than just literal data. A delimiter string that is followed by one of the specified characters is called a "delimiter-in-context". See Question 1.1.

**Current element**
The element that was most recently opened and still is open, at any point in a document. For example, at the end of "<SEC><ST>Introduction</ST>" the SEC is the current element.

**Data content notation**
A representation for data, for which a name is declared in an SGML DTD. Entities can then specify that their data is in the notation, so that an SGML processor can direct them to an appropriate processing program (whether or not that program is fully integrated with the SGML or HyTime system).

**Declared content**
The alternative to a content model in an element declaration; used when the element being declared cannot contain subelements but has some special, restricted kind of content (or no possible content). The three types of declared content are **CDATA**, **RCDATA**, and **EMPTY**.

**Delimiter**
Any of the 30-odd strings used in SGML to set off structural portions of a document. For example, the start-tag open delimiter is named **STAGO** and its default value (in the "reference concrete syntax") is "<". See also the appendix on SGML Delimiters.

**Delimiter in context**
An SGML delimiter string (such as "<") that occurs in a structural context where it will be recognized (such as in content and followed by certain characters). When not recognized, an SGML delimiter is treated as literal data. For example, "<" followed by a space cannot represent start-tag open, because space is not a name start character; therefore it is a literal less-than sign.

**Descriptive markup**
The principle of marking parts of document by names directly related to their purpose, significance, or function, rather than with names directly related to their formatting or other specific processing. Also known as "content," "generalized," or "generic" markup.

**Document instance**
An individual SGML document.

**Document Style Semantics and Specification Language** (DSSSL)
DSSSL is ISO/IEC standard 10179. It specifies a representation for the structure of SGML documents and other data objects, called "groves", and languages for transforming such structures and for formatting the information in them. Going beyond many other formatting languages, DSSSL supports complex but common publishing operations such as contextual formatting ("don't indent the first P in each SEC, except in the back matter"), transclusion ("grab the title of the SEC with **ID** SEC2.1 and insert it and the string 'See also'"), non-trivial kinds of numbering, and so on.

**Document tree**
A direct hierarchical representation of document structure, built from an SGML document and associated entities.

**Document type**
A kind or class of document as defined by a particular SGML DTD. See also "document type declaration."

**Document type declaration (or DTD)**
From Clause 4.103: "A markup declaration that contains the formal specification of a document type definition." This is the part of an SGML document that formally specifies what elements, attributes, entities, and notations can occur in it, and where. Typically, academic, industry, or other groups with a common interest define a DTD that describes the typical structure of documents of interest, and encourage use of that DTD to enhance portability and consistency.

**Document type definition (or DTD)**
From Clause 4.104: "Rules, determined by an application, that apply SGML to the markup of documents of a particular type..." This includes the formal SGML Document type declaration, as well as the related concepts, documentation, and other information that provide meaning to go with the SGML form.

**Electronic publishing**
The act of publishing documents in online form rather than on paper. This term can also refer to paper publication using computer tools at any point in the production process.

**Element content**
The content of an SGML element that contains no character data, but only subelements. See also "mixed content."

**Element instance**
An occurrence of an element of a particular type within an SGML document instance. The element extends from its start-tag to its end-tag (even if either or both is left implicit by minimization).

**Element structure information set (or ESIS)**
The information that an SGML parser passes back to typical "structure-controlled" applications. This includes where elements start and end, their attributes and content, etc. However, it does not include information about what syntax was used to express structures (such as whether a tag or attribute was implicit, the order attributes were specified, or where extraneous whitespace occurred inside tags). ESIS is defined in Annex A in the *Reference Application for SGML Testing* standard, ANSI X3.190 (which remarks that ESIS is "implicit" in SGML). It is very useful because it suggests a way to tell what aspects of an SGML document are conceptually, structurally, or logically significant. As defined, ESIS omits a few details that even many structure-controlled applications need, such as which elements are **`EMPTY`**, which attributes are **`ID`**s or **`IDREF`**s, and where SGML text entities begin and end. Most parsers therefore provide slightly more information than just the ESIS.

**Element type**
A defined class for components of a document, such as `CHAPTER`, `TITLE`, `LINK`, etc. Each type must be defined in the document's DTD. Processing is usually similar for all instances of an element type, and different for instances of different element types.

`EMPTY` **element**
An SGML element whose declaration specifies that it cannot have content, any subelements or an end-tag.

**End-tag**
A marker indicating the end of an element instance in an SGML document.

**Entity**
A unit of storage declared and given a name in an SGML DTD. An entity can be a literal string or an external data object such as a file, and may be in SGML or any other notation (so long as the notation name is declared and specified). Entities can be referred to in a document instance, for instance to assemble documents out of component parts.

**Entity reference**
An invocation of an entity within an SGML document instance, which will be replaced by the actual value of the entity (basically as if value had been there in place of the reference).

**Escape**
To prevent some character or string from having its special meaning in a computer language. For example, using some method to prevent "<" from being recognized as a start-tag open delimiter, so it is instead treated as a literal greater-than sign in content. One common method is to substitute an entity reference, such as "<". Most computer languages have some similar mechanism, such as putting "\" before a special character. See Question 3.7 for more on this notion.

**ESIS** (see "Element structure information set")

**Exclusion exception**
A list of tag names in parentheses after a content model in an element declaration, prefixed by the **MINUS** delimiters (normally "-"). This specifies elements that cannot occur *anywhere* within any instance of the element being declared or any subelements of such instances, and overrides any applicable "inclusion exceptions."

**Explainer**
A short explanation of the significance of a particular link end in a particular link, suitable for displaying as a caption to help readers determine whether they are actually interested in following the link. This idea and term were introduced by FRESS.

**Extended pointer**
A way of referring to locations in SGML and other documents, particularly locations that lack IDs but can be reached by searching, scanning around in document hierarchies, or other methods. This compact syntax for expressing locations is defined in the TEI Guidelines for the Encoding of Machine-Readable Texts, and is widely used in hypermedia documents.

**Formal public identifier (or FPI)**
A unique name by which an SGML document can refer to some other piece of data, in a certain format defined in ISO 9070 and used by SGML.

**Fully qualified generic identifier (or FQGI)**
The list of all the element types in the line of descent between the root of the document tree and some particular element. For example, a paragraph might have a FQGI of:

```
BOOK, CHAPTER, SECTION, PARA, FOOTNOTE, PARA
```

An FQGI does *not* uniquely identify an element instance, so cannot constitute a location for use in linking. However, it incorporates much of the contextual information required to process an element correctly for some purposes.

**General entity**
An SGML entity defined for use within a document instance, not within a DTD. Such entities are referenced via the **ERO** delimiter ("&"), not the **PERO** delimiter ("%"), which is used for "parameter entities."

**Generalized markup (or generic markup)**
Synonyms for descriptive markup.

**Generic identifier (or GI)**
The formal name for an SGML element type name such as `P`, `CHAPTER`, and so on. Commonly called the "tag name."

**Generic markup**
See "descriptive markup".

**Grove**
A way of representing the structure derived from an SGML document as a set of nodes representing elements, character content, processing instructions and so on, along with their relationships. Groves can represent the element structure tree of SGML documents as well as non-hierarchical connections such as between an **`IDREF`** and its destination `ID`. Groves were developed through cooperation between the HyTime and DSSSL committees and are formalized in the DSSSL standard. See also Question 5.11.

**Grove plan**
DSSSL does not specify exactly what kinds of nodes go into a grove, or how they must be related, because this varies from one application to another. A simple SGML application might specify grove plans that exclude DTD information, comments, processing instructions, or marked section boundaries. Even many sophisticated SGML applications would exclude details about whitespace inside markup. An application that built groves from vector graphic images might have completely different kinds of nodes: not elements and attributes, but polygons and line types. DSSSL and HyTime each specify a default grove plan.

**Hierarchical structure**
The division of documents into successive layers of structure, such as chapters, sections, lists with items, multimedia objects and their portions, on down to significant phrases, frames, or other components. DSSSL provides a formal description of the hierarchical structure of SGML documents in terms of "groves".

**HTML**
HyperText Markup Language, an application of SGML widely used to represent documents with links on the World Wide Web.

**Hyperlink**
A connection between discontiguous components in a collection of documents, typically intended to express a meaningful relationship between the connected data.

**Hypertext**
The practice of connecting portions of documents and other data objects together, such as by cross-references, quotations, annotations, and the like. Used especially when such connections are automated through the application of computers. This term uses "text" in the sense of "document," not in the sense of opposing letters to other media.

**HyTime**
ISO/IEC 10744, an international standard for hypermedia and time-based systems. HyTime provides tools for hypertext linking and for scheduling events (such as multimedia presentations) in space and time, using SGML as a representation language.

**`ID` and `IDREF` attributes**
Special declared values for SGML attributes. An attribute defined as an **`ID`** takes a value that must be a unique identifier for the element instance it appears on; the value may then be used to specify links to the element. An attribute defined as an **`IDREF`** takes the **`ID`**s of other elements in the same document as values, and so may serve as a link origin.

**Inclusion exception**
An option in SGML element declarations used to specify elements that can occur *anywhere* within any instance of the element being declared or their direct and indirect subelements. See also "exclusion exception."

**ISO**
The International Organization for Standardization, which undertakes to develop and promulgate standards in a wide variety of technical areas.

**Link**
See "hypertext link." The word "link" can also refer to an optional feature of SGML unrelated to hypertext, but it is seldom used in that sense in this book.

**Linkend**
A part of a hypertext link that points to some data object or portion of one (not the data that it actually points to, for which see "Anchor").

**Markup**
Information included in a document that is not properly part of the linguistic, graphical, or other content, but instead gives information *about* the content. SGML provides a standard syntax for including certain kinds of markup in documents.

**Minimal SGML document**
An SGML document instance that uses no minimization or other optional SGML features and uses the default syntactic settings.

**Minimization**
A blanket term for SGML methods for omitting or abbreviating markup when it can be inferred from context. A document that uses minimization is by definition *not* a "minimal SGML document."

**Mixed content**
An SGML model group in which both subelements and **#PCDATA** portions can co-occur. Proficient DTD writers avoid mixed content models except those that permit **#PCDATA** everywhere. See also "element content." See also Question 5.2.

**Model group**
Almost synonymous in SGML with "content model," however, the reserved word **ANY** is considered a content model, whereas only a parenthesized expression including generic identifiers is a true "model group."

**Name**
Certain SGML constructs are considered names, which means they can contain only certain characters (normally the unaccented Latin letters, digits, period, and hyphen) and be under a certain length (normally 8, though frequently increased). Among these constructs are element types, attribute names, many kinds of attribute values, entity names, and a variety of SGML keywords.

NDATA **entities**
"Notation data:" refers to SGML entities that are in representations or "data content notations" other than SGML. For example, graphic and multimedia objects are not typically represented in SGML, but may be referred to after identifying them and their notation in an **ENTITY** declaration.

**Nodes**
Any of the locations in the tree or grove that represents an SGML document's structure. They include SGML elements, pseudo-elements, data entities, attributes, and various other information units (DSSSL groves can be defined that also include other information as nodes).

NOTATION
See "data content notation."

**Occurrence indicator**
Any of the characters used to indicate how many times a structure can be repeated. These appear in SGML content models. Occurrence indicators include "?" (**OPT**) when the structure is optional, "*" (**REP**) when zero or more instances of the structure may occur, and "+" (**PLUS**) when at least one instance must occur. See also "connector."

**Ordered hierarchy of content-based objects (or OHCO)**
A name for the abstract document model used by SGML and some other representations. This model views documents as nested structures of components, each of which has a specified type that specifies the significance of its content for various kinds of processing. See DeRose, Durand, Mylonas, and Renear (1990).

**Parameter entity**
An SGML entity defined for use within a DTD, not within a document instance (with one exception: they can be used to specify the status keywords for marked sections). Such entities are referenced via the **PERO** delimiter ("%"), not the **ERO** delimiter ("&"), which is used for "general entities."

**#PCDATA**
"Parsed character data:" the name used in SGML element declarations (prefixed by "#", the **RNI** delimiter) to specify where within an element text content may occur. See also "**CDATA**" and "**RCDATA**."

**Processing instruction (or PI)**
A syntactic feature of SGML that permits inserting application-specific commands into a document. Processing instructions compromise portability of documents.

**Proper subelement**
An SGML element that is permitted in its containing element by virtue of the content model of its containing element, rather than because of any applicable inclusion exception.

**Pseudo-element (or pelement)**
A portion of an SGML document that is not properly an element, but constitutes a node in the document tree because it is a portion of character data with no internal markup. See also "**#PCDATA**."

**RAST**
RAST is the Reference Application for SGML Testing, which is closely related to "ESIS": a specification of what an SGML parser should return to an application for certain limited purposes. The RAST standard is listed in the Bibliography under American National Standards Institute (1992).

RCDATA **elements and marked sections**
"Replaceable character data:" the name used in element declarations to specify that an element can contain text content and entity references, but no subelements. Also applicable to marked sections. See also "**CDATA**" and "**#PCDATA**."

**Reference concrete syntax**
The "least common denominator" settings for SGML. When none of the SGML delimiters strings (such as "<" for start-tag open, etc.) are changed from their normal values, and none of the default size limits are changed, a document is said to use the reference concrete syntax and the reference quantity set.

**Regular expression**
A way of specifying pattern matches on character strings, popularized by various Unix tools and now available in many popular word processor "Find" commands as well. Regular expressions can search for exact strings, sets of characters, word boundaries, "everything up to" some character(s), and so on.

**Reserved name indicator** (**or** RNI)
A special delimiter string (normally "#") prefixed to some SGML reserved words to distinguish them from other tokens that could also occur in the same context. For example, the string **#PCDATA** is used instead of just "**PCDATA**" in content models to indicate where parsed character data is allowed. The **RNI** prevents conflict should there also be an element named PCDATA (though a DTD designer would be ill-advised to choose such a confusing element type name).

SDATA **entities**
"Specific character data:" a type of SGML entity most commonly used to represent special characters or other data that must be handled differently on different computer hardware, operating systems, or software applications.

**SDIF**
"SGML Document Interchange Format:" a method of collecting a DTD, a document instance, and any related SGML entities into a single bundle for transmission, for example across a wide-area network. SDIF is defined in ISO 9069 (ISO8824, ASN.1 "Abstract Syntax Notation 1" is a prerequisite).

**Semantics**
The meaning of expressions in a given language, as opposed to "syntax", which deals with how expressions are constructed.

**SGML**
The Standard Generalized Markup Language, ISO 8879.

**SGML application**
An SGML DTD, along with rules and documentation for the use of that DTD for processing documents appropriately for a given purpose. See also "SGML implementation."

**SGML declaration**
The first major component of an SGML document. It specifies the character set for the following document, any changes to the SGML delimiters and other syntactic settings, changes to name length limits, and so on.

**SGML implementation**
A computer program that can read SGML documents, find the boundaries of all their parts, and process them for some useful purpose. A single SGML implementation can typically support a wide range of SGML applications.

**SGML Open**
A consortium of companies that provide SGML software or services. Members of the consortium work together to enhance the interoperability of SGML systems and to promote the use of SGML.

**SGML text entity**
An SGML entity that will be parsed as normal SGML, with tags and other markup recognized. As opposed to **NDATA**, **SDATA**, **PI**, **CDATA**, and various other types of entities, for which the parsing rules are quite different.

**Start-tag**
A marker that indicates the start of an SGML document element, its type, and any attributes specific to the element instance.

**Status keyword**
Any of the keywords **IGNORE**, **CDATA**, **RCDATA**, or **INCLUDE**, that control how a marked section is parsed. Two control whether it is included, the others control what delimiters are recognized inside it. If multiple status keywords are present, the one occurring earliest in the list above applies (is "effective"). The other value, **TEMP**, is not called a "status keyword" (see Clause 10.4.2) and has no priority, nor any effect on parsing. It is seldom used.

**Stylesheet**
A specification of how to process various types of objects in a document on the basis of their types. Stylesheets are most commonly used to specify formatting, but the same idea is used in other kinds of processing such as information retrieval, sorting, searching, linking and navigation.

SUBDOC **entity**
A kind of SGML entity that represents an entire SGML document when it must be embedded in the midst of another SGML document (possibly with a different DTD).

**Subelement**
An element directly contained within another element (see Clause 4.309). Outside of the SGML standard, in common usage the term also refers to indirectly contained elements (such as a paragraph that is directly inside a section but only indirectly inside a chapter).

**Syntax**
Grammatical rules that govern what parts go where inside expression in a language. For example, the rules in English about where subjects and objects, nouns and verbs go. Or the rules in SGML about where delimiters and text, elements and attributes go. Distinguished from "semantics", which deals with the meaning of those expressions, rather than how they are expressed.

**Tag**
A marker for the start or end of an SGML element. See also "start-tag" and "end-tag."

**Text Encoding Initiative (or TEI)**
The Text Encoding Initiative is a major international effort that has established guidelines for the encoding and interchange of electronic texts. It includes representatives from many learned societies in the humanities and social sciences and the resulting DTDs and methods have been applied to a wide variety of major text collections. The TEI Guidelines are listed in the Bibliography under Sperberg-McQueen and Burnard (1994), along with pointers to online sources.

**Transclusion**
A term coined by Ted Nelson to refer to a particularly useful way of handling quotations in hypermedia systems. When a link is intended to be followed automatically, to retrieve some part of another document, and to display it in line without any user action to "follow" the link, the linked information is being "transcluded". There are many variations, for example in whether and how the reader is signaled that part of the text is not local, whether the transcluded text must also serve as a "gateway" by which the user can access its whole original document, and so on.

**Validation**
The process of checking an SGML document so that all formal errors are reported; obviously this will not catch conceptual errors, where the document is valid but incorrect, but it can catch a wide range of common errors.

**WG8**
Working Group 8 is the ISO committee that handles SGML, HyTime, DSSSL, and several others standards such a the Standard Page Description Language and some standards having to do with fonts. Its complete designation is ISO/IEC JTC1/SC18/WG8. In ISO, a Working Group consists of "individual experts", while balloting and national standards bodies are involved at the "SC" level.

**Whitespace**
A general term for characters such as space, tab, and newlines, used to separate words in many (but not all!) computer and human languages. In SGML such characters are collectively called separators, and there are four main types (see Clause 4.276 and Question 7.8).

**XML**
The eXtensible Markup Language, a small yet powerful subset of SGML developed by a committee of SGML experts sponsored by the World Wide Web Consortium.

# Index

MIX
Papier aus verantwortungsvollen Quellen
Paper from responsible sources
FSC® C105338

If you have any concerns about our products,
you can contact us on
**ProductSafety@springernature.com**

In case Publisher is established outside the EU,
the EU authorized representative is:
**Springer Nature Customer Service Center GmbH**
**Europaplatz 3, 69115 Heidelberg, Germany**

Printed by Libri Plureos GmbH
in Hamburg, Germany